PENGUIN CLASSICS

MICHELANGELO: POEMS AND LETTERS

MICHELANGELO BUONARROTI was born at Caprese in 1475, son of the local Florentine administrator (*podestà*). After an early apprenticeship to the painter Ghirlandaio, he attracted the attention of Lorenzo de' Medici who set him to study sculpture with Bertoldo di Giovanni. For almost forty years Michelangelo alternated between Rome and Florence working as sculptor, painter and architect for the Medici family, the Florentine Republic and a succession of popes. In 1534 he moved definitively to Rome where he died in 1564. Michelangelo is universally admired for masterpieces that are landmarks in the visual arts: the statues of *David* and of *Moses*, the *Captives*, the Medici Chapel, the Laurentian Library, the frescos in the Sistine Chapel. But he is also the most forceful Italian lyric poet of the sixteenth century, writing in a new and tough intellectual style. Often using metaphors borrowed from sculpture and painting, the poetry expresses the artist's deep love for Tommaso de' Cavalieri and Vittoria Colonna and sheds light on his intensely religious sensibility. The lively and sometimes truculent letters of Michelangelo provide essential documentation of his artistic career and his tense relations with his family. Few visual artists have ever left such a compelling self-portrait in words.

ANTHONY MORTIMER is Emeritus Professor of English Literature at the University of Fribourg, Switzerland. He has also taught in Italy, the United States and Germany and been Visiting Professor at the University of Geneva and Visiting Research Fellow at Merton College, Oxford. Among his recent publications are *Variable Passions: A Reading of Shakespeare's 'Venus and Adonis'* (New York, 2000) and, as editor, *The Authentic Cadence: Centennial Essays on Gerard Manley Hopkins* (Fribourg, 1992) and *Petrarch's Canzoniere in the English Renaissance* (Amsterdam, 2005). He has published widely on sixteenth- and seventeenth-century poetry and on Anglo-Italian literary relations. Anthony Mortimer's verse translations of Petrarch's *Canzoniere* appeared in Penguin Classics in 2002.

MICHELANGELO

Poems and Letters

Selections, with the *1550 Vasari* Life

Translated with an Introduction and Notes
by ANTHONY MORTIMER

PENGUIN BOOKS

PENGUIN CLASSICS

Published by the Penguin Group
Penguin Books Ltd, 80 Strand, London WC2R ORL, England
Penguin Group (USA) Inc., 375 Hudson Street, New York, New York 10014, USA
Penguin Group (Canada), 90 Eglinton Avenue East, Suite 700, Toronto, Ontario, Canada M4P 2Y3
(a division of Pearson Penguin Canada Inc.)
Penguin Ireland, 25 St Stephen's Green, Dublin 2, Ireland
(a division of Penguin Books Ltd)
Penguin Group (Australia), 250 Camberwell Road, Camberwell, Victoria 3124, Australia
(a division of Pearson Australia Group Pty Ltd)
Penguin Books India Pvt Ltd, 11 Community Centre, Panchsheel Park, New Delhi – 110 017, India
Penguin Group (NZ), 67 Apollo Drive, Rosedale, North Shore 0632, New Zealand
(a division of Pearson New Zealand Ltd)
Penguin Books (South Africa) (Pty) Ltd, 24 Sturdee Avenue, Rosebank, Johannesburg 2196, South Africa

Penguin Books Ltd, Registered Offices: 80 Strand, London WC2R ORL, England

www.penguin.com

Published in Penguin Classics 2007
005

Translation and editorial material copyright © Anthony Mortimer, 2007
All rights reserved

The moral right of the translator has been asserted

Set in 10.25/12.25 pt PostScript Adobe Sabon
Typeset by Rowland Phototypesetting Ltd, Bury St Edmunds, Suffolk
Printed in England by Clays Ltd, St Ives plc

ISBN: 978-0-140-44956-3

www.greenpenguin.co.uk

Penguin Books is committed to a sustainable
future for our business, our readers and our planet.
This book is made from Forest Stewardship
Council™ certified paper.

Contents

Acknowledgements

I should like to thank all those who have given me their support and encouragement and especially Colin Burrow, Edoardo Fumagalli, Guglielmo Gorni and Robert Rehder. Regina Schneider has been a most supportive colleague and Sonya Amacker has been smilingly meticulous in her attention to a manuscript that must often have seemed chronically unstable.

George Bull's admirable biography of Michelangelo and Christopher Ryan's lucid commentary on the poems have been constantly at my elbow. Useful comment on my work came from the readers of *Forum Italicum* and *Literary Imagination* and from audiences at the University of Fribourg, the University of Pavia and the annual conference of the Canadian Society for Italian Studies in Toronto.

My greatest debt is to Richard Waswo, my friend and accomplice for many years and the best reader that any translator could wish for. There is hardly a poem that has not benefited from his unerring insight and generous emendation. This would be a better book if I were always capable of following his advice.

I can only thank my wife by promising that I will now change the topic of conversation.

A.M.
Geneva, June 2006

Chronology

1475 6 March: birth of Michelangelo Buonarroti at small Tuscan town of Caprese where father Lodovico is Florentine-appointed administrator (*podestà*).

1481 Death of mother Francesca. Begins formal schooling, but shows stronger inclination for drawing and painting.

1488 Apprenticed to prominent Florentine painter Domenico Ghirlandaio.

1489–92 Trains as sculptor in the workshop of the Medici Garden of San Marco, directed by Bertoldo di Giovanni. Attracts attention of Lorenzo the Magnificent and comes into contact with humanist and Neoplatonist circle of Poliziano, Landino, Benivieni, Marsilio Ficino, Pico della Mirandola.

1492–4 Death of Lorenzo whose son Piero is less appreciative patron. Studies anatomy at Hospital of Santo Spirito. Works: *Battle of the Centaurs, The Madonna of the Steps* (relief sculptures), wooden crucifix for Santo Spirito.

1494–5 Travels to Venice and then to Bologna where he stays for a year. Medici expelled from Florence.

1496–1500 First stay in Rome at invitation of Cardinal Raffaello Riario. Brief visit to marble quarries of Carrara. Works: *Bacchus* for banker Iacopo Galli and *pietà* (now in St Peter's) for Cardinal Jean Bilhères de Lagraulas.

1501–5 Returns to Florence, now a republic under the leadership of the *gonfaloniere* (literally 'standard-bearer') Piero Soderini after theocratric interlude of Savonarola (executed 1498). Sculpts giant statue of *David*. Commissioned to fresco one wall of council chamber in Palazzo Vecchio; other wall assigned to Leonardo da Vinci. Fresco never completed, but cartoon, *Battle of Cascina* (now lost), is much admired and influences whole generation of Florentine painters. Other works: *St Matthew*, Doni *tondo* (only surviving easel painting), *Taddei Tondo*, Pitti *tondo*, Bruges *Madonna*. Earliest poems.

1505–7 Summoned to Rome by Pope Julius II who commissions him to build his tomb, originally intended for St Peter's. In April 1506 leaves suddenly for Florence after quarrel with pope. After six months in Florence, submits to pope in Bologna and makes large bronze statue of pontiff (later destroyed).

1508–12 Returns to Rome. Commissioned to fresco ceiling of Sistine Chapel which occupies him without a break from January 1509 to April 1512. Restoration of Medici in Florence.

1513–16 Death of Pope Julius II (1513). Makes second contract for the tomb with della Rovere family, heirs of Julius. Sculpts *Moses* and the *Captives*.

1516–19 Commissioned by new pope, Leo X, son of Lorenzo the Magnificent, to decorate façade of Medici family church of San Lorenzo in Florence. Arduous work in Carrara and Pietrasanta quarrying marble for the project which is eventually abandoned for lack of funds.

1519–20 Returns to Rome. Sculpts *Risen Christ* for Church of Santa Maria sopra Minerva.

1520–27 Back in Florence. Cardinal Giulio de' Medici (later Pope Clement VII) commissions more work in San Lorenzo, this time the Medici Chapel (new sacristy) for the family tombs, and later the Laurentian Library.

1527–30 Medici expelled and republic restored in Florence. Charged with overseeing fortifications of city. Death of beloved brother Buonarroto (1528). Military mission to Ferrara where Alfonso d'Este commissions painting of *Leda and the Swan* (now lost). Flees briefly to Venice in 1529, but soon returns to Florence and remains at his post until city surrenders to Medici.

1530–33 Pardoned by Clement VII for his adherence to the republic, resumes work in San Lorenzo. Also signs third

contract with heirs of Julius for modified and reduced version
of the tomb. During visit to Rome in winter 1532–3 meets
and falls in love with young nobleman Tommaso de'
Cavalieri. Beginning of most productive period for poetry
which lasts until 1547. Works of this last Florentine period
include the Laurentian Library, the statues in the Medici
Chapel (Dukes Lorenzo and Giuliano, *Night, Day, Dawn,
Dusk*), four *Captives* (now in the Accademia), the *Victory*
and several presentation drawings.

1534–41 Death of father Lodovico and definitive move to
Rome (autumn 1534). Freed from obligations of tomb by
new pope, Paul III, who commissions fresco of *The Last
Judgement* on east wall of Sistine Chapel, begun 1536 and
completed 1541. Meets Vittoria Colonna who becomes
second great addressee of his major poetry. Friendships with
Florentine political exiles such as Luigi del Riccio and Donato
Giannotti. In 1540 begins regular correspondence with
nephew Lionardo. Sculpts bust of *Brutus*.

1542–6 Signs fourth and last contract for the Julius tomb.
Begins work on frescos of Pauline Chapel (*Conversion of
St Paul* and *Crucifixion of St Peter*). With help of Riccio and
Giannotti prepares collection of poems, though not neces-
sarily for publication. Death of Riccio.

1547 Death of Vittoria Colonna. Poetic production becomes
more sporadic. Benedetto Varchi's lecture (published 1549)
on Sonnet 151. Assumes responsibility for construction of
St Peter's. Completes construction of Palazzo Farnese (left
unfinished by Antonio da Sangallo).
Much-reduced Julius tomb unveiled in the church of San
Pietro in Vincoli.

1548 Begins work on Florence *pietà*. From now on works
mainly as an architect, redesigning St Peter's, the Capitol,
Porta Pia.

1550 Publication of Vasari's *Lives*.

1553 Publication of Ascanio Condivi's *Life of Michelangelo
Buonarroti*.

1555 Much affected by death of Francesco Amadori (Urbino)
who had served him for twenty-six years. Defect in marble

forces him to abandon Florence *pietà*. Begins work on Rondanini *pietà*.

1564 Still working on Rondanini *pietà*. Dies 18 February, comforted by his pupil Daniele da Volterra and by Tommaso de' Cavalieri. Buried in Santa Croce, Florence, with imposing funeral ceremonies organized by the city's artists.

Introduction

THE LITERARY REPUTATION

The long life of Michelangelo Buonarroti (or 'Michelagniolo' as he usually signed himself) spans the period between the heyday of Florentine humanism and the advent of the counter-reformation. He was born in 1475, six years after Lorenzo the Magnificent had assumed power in Florence; he died in Rome in 1564, a year after the conclusion of the Council of Trent which had given a decisive impulse to the renewal of the Catholic Church. Given those dates, it is tempting to read the whole career as representative of a major cultural shift ideally imaged in the contrast between the adolescent sculptor copying ancient pagan statues in the Medici garden and the disenchanted old man of the penitential sonnets lamenting the error that has lured him into making 'an idol and a tyrant out of art' (285).[1] It was, however, from a relatively early age that Michelangelo struggled to reconcile the cult of beauty with a strongly religious and ascetic temperament. From the great humanists of the Medici circle that he frequented in his youth – men like Angelo Poliziano (1454–94), Pico della Mirandola (1463–94) or Marsilio Ficino (1433–99) – he aborbed Neo-platonic ideas about physical beauty as a manifestation of the ultimate beauty of the Good; but we know that by the time he was twenty he had already been impressed by the fiery sermons of the austere Florentine reformer Girolamo Savonarola (1452–98), who burned secular art upon the Bonfire of the Vanities and for whom any celebration of the body was to be condemned as a form of idolatry. The tension to which so much of

Michelangelo's poetry bears witness should not be simplified: the aesthetic and spiritual imperatives coexist in a shifting relation of confluence and conflict. This is not so much the traditional clash between the flesh and the spirit, but rather an unresolved debate between two forms of spirituality, one of which has a place for physical beauty that the other rejects. That in Michelangelo's case the beauty involved was predominantly masculine could only exacerbate the issue. It is no accident that the poem in which he makes the most extravagant claim for beauty as the *only* way to God (83) is also one in which he feels obliged to defend himself against accusations of sexual immorality.

To Michelangelo fame came early; it lasted throughout his career. Still in his twenties, he was already celebrated as the rival of Leonardo da Vinci in the cartoons for the Council Chamber of Florence and as the creator of the monumental statue of *David* that symbolized the city's republican spirit. At the time of his death, when he was almost eighty-nine, he was in charge of the construction of St Peter's, working on a number of other architectural designs and still chipping away at the Rondanini *pietà*. In the sixty intervening years he had been occupied with the Sistine Chapel, the tomb of Pope Julius II, the library and sacristy of San Lorenzo and a number of ambitious but frequently unfinished projects. Under the circumstances, it is hardly surprising that his life should be better documented than that of any other Renaissance artist, but the sheer extent of that documentation is nonetheless extraordinary. Our information comes from a wide variety of sources: the biographies written and published in his lifetime by Giorgio Vasari (1511–74) and Ascanio Condivi (1525–74), the conversations recorded by Donato Giannotti and Francisco de Hollanda, a correspondence that includes almost 500 letters by the artist himself, and finally the poetry. Michelangelo is the first visual artist to leave a significant body of literary work, and it is inevitable that we should read the poems in the hope of gaining greater insight into the workings of such a powerful and productive mind; indeed one of the things that distinguishes Michelangelo's poetry from that of his more conventional contemporaries is surely the sense of an intensely lived experience behind the literary text. Yet the poetry is likely to be both misunderstood and underestimated if we value it primarily or exclusively as direct self-revelation. Thomas Mann may have seen the emotional outbursts of a great soul rather than poems in the strict sense of the word,[2] but this does less than justice to Michelangelo's conscious artistry and neglects the influence of tradition and genre in shaping the poetic persona that Michelangelo projects in his verse. It would be pretentious and counterproductive to suggest that we ought to read the poetry without reference to the life, but we cannot entirely evade the question of whether it could stand on its own merits if we did not already know the author as sculptor, painter and architect.

The problem is, to some extent, already posed by Michelangelo himself. His explicit attitude towards his poetry is almost invariably self-deprecatory. He protests that writing is not his profession, asks a presumably more literary friend to polish up one of his madrigals, dismisses yet another poem as 'a poor thing' and jokes wryly with Vasari about the absurdity of an ageing artist devoting himself to sonnets. Manuscript evidence might at first seem to confirm this image of the casual amateur. As we see these poems, as often as not unfinished, jotted down next to some anatomical study, on the edge of some rapid architectural sketch or on the back of a bill, it is easy to get the impression that verse was quite literally a marginal activity for a mind and a hand that simply could not remain idle. But some of his finest poems, far from being tossed off in the spare time of which he had so little, are the result of five or six laborious reworkings.[3] Moreover, in his most productive period, between 1532 and 1547, he produced about 200 poems, enough to suggest that verse, at this stage, was a more or less constant concern. The collection of about a hundred poems (mostly madrigals), compiled with the help of his friends Luigi del Riccio and Giannotti between 1542 and 1546, may or may not have been intended for publication, but it surely shows that the artist took his verse seriously enough to have it ordered and preserved for posterity. As for Michelangelo's literary reputation in his own time, we find the burlesque poet Francesco

Berni (1497–1535) contrasting Michelangelo's intellectual substance with the merely verbal elegance of conventional Petrarchists ('He says things and you say words')[4] and the humanist Benedetto Varchi (1503–65) devoting a celebrated lecture to Poem 151.[5] Less than a dozen poems, however, saw print in the poet's lifetime. The elaborate staging of Michelangelo's funeral ceremonies in July 1564 included the erection of four female figures to represent painting, sculpture, architecture and poetry; but when the tomb was finally erected ten years later the muse of poetry had disappeared.

It was not until 1623 that a selection of the poems was finally published by his grand-nephew Buonarroti the Younger (1568–1646). This edition, while it had the merit of reminding posterity that Michelangelo was indeed a poet, went a long way towards obscuring the qualities that made the poems worth reading in the first place. Not only did Buonarroti the Younger limit his selection to less than half of the poems we know today, but he gave his grand-uncle's work a thorough cosmetic overhaul to make it fit the etiolated Petrarchan taste of the period: jagged fragments were blithely and tacitly completed, colloquialisms banished, metrical irregularities ironed out and tortuous syntax rendered straightforward; even the pronouns in the Cavalieri poems were changed to avoid any suspicion of homoeroticism. It was in this blandified and bowdlerized version that Michelangelo's poetry survived the next two centuries, while critical appreciation was reserved for a select group that included such major figures as Ugo Foscolo (1778–1827) and Wordsworth. Only in 1863, with the edition of Cesare Guasti, were readers finally given access to a text that derived from a scrupulous inspection of the poet's manuscripts. This was further improved by Carl Frey (1897), and in 1960 Enzo Noè Girardi produced the text that has remained the basis of all modern editions.[6]

This brief textual history has been necessary because it may help to explain why the status of Michelangelo as a poet has remained uncertain for so long. Even the emergence of an authentic text did not, in fact, have the automatic effect of reviving the reputation of the poetry. The edition of Buonarroti the Younger, precisely because it conformed to the traditional standards of Italian versifying, had at least been readable. What readers now discovered was a text that challenged their expectations, a rough surface that seemed to defy penetration to such an extent that, a hundred years after Guasti, Girardi still felt obliged to follow his example and provide each poem with a prose paraphrase. Thus, for much of the twentieth century, the sense remained of a genius working against his natural bent in a medium that he found uncongenial; and the result has been an unfortunate divorce between style and content. Dubious analogies with sculpture have been allowed to suggest poems hacked out of recalcitrant material. A slightly more sophisticated approach (echoing Berni's comment) has insisted on a body of work where intellectual power takes precedence over lyrical impulse – in Benedetto Croce's words, 'strong prose rather than song'.[7] But what we are now beginning to understand is that the power of these poems lies not so much in the ideas themselves (which, in paraphrase, are usually commonplaces of Renaissance thought) as in a profoundly innovative way with language that recreates those ideas as experience.

LANGUAGE AND FORMS

The language of sixteenth-century lyric poetry in Italy remained essentially that created by Petrarch (Francesco Petrarca, 1304–74) in his famous *Canzoniere*. This poetic sequence presents the poet's love for Laura in a language whose vocabulary is both central and restricted, avoiding the extremes of colloquial and erudite, carefully balanced between the concrete and the abstract. The syntax is relatively straightforward and the primary meaning plain. Above all, Petrarch's poetry is characterized by a remarkable unity of tone, a firmness of structure and an overriding musicality that provide at least aesthetic resolution to the conflicts that are its subject matter. Like other lyric poets of his time, Michelangelo inherited from Petrarch a whole battery of rhetorical devices and set phrases that have become known (often with unfairly negative connotations) as the 'Petrarchan conventions'. To take a few poems at random, sonnets 72, 76 and 77, according to a recent annotated edition, contain at least a dozen phrases that are obviously reminiscent of the *Canzoniere*. If Michelangelo stands apart from the prevailing Petrarchism of his time, it is not (as his admirers sometimes claim) that he is 'anti-Petrarchan', but rather that he has a more creative response to Petrarch than any of his contemporaries. Where then do the differences lie?

The first thing that strikes a reader who moves from Petrarch to Michelangelo is the sheer difficulty of reading. In the *Canzoniere* the wonderfully smooth surface offers such little resistance that, on a first reading, one is hardly aware of the text's underlying complexity. With many of Petrarch's less talented followers the smooth surface is all there is. With Michelangelo, on the contrary, the reader is frequently held up, obliged to struggle through inhabitual contractions, all-purpose conjunctions, dubious grammar, abrupt parentheses and generally tortuous syntax. The result, when it is not simply confusion, is a feeling for the importance of what is being said precisely because the saying cannot be taken for granted. Any plain affirmation that finally emerges does so with the explosive force of a flow that has been obstructed. Significantly, it is often when Michelangelo borrows imagery from his own profession that the resistance is most strongly felt. Take, for example, the opening of 153:

> It is not just the mould,
> empty of art, that waits to be full filled
> from the fire with molten silver or gold,
> and must be shattered for the work
> to be brought forth;

The Italian text has:

> Non pur d'argento o d'oro
> vinto dal foco esser po' piena aspetta,
> vota d'opra prefetta,
> la forma, che sol fratta il tragge fora.

If one were to attempt the impossible task of preserving the original word order, this would translate as something like: 'Not just, with silver or gold / conquered by fire, waits to be filled, / empty of completed work, / the mould which only broken brings it forth'. It takes some time to understand that the subject of the sentence is 'the mould' and that 'it' refers to 'the completed work'. As Christopher Ryan has pointed out, what the syntax does is almost to reverse the natural chronological order which would have given us the mould, empty of work, waiting to be filled by the molten metal.[8] The syntax enacts the arduous step-by-step retracing of a painful creative process back to its beginning. The heavy stresses on *sol fratta* (only broken) are mimetic of the violent effort needed to liberate the form. It is not inappropriate to remember the serious problems that Michelangelo had in casting the bronze statue of Pope Julius II.

This kind of reading, of course, does not always work with a poet as uneven as Michelangelo, since it is often difficult to distinguish between poems where the resistant texture is the result of conscious artifice or intuitive strategy and those where it is simply evidence of incompetence. A negative example would be 46, where impossibly vague pronominal reference destroys a promising analogy between the shaping force of the sculptor's hammer and the moral influence of his brother Buonarroto. And yet, when all due reservations have been made, there is a substantial body of poetry that justifies A. J. Smith's perceptive summing-up: 'What the obstructed text creates is the mood of the utterance – effort, struggle, the plea bursting out in the face of its own recalcitrance ... A very little attention to the arrangement of clauses will show how carefully the syntax has been managed to catch not merely the balances and emphases but the cadences, nuances, pitch of the mood.'[9]

Similar difficulties in distinguishing between artifice, intuition and inefficiency arise when we turn from Michelangelo's language to his handling of traditional forms and to the problem of the fragments. Though there are excursions into other forms such as the quatrain, the *ottava rima* stanza or the *terza rima* piece known as *capitolo*, the vast majority of the poems (over

200 out of 301) are either madrigals or sonnets. With the
madrigal, a relatively free-rhyming arrangement of long and
short lines (eleven and seven syllables), Michelangelo obviously
had little trouble; but the stricter form of the Italian sonnet,
with its structure of octave and sestet, appears to have been less
easily mastered. This, at any rate, is what might be deduced
from the fact that, along with the seventy-nine completed
sonnets, we find no less than thirty-seven poems that are usually
considered as unfinished or partial sonnets. But what are we to
make of a poem like 32?

> I live to sin, dying to myself I live;
> my life's not mine, but that of sin alone:
> heaven gave my good, my evil is my own,
> by my free will that I no longer have.
> My liberty has made itself a slave,
> my mortal part a god. O wretched man!
> to what a life, what misery was I born!

Since there is no established Italian form that corresponds to
this seven-line piece, it is hard to see it as other than the incom-
plete octave of a sonnet; and yet the thought is so complete in
itself that few readers will want to judge the poem as unfinished
on the basis of a purely formal criterion. Many critics have
been tempted to relate such poems to sculptures like the famous
Captives where the figures seem to be struggling to emerge from
a base of uncarved stone;[10] but, in fact, that analogy seems
more appropriate to the kind of resistant texture we looked
at in 153 than to the incomplete sonnets. We have, perhaps,
overestimated the importance of the fragments. If incompletion
is not always the vice the older critics thought it was, neither is
it the virtue that modern theory often takes it to be. Whatever
the case with his sculpture, there is little in the poetry to justify
the idea that Michelangelo cultivated anything like an aesthetics
of the unfinished. What the best of these supposedly incomplete
pieces do suggest is a fundamental artistic integrity that, con-
sciously or intuitively, will not allow a poetic statement to be
padded out in order to fit a pre-established form.

The poems of Michelangelo can be grouped in various ways according to the reader's focus of interest. Historians of Renaissance literature, for example, might well think in terms of his favourite forms: sonnet, madrigal, burlesque *capitolo*, elegiac quatrain, etc. Art historians and biographers might opt for a chronological division that would give us three periods: 1503–32, the relatively scarce production previous to the artist's definitive transfer to Rome; 1532–47, the great and prolific maturity that begins when he meets Tommaso de' Cavalieri (*c.* 1509–87) and ends with the death of Vittoria Colonna (1490–1547); 1547–60, an old age of sporadic though still powerful creation. But for the readers envisioned by this volume the most useful categorization is probably along the following broadly thematic lines.

1. Love poetry: a) for Tommaso de' Cavalieri; b) for Vittoria Colonna; c) for 'the beautiful cruel lady'
2. Religious poetry
3. Miscellaneous poems

The divisions are by no means hard and fast. The love poems are suffused with religion and the subdivision in terms of addressee is not always easy to establish. The same poem might serve equally well for Cavalieri or for Colonna, and even 'the beautiful cruel lady' could be Colonna in another guise. When all due caveats have been entered, however, the majority of the poems can still be clearly assigned to one of the three groups.

LOVE POETRY

In his late fifties Michelangelo met and fell in love with the handsome, cultured and impeccably virtuous Roman aristocrat Tommaso de' Cavalieri who was then in his early twenties. That Michelangelo's sexual orientation was what we would now call homosexual cannot be doubted; less clear are the implications of this for a deeply religious artist in sixteenth-century Rome. Sexual acts between men were strongly condemned and punished, but homosexuality as a concept did not yet exist. Men could, and did, express admiration for male beauty and passionate love for other men without exciting disapproval. Thus, though there is no sign that his affection for Michelangelo had any erotic component, Cavalieri still felt able to accept the older man's ardent homage with a good grace and with only an occasional hint of embarrassment. And yet malicious rumours about the nature of Michelangelo's relations with young men certainly did circulate in Rome since both the artist himself and his contemporary biographers go out of their way to refute them. We can only speculate about the truth behind those rumours, but it is hardly to be supposed that Michelangelo failed to recognize or was untroubled by the transgressive potential of his sexuality. Neoplatonism came to his rescue by teaching that love of beauty is a profoundly spiritual experience, since all transient human beauty is a reflection and creation of the eternal beauty of the Good which is to be identified with God. Moreover, love between men could be seen as possessing higher spiritual qualities than love between men and women, precisely because, in the natural order of things, it would be denied physical consummation (see sonnet 260). Michelangelo was not a philosopher and there is no real evidence to suggest that he was widely read in Neoplatonist thought, but we can be sure that the Neoplatonism he did absorb was essential to his self-definition and justification as lover and artist. It is a lived Neoplatonism, constantly put to the test by hard experience. Sonnet 83 is a striking blend of rapture and anxiety.

> Here in your lovely face I see, my lord,
> what in this life no words could ever tell;
> with that, although still clothed in flesh, my soul
> has often already risen up to God.
> And if the foolish, fell, malevolent crowd
> point others out as sharing their own ill,
> I do not cherish less this yearning will,
> the love, the faith, the chaste desire of good.

> To wise men there is nothing that we know
> more like that fount of mercy whence we come
> than every thing of beauty here below;
>   nor is there other sample, other fruit
> of heaven on earth; he who loves you with faith
> transcends to God above and holds death sweet.

The poem evokes eternity by its circular shape; both beginning
and ending with the soul that rises to God through the contem-
plation of Cavalieri's beauty. But intruding on that eternity,
like sneering echoes of the time-bound world, come the voices
of the crowd who read their own vices into the poet's ardour.
It is surely the anxiety aroused by those voices that provokes
the poet into his most extreme justification of the cult of beauty.
Beauty is not just a reflection of God's goodness and perfection;
it is a better reflection than anything else ('there is nothing that
we know / more like that fount of mercy'). And, not content
with seeing beauty as the best way to God, the poem goes on
to suggest that it is, indeed, the only way ('nor is there other
sample, other fruit / of heaven on earth'). At this stage, it might
look as if the progress of the poem has been from the particular
to the general, but the poem cannot be completed without a
return from meditation on beauty in the abstract to its starting
point in love of the specific beauty of Cavalieri: 'he who loves
you with faith / transcends to God above'. Though 'love with
faith' may be a perfectly conventional phrase, in this context it
has a faintly disturbing resonance, as if the poet were transfer-
ring to Cavalieri the love he owes to God and thus destroying
transcendence in the very moment when he proclaims it.

Sonnet 83 is not the only poem to reveal the problems
inherent in the relationship. Sonnet 58 suggests that he has been
'barred the precious company' of Cavalieri by the lying voices
of 'those who in others only see themselves'; and 60, with its
extraordinary stuttering start ('You know, my lord, that I know
that you know'), laments a situation that prevents the two
men from 'exchanging greetings'. Apart from the ending of 72,
where he longs to fold Cavalieri in 'these unworthy ready arms',

and the queasily jocular 94 in which he dreams of his skin being used as clothing for the one he loves, the poetry steers clear of anything like direct expression of physical desire.

Yet ultimately, despite the recurrent need to repel slanders and despite occasional doubts about the adequacy of his own response to the transcendent force of such beauty (77), the dominant mood of Michelangelo's poems for Cavalieri must still be seen as buoyant and optimistic. It is Cavalieri who enables him to proclaim 'I hold myself more dear than once I did' and whose love invests the poet with magical talismanic powers (90). Images of flight and elevation abound (59, 61, 62, 89). Above all, the vision of Cavalieri provides access to the universal and immortal form (105, 106) of the Beautiful and the Good. To a passionate temperament, starved until middle age of strong emotional attachments, the love for this young man (even if not reciprocated with the same intensity) must have seemed the fulfilment of his long yearnings and the living demonstration of the truth of the Neoplatonic doctrines that he had absorbed in his youth.

About five years after his first meeting with Cavalieri, Michelangelo came to know the second great object of his love poetry, Vittoria Colonna, Marchesa di Pescara, a widow in her late forties, known both for her literary talent and for her austere piety. With Colonna Michelangelo developed a profound spiritual and intellectual relationship that lasted until her death in 1547. The poems that he wrote for her are not, at first sight, significantly different from those addressed to Cavalieri. There is the same Neoplatonic insistence on the Beautiful as a way to God, the same concern for his own unworthiness, the same Petrarchan repertory of antitheses to express the emotional extremes of suffering and exaltation. Closer reading, however, suggests a subtle but unmistakable change of emphasis that may be illustrated by the madrigal 152:

> By what we take away, lady, we give
> to rugged mountain stone
> a figure that can live

and which grows greater where the stone grows less;
so, hidden under that excess
which is the flesh, the trembling soul
still contains some good works
that lie beneath its coarse and savage bark.
You only can extract them still
and free them from this outer shell
for in myself I find no strength or will.

Whereas Cavalieri brings ecstatic and transcendent vision, Colonna is seen more often as a reforming influence, shaping the poet's moral life. Here the poet is the matter from which she extracts a better form; elsewhere he is the rough model that she perfects (236) or the blank page on which she writes (162). Where Cavalieri had been celebrated for raising the poet in flight, Colonna is asked to descend towards him (156), to meet him halfway, as if it were consolation and companionship that he seeks rather than rapture. This new sense of dialogue and exchange may be suggested by Michelangelo's readiness to use the imagery of his own profession while at the same time borrowing some of the theological terminology ('good works') that was current in Colonna's reformist circle. After the Cavalieri poems, one may feel a certain slackening of nervous intensity, but this is accompanied by a considerable gain in contextual richness.

Finally, we have a somewhat loose grouping of love poems, some of which are usually described as being for 'the beautiful cruel lady'. Given Michelangelo's homoerotic leanings, it is highly unlikely that such a woman ever existed and one is tempted to dismiss her as a mere pretext for ingenious exercises in a late Petrarchan vein. This is, however, to overlook poems like the madrigal 263 with its violent opening ('A woman's beauty yet again / unleashes, lashes, spurs me on') and its bitter, disenchanted conclusion that old age is no protection against the assaults of sensuality ('once he has heard an echo of its voice, / being old won't help him without grace'). There is a toughness here that is more reminiscent of Dante's spiky rhymes

for the Stony Lady than of Petrarch's suave harmonies. We are
reminded that Michelangelo is one of the very great poets of
old age – its physical humiliations, its hard-learned renunci-
ations, its sudden destructive returns of lust and its weary
spiritual yearning.

RELIGIOUS POETRY

The religious poetry of Michelangelo's last creative period
(1547–60) is marked by the apparent rejection of love and art,
the two passions that are born of the poet's sensibility to human
beauty. The rejection of love need hardly surprise us and the
poet's feeling of guilt, though it may have been exacerbated by
his homosexuality, is certainly not determined by it. This kind
of recantation is, after all, a tradition that can be traced in
Renaissance poetry from the penitential sonnets of Petrarch
down to such English examples as Sir Philip Sidney's 'Leave
me, O love, that reacheth but to dust'. More puzzling to the
modern reader is the apparent rejection of art in poems 282,
283, 285 and 288, especially if we remember that Michelangelo
did, in fact, continue to exercise his profession until the last
weeks of his life. What Michelangelo is saying about art cannot,
in fact, be fully understood outside the theological context
of the Reformation debate over faith and good works. Both
Catholics and Lutherans agreed that no man could escape
damnation without faith in the saving grace that flows from
Christ's passion; but, whereas Catholics allowed good works a
secondary role, Luther had famously insisted on faith alone.
The devout reformist circle around Vittoria Colonna tended
towards the latter doctrine and its influence can be felt in many
of Michelangelo's later poems (280, 289, 292, 296), even if the
poet stops short of anything that could be construed as an
explicit challenge to Catholic orthodoxy. In the light of this
special emphasis on faith, art is rejected not because it is
inherently sinful, but because it risks becoming one of those
'good works' in which men place a misguided trust.

At the level of explicit statement, the final religious poems

present a bleakly pessimistic picture of a man who has lost
confidence in the virtues of his own profession, who is threat-
ened by the 'two deaths' of body and soul, and who is deeply
convinced of his own guilt and far from certain of grace. And
yet there is something in the manner of these poems that
counteracts the gloom they proclaim. This can, perhaps, be
demonstrated by juxtaposing a late religious poem (285) with
one written about twenty years earlier (87). The earlier poem
begins with a tangle of conflicting intentions that seems to make
clear statement impossible:

> I wish I willed what I will not, O Lord:
> a veil of ice hid between heart and fire
> quenches the flame and makes my page a liar;
> the pen is fruitless, by the works denied.

This recalls one of the poems addressed to Cavalieri ('You
know, my lord, that I know that you know', 60) and develops
a similar plea for a loving violence that will break down all
barriers to communion: 'You rend the veil, Lord, you break
down that wall'. It is not simply the image but the sheer nervous
energy that will remind the English reader of Donne's 'Batter
my heart, three-personed God'. Poem 285, by contrast, has a
clear, calm and unobstructed movement.

> Through stormy seas and in a fragile bark
> my life has reached at last the common port,
> where all must come to render their report,
> accounting for each good and evil work.

The Petrarchan navigation image has a reassuringly familiar
ring and the 'common port' speaks of a universal and compre-
hensible human condition rather than some inexplicable and
inextricable knot of emotions peculiar to the speaker. Certainty
of death and fear of damnation there may be, but there is no
veil or wall between the poet and his God 'whose arms were
opened for us on the cross'. It is not, however, the details of
the imagery that ultimately make the difference: the feeling of

assurance comes less from what is said than from the hard-won plainness of its saying.

MISCELLANEOUS POEMS

The poems that are habitually grouped in this holdall category are not numerous, but they show a readiness to experiment with a surprisingly wide variety of genres. It is clear, however, that Michelangelo has trouble with the longer forms. The mock-rustic love poem in the manner of Lorenzo de' Medici (54) has some genuinely funny passages, but is curiously uneven in tone; an ambitious attempt at an allegorical poem in *ottava rima* (67, not translated here) peters out after fourteen stanzas; the unfinished *terza rima* elegy on the death of his father (86) has an obvious biographical interest, but the sporadic moments of self-revelation hardly suffice to relieve what looks like a purely conventional filial piety. Modern readers are not likely to feel much more in tune with the forty-eight elegiac quatrains (nine translated here) that Michelangelo wrote on the death of Cecchino Bracci to please the boy's uncle, Luigi del Riccio, his own good friend and financial advisor. Though these poems often have a certain formal elegance, they are fatally repetitive and the strangely jocular comments that accompanied their sending ('For the salted mushrooms, since you don't want anything else'; 'This awkward thing, already said a thousand times, for the fennel') seem designed to distance the poet from any emotion that they might convey.

That leaves us with three small groups that might be described as poems of politics, poems of friendship and self-portraits. The first of these groups includes a vigorous denunciation of Roman corruption (10), a dark allegorical vision of Florence under the autocratic regime of Cosimo de' Medici (249), and the celebrated bitter reply to the minor poet Giovanni di Carlo Strozzi's compliment on the statue of *Night* in the Medici Chapel (247). Under poems of friendship one might want to place the insider joking with Berni and Sebastiano del Piombo (85), but more obvious examples are the two sonnets to Vasari (277, 299) and what is probably Michelangelo's last completed poem, the sonnet to Ludovico Beccadelli (300), which also pays moving tribute to the artist's faithful servant, Urbino. After the passion and profundity of his relations with Cavalieri and Vittoria Colonna, the sheer ease and urbanity of these poems show a Michelangelo refreshingly capable of milder emotions. Finally, separated by about forty years, are the two extraordinary self-portraits (5, 267), both of which may be seen as wry attempts to demystify the heroic figure of the artist that Michelangelo himself did so much to create. The first involves a graphic description of the physical difficulties of painting the Sistine Chapel and it is difficult not to think of the contrast between the triumphant nudities on the ceiling and their wretched hunchbacked creator with his paint-blotched face. The second is a violently scatological portrait of the artist as an old man. In both poems the deep resentment that has been controlled by Michelangelo's talent for grotesque comedy is allowed to emerge in the conclusion – 'this is no place for me, and I'm no painter' (5); 'poor, old and servant to another's will' (267).

In sonnet 84 Michelangelo makes explicit reference to the contemporary literary theory of the three styles, 'the high, the low, the middle'. The bulk of his verse is clearly in the high style suited to its elevated emotions; but the miscellaneous poems do more than enough to demonstrate his mastery of the other two and thus his thoroughly professional approach to the craft of poetry.

POETRY AND ART

Attempts to relate Michelangelo's poetry to his achievements as a visual artist are fraught with difficulty. The few poems that do refer to specific artworks (5, 14, 247) contain no information as to the artist's thematic choices or aesthetic options. Nor does the comparison of imagery take us very far. Flight is so obvious a metaphor for rapture (59, 61, 89) that there is no reason to connect it with the *Ganymede* drawing that Michelangelo gave to Cavalieri; the sheer weight of tradition would have made the arrows of love (59, 90, 272) and the bondage of the lover (25, 98) inevitable, even without the sketch of *Archers Shooting at a Herm* or the statues of the *Captives*; a devout Christian did not need to have painted the Sistine *Last Judgement* to think of God's 'stern arm' (290) being raised against sinners. Michelangelo was not a highly visual poet and most of his images are drawn from a stock of conventions that renders any significant connection with his visual art most unlikely.

Far more interesting is Michelangelo's use of sculpture as a metaphor, but the relevant poems have been ill-served by commentators who insist on reading them as a manifesto of art theory. The celebrated sonnet 151 is a case in point:

> The best of artists can no concept find
> that is not in a single block of stone,
> confined by the excess; to that alone
> attains the hand obedient to the mind.
> Noble and gracious lady, most divine,
> the evil that I flee and good I crave
> thus hide in you; but, that I may not live,
> my art proves contrary to my design.
> Not love then, nor your beauty or disdain,
> your harshness or my fortune or my fate
> or destiny is guilty of my pain,
> if in your heart at once you carry both
> mercy and death, and if my lowly wit,
> burning, draws from it nothing else but death.

I have quoted the whole poem precisely because nearly all the commentators, from Benedetto Varchi onwards, have limited their attention to the first quatrain, seen as a straightforward expression of the idea (more Aristotelean than Neoplatonic) that the artist, by revealing the hidden form, fulfils nature's unachieved potential. But what makes the poem interesting and moving is that, once stated, this idea of a single form inherent in the matter is called into question. Plurality takes over. If the lady is like a stone, then this stone hides an infinity of forms ranging from 'the evil that I flee' to 'the good I crave'; and so what finally emerges depends, after all, on the artist's own 'lowly wit'. It follows that either the theory in itself or the analogy between carving a stone and writing a poem for Vittoria Colonna must be false. No less than in Shakespeare's *Sonnets*, 'false compare' is a real issue. Michelangelo is not using poetry to make statements about art theory; he is using art theory to make poetry.[11]

THE LETTERS

Michelangelo wrote very few letters with any literary pretentions and was not usually concerned to express his intimate feelings outside his poetry. It is probably no accident that so few letters to Cavalieri or Vittoria Colonna have survived (Letters 29, 30, 40, 41). The letter was an essentially practical instrument to be used in the service of the two great constant concerns of his life: his professional work as an artist and the promotion of his family fortunes. Only with reluctance does he write about art theory (Letter 45 is the reply to a request he could hardly refuse) and he almost never says anything about the intentions behind a specific work. There are only occasional moments of jubilation when something turns out well or when he feels challenged by a new project. The casting of the bronze statue of Pope Julius II, after the expert Bernardino had tried and failed, produces a self-congratulatory 'in the hands of anyone else it would have turned out badly' (Letter 6), and the prospect of working on the façade of San Lorenzo excites him to claim 'it will be the mirror of all Italy for both architecture and sculpture' (Letter 15). The completion of his four-year stint on the Sistine Chapel ceiling, however, seems to deserve only a relatively downbeat comment: 'I have finished the chapel I was painting: the pope is very happy with it, but other things haven't turned out as well as I hoped' (Letter 11).

What the letters do document very fully are the complex vicissitudes of a career that saw Michelangelo coveted by both Rome and Florence, torn between the conflicting demands of

pope and duke, dogged by financial wrangles and frustrated by
large-scale projects that were later abandoned, like the façade
of San Lorenzo, or seriously sized down, like the tomb of
Julius II. Michelangelo, no doubt, must bear his own share of
blame for these disappointments: he seems to have had an
inveterate habit of biting off more than he could ever have time
to chew; if not actively dishonest, he was somewhat disingenu-
ous about money matters; he was notoriously cantankerous
and quick to take offence. Nevertheless, even if we need not
trust every word in the important self-justifying letters (Letters
3, 20, 24, 37), it is clear that he was often the victim of patrons
who embarked on ambitious projects and then modified or
dropped them as soon as the going got financially tough.
Michelangelo himself could certainly not be accused of shirk-
ing. The physical hardships he was prepared to undergo and
his sheer commitment to the work in hand are evident in the
remarkable series of letters (Letters 15–20) that recount his
toils in the quarries of Carrara and Pietrasanta, the dangers of
the excavation, the building of roads to bring the marble down
from the mountain and the hiring of barges for its shipment up
the Arno to Florence. As a master, Michelangelo appears to
have been demanding but fair, asking no more of others than
of himself. He complains bitterly about a 'little shit of a boy'
who is not cut out for the job and then characteristically calms
down in the postscript: 'If you speak to the boy's father, put it
to him nicely; say that he's a good boy, but too refined' (Letter
14). He denounces two workmen who have tried to cheat him
(Letter 4), but pays moving tribute to the faithful Urbino (Letter
62) and takes steps to support his widow.

His precocious fame and considerable earning power made
Michelangelo, by the age of thirty, the financial mainstay and
effective head of the Buonarroti family, deciding on investments
and the purchase of property, supporting his chronically un-
employed father and attempting to set up his brothers in the
wool trade. The letters show how seriously he took these res-
ponsibilities and how temperamentally ill-equipped he was for
them. The unrelenting practicality of their content is often
rendered even more indigestible by the nagging, self-pitying

tone, and it comes as a relief to the reader when the artist breaks out into violent denunciation of his unreliable father (Letters 22, 23) or his ne'er-do-well brother Giovansimone (Letter 8).

Relations with the family continued to be both close and tense right to the end when the recipient of the letters became his long-suffering nephew Lionardo. Lionardo is reproached for his bad handwriting, ticked off for sending a brass rule ('as if I were a mason or a carpenter', Letter 47) and even accused of wishing his uncle's death (Letter 38); he is also advised on the choice of a wife, commiserated on the death of a child and thanked for his gifts of food and wine.

Michelangelo's letters are written rapidly, under the pressure of events. The vocabulary is colloquial, the grammar slipshod and the sentences composed of loosely connected strings of main clauses. Grotesque humour rubs shoulders with pithy proverbial wisdom. Openings on to the emotional depths are rare, but when they do come they have an unguarded simplicity and force: a passing reference to Cavalieri provokes the comment 'if he faded from my memory, I think I should drop down dead' (Letter 31) and Vittoria Colonna is remembered as one 'who was devoted to me, and I no less to her. Death robbed me of a great friend' (Letter 53). Michelangelo could write a formal and decorous prose when he had to, but it would be hard to find another letter-writer in the period who gives us a such a strong sense of the living speaking voice.

VASARI'S LIFE OF
MICHELANGELO (1550)

A competent if unoriginal painter and architect, Giorgio Vasari owes his fame to his pioneering *Lives of the Most Excellent Italian Architects, Painters and Sculptors from Cimabue down to the Present Day* (1550), a work that has guaranteed his status as one of the founding fathers of art history. That Michelangelo, the only living artist included, should be chosen to conclude the book is not simply a matter of bringing the story up to date. Vasari, as the majestic opening to the Life of Michelangelo reminds us, sees the history of Italian art as a development that begins in the thirteenth century and leads up to God's merciful gift to the world of a genius capable of bringing all the visual arts to their final perfection. It is not a context that inspires any great faith in the historian's objectivity and, indeed, the Life needs to be read with considerable caution. The account of Michelangelo's flight from Rome in 1506 can be dismissed as largely fanciful; the long-drawn-out wrangle over the tomb of Pope Julius is downplayed; other aspects of the career are misrepresented to avoid offending Vasari's Medici patrons; dates are sometimes inaccurate. And yet the Life remains essential for any serious student of Michelangelo. It tells us, for example, a great deal about the specific qualities of his art that excited the admiration and wonder of his contemporaries: the anatomical precision of the figures in the Medici Chapel, the expressivity of gesture in the prophets and sibyls of the Sistine Chapel, the awesomeness (*terribilità*) of the statues of *Moses* and Pope Julius II, the sense of movement in the *Battle of Cascina* cartoon (especially the soldier pulling on his hose), the technical difficulties overcome in the painting of Jonas leaning backward on a vault that curves inward. It also offers a rich selection of anecdotes that give us a real sense of Michelangelo's growing reputation as the eccentric and asocial artist-hero. The splendid story of the painter throwing planks at the pope is certainly untrue, but what counts is that it is the sort of thing people said and believed about Michelangelo.

Michelangelo was flattered by the Life and grateful to its author who became a good personal friend (277, 299), but he was not entirely satisfied with its account of his career. As we can see from the Letters, he had a compulsive need to justify himself, especially with regard to the convoluted history of the Pope Julius tomb. As a result, we have the Life that Ascanio Condivi published in 1553 and which seems to have been largely authorized if not dictated by the artist himself. Vasari's second edition of the *Lives* (1568) provided a much-extended account of the Life of Michelangelo and made certain corrections in the light of Condivi's biography. I have, however, decided to use the 1550 version and this for a number of reasons. The 1568 Vasari text is too long to fit comfortably into a volume whose primary purpose is to offer a selection of Michelangelo's own writings, and it is, in any case, readily available in English, whereas the 1550 version has been unaccountably neglected. Moreover, the 1550 version has a value of its own: it was designed to be the conclusion of a monumental enterprise (a position it loses in 1568) and it has a special status as the world's first biography of a living artist. It thus marks, as neither Condivi nor the 1568 text can, the first and most important step in the literary creation of the Michelangelo legend.

NOTES

1. Numbers in brackets refer to Michelangelo's poems.
2. Thomas Mann, *'Michelangelo in seinen Dichtungen'* ('Michelangelo in his Poems'), first published in the Zurich review *Du*, 1950.
3. For a discussion of these revisions, see Glauco Cambon, *Michelangelo's Poetry: Fury of Form* (Princeton, 1985).
4. The phrase quoted occurs in a verse-letter from Berni to which Michelangelo replied. See note to poem 85.
5. Benedetto Varchi, *Due lezzioni* (*Two Lectures*, 1549), trans. in John Addington Symonds, *The Renaissance in Italy*, vol. 2 (New York, 1893).
6. *Le Rime di Michelangelo Buonarroti*, ed. Cesare Guasti (Florence, 1863); *Die Dichtungen des Michelagniolo Buonarroti*, ed. Carl Frey (Berlin, 1897); *Michelangiolo: Rime*, ed. Enzo Noè Girardi (Bari, 1960).
7. Benedetto Croce, *'La lirica cinquecentesca'*, *La letteratura italiana*, ed. Mario Sansone (Bari, 1963), vol. 1, p. 363.
8. Christopher Ryan, *The Poetry of Michelangelo* (London, 1998), p. 151.
9. A. J. Smith, *The Metaphysics of Love: Studies in Renaissance Poetry from Dante to Milton* (Cambridge, 1985), p. 173.
10. There are four of these *Captives* in the Accademia, Florence, and one in the Casa Buonarroti, Florence. These are not to be

confused with the two far more finished statues of *Slaves* in the Louvre, Paris.

11. For my reading of sonnet 151 I am much indebted to Colin Burrow for his essay 'Why Shakespeare is not Michelangelo', *Thinking with Shakespeare: Comparative and Interdisciplinary Studies*, ed. William Poole and Richard Scholar (Oxford, 2007).

Further Reading

Translations

Bull, George, 'Life of Michelangelo Buonarroti', in *Giorgio Vasari: Lives of the Artists* (Harmondsworth, 1987). The most readable translation of the 1568 *Lives*.

—, 'Ascanio Condivi: Life of Michelangelo Buonarroti', in *Michelangelo: Life, Letters, Poetry* (Oxford, 1987). An essential complement to the Vasari biography.

Clements, Robert J., *Michelangelo: A Self-Portrait* (New Jersey, 1963). Useful anthology of extracts from contemporary accounts and from Michelangelo's own writings; arranged thematically and translated by various hands, including Clements himself.

Ramsden, E. H., *The Letters of Michelangelo*, two vols. (London and Stanford, 1963). Monumental scholarly edition with excellent appendixes that situate the letters in their biographical, cultural and social context.

Ryan, Christopher, *Michelangelo: The Poems* (London, 1996). Bilingual edition. A lucid and scrupulous prose translation of the entire corpus.

Saslow, James M., *The Poetry of Michelangelo, An Annotated Translation* (New Haven, 1991). Bilingual edition. Stimulating introduction and abundant notes compensate for a translation that hovers uneasily between verse and prose.

On the Poetry

Cambon, Glauco, *Michelangelo's Poetry: Fury of Form* (Princeton, 1985). Not a book for the beginner, but valuable for its perceptive analysis of Michelangelo's revisions.

Clements, Robert J., *The Poetry of Michelangelo* (New York, 1965). A pioneering study of the poetry, still useful despite Clements' strange recourse to some wildly inaccurate and disparate English translations.

Ryan, Christopher, *The Poetry of Michelangelo* (London, 1998). Combines a firm grasp of the context with illuminating close readings of individual poems. Especially informative on the theological background.

Smith, A. J., 'Matter into grace: Michelangelo the love poet', in *The Metaphysics of Love: Studies in Renaissance Love Poetry from Dante to Milton* (Cambridge, 1985), pp. 150–76. The best brief introduction for an English reader of Michelangelo's poetry.

General

Bull, George, *Michelangelo: A Biography* (London, 1996). The standard English biography.

Hibbard, Howard, *Michelangelo*, 2nd edn. (Harmondsworth, 1985). Well-written overview of the art with useful passing reference to the poetry.

King, Ross, *Michelangelo and the Pope's Ceiling* (London, 2002). Lively, well-researched and refreshingly iconoclastic account of the creation of Michelangelo's famous fresco.

Murray, Linda, *Michelangelo* (London, 1980). Good on the symbolism of the major works.

Salmi, M., ed., *The Complete Work of Michelangelo*, two vols. (London, 1966). Essays by various scholars to mark fourth centenary of the artist's death. Lavishly illustrated.

Summers, David, *Michelangelo and the Language of Art* (Princeton, 1981). Examines significant words and concepts used by Michelangelo's contemporaries to discuss his art.

Tolnay, Charles de, *The Art and Thought of Michelangelo* (New York, 1964). Digest of a lifetime's work by the greatest of modern Michelangelo scholars.

A Note on the Texts

In a letter of 1805 Wordsworth pointed out the three major difficulties that face any translator of Michelangelo's poetry: the obscure and contorted syntax which is 'most difficult to construe', 'the majesty and strength' that Michelangelo shares with Dante and that is so different from the smooth musicality of the Petrarchan tradition, and, finally, the sheer compression of the utterance: 'so much meaning has been put by Michael Angelo into so little room, and that meaning so excellent in itself that I find the difficulty of translating him insurmountable'.[1] The comment is so perceptive that the modern translator can supply little more than a wry nod of agreement. Michelangelo is a difficult poet even for Italians and in trying to make him accessible in English one is always threatened by the twin devils of paraphrase and periphrasis. I have tried to produce readable and comprehensible English verse without entirely eliminating that feeling of a resistant text which is central to our experience of Michelangelo's poetry.

Rhyme is always a problem for English translators, but forms like the sonnet and the madrigal tend to dissolve once it has been abandoned. Here, as in my earlier translations of Petrarch, I have opted for the compromise solution of blending full rhyme with every possible variety of consonantal or assonantal echo. Where I have found the original rhyme scheme too constricting I have felt free to modify it or even to allow myself the occasional unrhymed line. It is the overall feel of the rhyme scheme that I have sought rather than its faithful reproduction.

With the letters I have gone further than previous translators in the direction of contemporary colloquial speech, while with

Vasari I have preserved as much of the sometimes magniloquent syntax as is compatible with respectable modern usage.

For the text of the poems I have relied on *Michelangiolo Buonarroti: Rime*, ed. Enzo Noè Girardi (Bari, 1960). Numbering and division into poems and fragments follow this edition.

The standard text of the letters is in *Il Carteggio di Michelangelo*, ed. Paola Barocchi and Renzo Ristori, five vols. (Florence, 1965–83). A more accessible edition is *Michelangiolo Buonarroti: Lettere*, ed. Enzo Noè Girardi (Arezzo, 1976). Fuller annotation than is given here can be found in the two-volume Ramsden translation (see Further Reading). Material within square brackets is editorial. I have numbered the letters consecutively. Ramsden and Girardi numbers (R and G) are given after each letter.

The 1550 text of Vasari's Life of Michelangelo is in *Giorgio Vasari: Le Vite de' più eccellenti architetti, pittori, et scultori italiani, da Cimabue, insino a' tempi nostri*, ed. Luciano Bellosi and Aldo Rossi, two vols. (Turin, 1986).

NOTES

1. *The Letters of William and Dorothy Wordsworth*, ed. E. de Selincourt, Rev. Chester L. Shaver, Mary Moorman and Alan G. Hill (Oxford, 1967), vol. 1, pp. 628–9.

POEMS

POEMS

How joyful is the garland finely tressed
with flowers linked to crown her golden hair,
each pressing close upon the one before
to kiss her head, vying to be the first!
    Happy all day the gown that clasps her breast   5
and then below floats freely to the air,
and that spun gold, the net delighting where
it touches cheeks and neck and never rests.
    But surely happier the ribbon placed
with golden tips in a such a lucky manner   10
to press and touch the breast where it is laced.
    And round her waist the simple girdle seems
to whisper low: here let me cling forever.
Just think what I could circle with my arms.

1507

5

I've got a goitre from this job I'm in –
bad water does it up in Lombardy
to peasants, there or in some other country –
because my belly's shoved against my chin.
    Beard skyward, nape of neck pressed back upon   5
my hump, I'm hollow-chested like a harpy;
the brush keeps dripping till my face looks gaudy,
more like mosaic than anything you'd tread on.
    Somehow my loins have climbed into my gut,
and as a counterweight I use my arse,   10
and where my feet are going eyes don't know.
    In front my hide is all stretched out and tight,
behind my bending makes it floppy loose,
and I'm as curved as any Syrian bow.
        No wonder that my mind is so   15
far out of joint that it gets nothing right;

show me the crooked barrel that shoots straight.
        Giovanni, now you know my state,
defend my poor dead painting and my honour;
20   this is no place for me, and I'm no painter.

                                        1509–12

6

My lord, if one old proverb's true, it's this:
nobody wants to do the thing he can.
You listen to mere words and fabling men,
rewarding those who are truth's enemies.
5   I am your old true servant, always was,
bound to you as the rays are to the sun,
and you heed not the time I spend in vain,
and still the more I strive the less I please.
        Once, through your highness, I had hoped to ascend
10   to where, at need, just scales and potent sword,
and not an echoing voice, would answer me.
        But now it must be heaven that scorns to send
virtue into the world, if it asks men
to pluck the fruit from such a withered tree.

                                        C.1511

10

From chalices they're forging helm and sword,
Christ's blood is sold in buckets, and round here
the cross and thorns become the shield and spear,
yet for all this Christ's patience has endured.
5   But let him come no more down this old road
to see the sky-high price his blood would bear,
since here in Rome they sell his skin so dear,
and every way is closed to every good.
        If ever I sought ruin, now's the time;

my work's all gone, and he who wears the mantle   10
can play Medusa's petrifying game;
   but if high heaven is pleased with poverty,
can our great restoration ever come
under a sign that quells the life to be?

Date uncertain

14

Day and Night speak and say – With our rapid course we have
brought to death Duke Giuliano; it is only right that he should
take revenge on us as he does. And the revenge is this: that
since we killed him, he has taken the light from us, and by
closing his eyes he has sealed ours, which no longer shine upon
the earth. What, then, would he have done for us, had he lived?

c.1524

18

Countless the soul tries remedies in vain:
since I was taken from the ancient road,
it strives and fails to find the path again.
The sea, the mountain and the fiery sword:
amid all these, surrounded, I live on.   5
The mountain is denied to me by one
who took away my reason and my mind.

1522

21

Whoever's born on earth arrives
at death with time that passes on;
the sun leaves nothing here alive.
Pleasure is past and pain is gone,

5   and all the thoughts and words of man,
           and all the glories of his line,
           mere smoke and shadows in the sun.
           Men you are, and so you must
           be sad and happy, as were we;
10   what we now are, come and see;
           dirt in sunshine, lifeless dust.
                   All things come to death at last.
           Once these eyes were round and full,
           their sockets held life's light and prime;
15   now black holes in a horrid skull,
           and this is the great work of time.
                                                    Date uncertain

25

Bound by a cruel lord in bitter chains,
a servant hopeless in captivity,
inured by habit to such misery,
would hardly ask for liberty again.
5   Tiger and serpent too habit restrains,
and the fierce lion in the forest born;
and the young artist, overworked and worn,
through sweating habit double strength obtains.
          But fire knows no such law; for though it will
10   consume the sap in green and growing wood,
it feeds the dry old stick and warms his chill,
          urges him back at last to his green youth,
renews, rejoices and inflames him still,
wrapping his heart and soul in love's sweet breath.
15   And should someone in mirth
jeer that to love a thing divine brings shame
if one is old, it is a lying claim.
          The soul that does not dream
commits no sin in loving things of nature,
20   weighing them well with due restraint and measure.
                                                    Date uncertain

32

I live to sin, dying to myself I live;
my life's not mine, but that of sin alone:
heaven gave my good, my evil is my own,
by my free will that I no longer have.
    My liberty has made itself a slave,   5
my mortal part a god. O wretched man!
to what a life, what misery was I born!

                                      1525

34

This love I live is nowhere in my heart,
my love for you with heart can have no share;
it cannot stay with what is mortal, where
it meets with error and with evil thought.
    When both our souls left God, in you Love
        wrought   5
splendour and light, in me a perfect eye;
my great desire cannot fail to see
God living in, alas, your dying part.
    Heat cannot be divided from the flame,
eternal beauty from my vision, which   10
exalts those who resemble whence it came.
    Since in your glance you hold all paradise,
I burn to go back where I loved you first,
and run to find myself before your eyes.

                                        1526

37

In me is death, in you my life must be;
you mete and measure and determine time;
my life is short or long as you decide.
    And I am happy in your courtesy.
Blest is the soul in which there runs no time,
being formed by you for contemplating God.
                                    Date uncertain

41

Spirit well born, the mirror where is seen,
in your chaste limbs, so lovely and so dear,
what nature and heaven can accomplish here
when they create a work that yields to none:
    fair spirit, where we trust to find within
those qualities that in the face appear,
love, kindness and compassion, things so rare,
never before with beauty thus made one:
    Love seizes me and beauty binds me fast;
kindness, compassion, in your sweet regard,
appear to give the heart firm grounds for trust.
    What custom or what law on earth,
what cruelty now or ever could forbid
that such a lovely work be spared by death?
                                    1529–30

42

I beg you, Love, to tell me if my eyes
see truly the true beauty that I seek,
or if it's here within, for when I look
I see carved everywhere that woman's face.
    You must know this; to take away my peace,

you come along with her, at which I break
out into anger; yet I would not lack
a single sigh or wish a fire less fierce.
   – The beauty that you see does come from her,
but in a better place it learns to grow,   10
ascending to the soul through mortal eyes.
   There it becomes lovely, divine and pure,
like the immortal part that wills it so:
this and not that now comes before your eyes.

1529–30

46

If my rough hammer shapes from the hard stone
some human form, it is the master who
gives it that movement, guides and holds it too,
so it proceeds with motion not its own.
   But with its working one in heaven divine   5
makes others beautiful, itself more so;
a hammer makes a hammer, there is no
hammer not made by that first living one.
   And since the blow has more effective might
the higher it is lifted at the forge,   10
so this has risen to heaven above my own.
   Thus mine will fail and cannot be complete,
unless the heavenly smithy lend him force
to make it so, who worked on earth alone.

1528

48

As flames flare higher, buffeted by wind,
so every virtue that is prized by heaven
will shine the more the more it is maligned.

Date uncertain

49

Your beauty, Love, is not a mortal thing:
there is no face among us that can match
the image in the heart you rule and touch
with other fire, move with other wings.

1527–30

52

If in the world self-slaughter were allowed
for any hoping to gain heaven through death,
it would be just for one who with such faith
lives in a sad and wretched servitude.
But since man is no phoenix, not restored
to the sun's light, reborn and coming forth,
my feet are sluggish and my hand is loath.

1531

53

A man who rides at night by daytime should
refresh himself sometimes with rest and slumber:
I trust to see my life and soul restored,
after so many trials, by my master.
No evil lasts where there's no lasting good,
but one is often changed into the other.

1531

54

I do believe, if you were made of stone,
loved with a faith like mine, you would awake,
jump to it, come and join me at a run;

if you were dead, then I would make you speak,
and if you were in heaven I'd pull you down   5
with sighs and tears and all the prayers I'd make.
But since you're here in flesh and blood, alive,
when can your loving servant hope to thrive?

I can do nothing else but follow you,
a noble quest, I don't regret the bother.   10
You're not some tailor's dummy put on view,
where they move first one part and then another;
if reason guides you, as it ought to do,
you'll make me happy one day or the other:
for honest service heals the serpent's bite,   15
like sour grapes that put the toothache right.

There's nothing that withstands humility,
love has a force no cruelty can resist;
harshness is always overcome by pity,
as joy will conquer sorrow at the last;   20
without a heart to match, a noble beauty,
new to the world like yours, could not exist;
a sheath that looks dead straight and fairly made
can't be the scabbard for a crooked blade.

I've done you such good service, it can't be   25
that you're not pleased a bit or just don't care;
look anywhere you like and you will see
that faithfulness in friends is something rare;
[. . .]
[. . .]   30
[. . .]
[. . .]

When I'm without you for a single day,
wherever I may be, I get no rest;
I see you and I get the gripes the way   35
a starving man does when he sees a feast.
[. . .]

[. . .]
like emptied bowels when a man can't wait,
40   there's greater ease because the pain was great.

There's not a single day when I don't greet
and see and hear her in my mind at will;
no furnace or no oven has a heat
that my sighs couldn't blow far higher still;
45   and if she comes around where we might meet
I start to give off sparks like molten steel;
then there's so much to say and I'm so worried
that I say less than if I weren't so hurried.

If sometimes she unbends with half a smile
50   or greets me in the middle of the road,
ignited like a cannon or a pile
of gunpowder, I suddenly explode;
one question from her and I'm gasping, while
my voice is blocked with all that should've flowed
55   in my reply; and then I lose all hope,
desire gives up because I just can't cope.

I feel within myself a love so great
that it could lift me to the stars above,
but when I sometimes try to bring it out,
60   no hole that's in my skin proves large enough
to stop love seeming smaller than I thought
and less than marvellous my rhyming stuff:
for grace alone gives love one can express;
whoever flies the higher says the less.

65   I think a lot about my past, my prime,
and how I was before I fell in love:
nobody thought that I was worth his time,
I mooched about all day from morn to eve;
did I think then that I would take up rhyme
70   or snub the common crowd and take my leave?
But now it seems my name is everywhere;
for good or ill, at least men know I'm there.

You entered me through weeping eyes just like
a bunch of sour grapes that's crammed inside
a bottle with a very narrow neck   75
and then expands because the belly's wide;
and so in me your image goes to work
like inner fat stretching a swelling hide:
and since you came through such a slender spout,
I hardly dare to think how you'll get out.   80

Think about air inside a ball – how, when
the valve's blown open from outside, the same
breath on the inside closes it again:
just so, I feel, your lovely image came
in through the eyes it opened up and then   85
locked itself in my soul by closing them:
think how a ball, struck at first bounce, will rise;
I'm bounced to heaven by your striking eyes.

Praise from one lover never satisfies
a lovely woman, she will always fear   90
that with her death her fame for beauty dies;
for all the love and reverence I bear,
the lame can't follow where the slowcoach flies,
and all my skill's too cheap for worth so dear:
the sun does not revolve to bring its light   95
to one man only, but for all men's sight.

How you can burn my heart I still don't know,
passing through eyes so wet they should put out
your burning glances and a bonfire too.
All that I try in my defence falls short: 100
if fire burns water, nothing else will do
to heal the ill that I desired and sought
but fire itself. How often, strange but sure,
a fire-scorched heart needs fire for its cure!

c.1531–2

55

I've bought you something simple that they sell
at no small cost because it smells so sweet;
I often find my way around by smell.
So if, while I'm away, you wanted out,
I'd pardon you, for I could always tell
your hiding place without the slightest doubt:
just keep this with you, and make up your mind:
I couldn't fail to find you, even blind.

1530–31

58

If the immortal wish that guides above
the thoughts of men could make mine manifest,
it might raise pity in the pitiless
lord who alone rules in the house of Love.
But since by law divine the soul must live
while body shortly dies, the senses miss
the soul's true value and cannot express
full praise of fullness they do not perceive.
Alas, how therefore shall the chaste desire
that burns within my heart be ever heard
by those who in others only see themselves?
I'm barred the precious company of my lord
who heeds their lies; because, in truth, the liar
is one who, hearing truth, still won't believe.

For TC. 1532–3

59

If one chaste love, one pity pure, sublime,
should link two lovers in a single fate,
if one harsh destiny affects two hearts,
and if one will, one spirit, governs them;
    if one soul in two bodies can become   5
eternal, so that both are raised in flight
to heaven on like wings, if love's gold dart
searches their reins and strikes them with its flame;
    if neither loves himself, but each the other
with one delight, one relish, and both set   10
their wills towards one single end forever:
    this multiplied by thousands would not make
one hundredth of our faith, our love's true knot,
that only scorn can still untie or break.

For TC. 1532

60

You know, my lord, that I know that you know
that here I come more closely to enjoy you,
and who I am you know I know you know:
what keeps us from exchanging greetings then?
    If all the hope you give me be not vain,   5
not vain the great desire you bestow,
let the wall break that stands between the two,
for hidden troubles breed a double pain.
    If, my dear lord, in you I only love
what in yourself you love, show no disdain: 10
one spirit's love is by another blest.
    What in your lovely face I learn and crave,
what human minds can scarcely understand –
whoever would know this must know death first.

For TC. 1532

61

If I had thought when first I saw the sun
of that blest phoenix I should be renewed
by the same fire that wastes me, like the bird
who in old age is burned to be reborn,
as a swift leopard, stag or lynx will run
to flee a danger or to seek some good,
to his fair motions, words and smile I would
have sped, but now am prompt yet slow to turn.
But why should I still mourn, since I have seen
that only in this blithe angel's eyes there live
my peace, my rest and my salvation's light?
Perhaps in earlier days it would have been
worse to have seen and heard him; now he gives
me wings like his to follow his strong flight.

For TC. 1532

62

Only with forging fire can the smith bend
the loved work to his concept's mastery,
nor without fire can the artist see
the gold into its purest state refined;
nor could the phoenix, unless first it burned,
be born again; thus if I burn and die,
I hope to rise with that bright company
whom death exalts and time does not offend.
This fire I speak of, by good fortune, lies
within me still with power to renew
one who is almost numbered with the dead.
Since fire to its own element must rise
by nature, and since I am fire too,
how can it fail to bear me to the skies?

For TC. 1532

63

Cold stone and inner fire are two such friends
that if, once fired by the spark it gives,
the stone is burned and broken, still it lives
as that by which eternal stones are bound.
If it survive the furnace, it will stand   5
through summer and winter and more precious
      prove,
like some new soul among the blest above,
purged of its sins, from hell to heaven returned.
So with my fire that plays its secret game;
if it burst out, then I must be dissolved,   10
and yet, thus burned and spent, more life I hold.
And if, reduced to smoke and dust, I live,
I shall be made eternal in the flame,
being struck not out of iron, but of gold.

For TC or VC. Date uncertain

64

If fire makes iron melt and shatters stone,
being child of that same hardness, how much more
will hotter fire than hell's consume and burn
a weaker foe, this sheaf of dried-up straw?

Date uncertain

66

Perhaps so others might awake my pity,
that others' faults I should no more deride,
through trusting my own strength, no other guide,
my soul is fallen that was once so worthy.

5   Fighting for mere escape, not victory,
     unless your power comes to take my side,
     I know not in what flag I should confide
     against the crowding, shouting enemy.
         O flesh, O blood, O wood, O ultimate pain,
10   in you may all my sin be justified,
     sin I was born to as my father's seed.
         Sole good, may now your supreme pity deign
     to succour my predicted evil state,
     so near to death and yet so far from God.

                                              1532

                          71

     Yes, I received it, thank you for your pains,
     and twenty times I've read all you have written.
     May nature give you teeth, for what you've bitten
     you still can't chew, but spit it out again.
5   Since we last met I've learned, in fact, that Cain
     was the great founder of your family tree,
     and you're no bastard offspring, since you see
     as your own loss whatever others gain.
         Like all proud envious enemies of heaven,
10   you cannot bear your neighbours' charity
     and only seem in love with your own ruin.
         Think of the Poet, what he had to say
     about Pistoia, that's enough; and even
     if you praise Florence you're not fooling me.
15   A precious jewel, I agree,
     but one that vulgar minds can't comprehend,
     and not a place that needs you for a friend.

                                            1532–4

72

If, when we look into a face, we find
that eyes reveal the heart, then nothing shows
my flame more clearly; so let this suffice,
dear lord, to ask for mercy at your hand.
  Your soul, perhaps, more willing to respond   5
than I dare hope to the chaste fire that glows
within me, will have pity and draw close,
since, for all those who ask it, grace abounds.
  If this be true, then O the happy day!
Let time suspend its days and hours that moment,   10
the sun stop short upon its ancient way;
  that I may have, and not for my own merit,
my sweet and longed-for lord forever stay
folded in these unworthy ready arms.

For TC. 1533

76

I do not know if what the spirit feels
is its first maker's long-desired light,
or if the glimmer of some beauty caught
amid the crowd is what the heart recalls;
  or whether fame or dreaming now reveals,   5
before my eyes and present to the heart,
someone – who knows? – some lingering burning
          smart,
and this is why my tears begin to fall.
  All that I feel and seek and who may lead
me there is quite beyond me, not to be found,   10
though someone else may show me where it lies.
  Here's how I am since I saw you, my lord,
moved by a bitter sweet, a yes and no:
the cause, of course, can only be your eyes.

For TC. 1533

77

If fire were equal to the loveliness
that burns in your bright eyes from whence it came,
the coldest regions of the world would flame
like fiery arrows flaring as they pass.
5   But heaven, ever pitying our distress,
for all the beauties that in you it frames
has made our power of vision weak and lame,
so as to soothe life's mortal bitterness.
No fire can match the beauty heaven sends,
10   for man can only be inflamed to love
as much of beauty as he comprehends.
So, in old age, it is with my desire:
if I seem not to burn and die for you,
my partial vision lights a feeble fire.

For TC. 1533

78

From sweet lamenting to a suffering smile,
from an eternal to a passing peace
now am I fallen: for when truth has ceased
to speak, the senses rule the severed soul.
5   I know not where the blame lies for this ill
which, as it grows more fierce, displeases less,
whether in my own heart or in your face
or in the eyes that fire from heaven stole.
Your beauty is not mortal, but was made
10   in heaven to give us proof of work divine;
thus, though I yearn and burn, there's comfort too
that I could do no other at your side.
If arms to kill me are of heaven's design,
who, if I die, could put the blame on you?

For TC. 1533

79

O happy spirit, who with eager flame
quicken my heart already ripe for death,
and, amid all the joys that bless your youth,
greet me alone before more noble names;
as once to eyes, now to the mind you come   5
and bring me solace through another's breath,
thus hope the wakeful suffering may soothe
that's no less felt than is desire's dream.
Since he who speaks for me finds grace for me
in you, despite the world of cares you have,   10
now he who writes to you must thank your grace.
For it would be disgraceful usury
to give you some base pictures and receive
a lovely living person in their place.

For TC. 1533

80

I thought that day when first I saw displayed
so many beauties, singular each one,
my eagle eyes might gaze upon the sun,
fixing the least of all that I desired.
But then I learned how I had sinned and erred: 5
to follow wingless where an angel's flown
would be as vain as casting seed on stone,
words on the wind and the mind on God.
If infinite beauty then cannot abide
the heart so near, while dazzling the eyes,   10
and yet from far does nothing to relieve me,
what will become of me? and in what guide
shall I find help to deal with power like yours,
burning when near and killing when you leave me?

Possibly for TC. 1533

81

All that I see gives counsel and implores
and forces me to follow you and love;
since all that is not you is not my good.
Love, who scorns every other marvel, for
5   my own salvation's sake bids me to crave
you as sole sun; and thus the soul's deprived
of all high hope and all the strength I own;
yet not for you alone
Love wills that I should burn, but for whoever
10   has eyes or brows like yours, at least in part.
And anyone who departs
from your fair eyes, my life, will have no light;
for there can be no heaven where you are not.

                                               1526–34

82

I cannot think so high as to bring forth
some other image of such loveliness,
bodiless shade or else in earthly dress,
to arm my will against your beauty's strength.
5   For when I leave you I sink down to depths
where Love despoils and strips me of all force;
so, while I hope to make my sufferings less,
he doubles them and comes to bring me death.
         And therefore it is vain for me to spur
10   my flight from hostile beauty, doubling pace;
the slow can't stop the swift from drawing near.
         But Love with his own hands shall dry my tears,
promising that my toils must still be dear;
for he who costs so much cannot be base.

                                       For TC. c.1533–4

83

Here in your lovely face I see, my lord,
what in this life no words could ever tell;
with that, although still clothed in flesh, my soul
has often already risen up to God.
And if the foolish, fell, malevolent crowd   5
point others out as sharing their own ill,
I do not cherish less this yearning will,
the love, the faith, the chaste desire of good.
To wise men there is nothing that we know
more like that fount of mercy whence we come   10
than every thing of beauty here below;
nor is there other sample, other fruit
of heaven on earth; he who loves you with faith
transcends to God above and holds death sweet.

For TC. 1534

84

As in the very pen and ink we find
all styles exist, the high, the low, the middle,
and marble holds an image, mean or noble,
drawn out according to our making mind;
so, lord, there may be, in your breast confined,   5
not only pride but motions sweetly humble;
and yet whatever I draw forth resembles
my inner self, and in my face it's signed.
Whoever sows deep sighs and tears and pain
(to various forms the various seeds on earth   10
convert the single pure and heavenly rain)
will reap that sorrow and those tears again:
high beauty gazed on by deep grief brings forth
a crop of sufferings, sure and bitter pain.

For TC. 1534

85

No sooner was your letter given me
than I sought out a clutch of cardinals
and passed your greetings to the chosen three.
    The greatest Medico of all our ills
5 laughed so much at the message that he blew
his nose too hard and broke his spectacles.
    The reverend holy man who's served by you
both here and there – that's what you say, at least –
liked it so much he burst out laughing too.
10   I haven't seen the one who knows the best-
kept secrets of our Medico the Less,
but it would fit him if he were a priest.
    And there are many others who would curse
the name of Christ to have you here again;
15 no harm in that, nobody thinks them worse
    for lack of faith. I'll use your letter then
to root out all this lust for you, and let
the hangman drown anyone who complains.
    The Carnesecchi, dried and salted meat,
20 (but tender as a cutlet that one fries)
forgets himself; you're all he thinks about.
    By Buonarroti you're so idolized,
trust me, that ever since your letter came
he seems uplifted higher than the skies,
25   and says that he could never give your name
eternal life, for all his skill with stone,
the way your heavenly songs have done for him:
    summer and winter pass, but they remain
unharmed, untouched by cruel death and time,
30 which cannot conquer virtuous renown.
    And then he said, as your good friend and mine:
'See votive offerings hung and candles lit
before the paintings at a holy shrine;
    among such paintings I must surely fit,

but as a worthless botch some dauber makes,   35
sploshed with a clumsy brush from dirty pots.
    Thank Berni with my love, for what I'm like
in honest truth is known to him alone:
to praise and puff me is a bad mistake.
    But by his teaching I can still be shown   40
the light; and what a marvel it would be
to make a real man from a painted one!'
    That's what he said; and I most heartily
commend him to you as the man assigned
to give this letter safe delivery.   45
    As I write out these verses line by line,
I blush to think who will receive this scrawl,
this rude crude stuff; poetry's not my line.
    But nonetheless I shall commend as well
my own poor self and say that I am ever   50
and always yours; and now I think that's all.
    To you, whom I account most rare, I offer
all that I am; and even if I lost
my cowl, you must not think that I would waver.
    That's what I say and swear, and you may rest   55
assured I'd serve you better than myself;
don't look on me, a brother, with disgust.
    Command me, sir: and then do it yourself.

                                        1534

86

My heart already was oppressed with grief,
and I was thinking that to give free rein
to tears and weeping would bring some relief,
    when fortune came to swell the roots and veins
of all that water at the very source   5
– with death and not some lesser woe and pain –
    at your departure; so when I discourse
of you I must distinguish tears, pen, voice

from those that mourn your son, the earlier loss.

10   He was my brother, you were father to us:
to him by love, to you by duty bound,
I know not which affliction is the worse.

My brother's painted by my memory's hand,
but you it sculpts alive within my heart –
15   the more my heart is hurt and my face stained.

And yet there's comfort knowing that the debt
my brother paid unripe you paid full-grown;
when old men die it pains us less to part.

The sufferer's loss should be to him less keen
20   the more it is judged needful in that place
where, safe from sense, the truth at last is known.

But who is there that would not weep the case
of his dead father? – not to see again
that endlessly endeared familiar face.

25   The selfsame troubles bring a different pain
to different men; what counts is how they feel:
how I am touched, O Lord, you know alone.

And even when soul bows to reason's rule,
the yoke's hard burden bends my neck so low
30   that afterwards to greater grief I fall.

And were it not that I keep thinking how
a man who dies well laughs in heaven above
to see how we fear dying here below,

my sorrow would be greater; but my grief
35   is tempered by my faith that in death's nest
all those who have lived well find sweet relief.

Our intellect so deeply is oppressed
by our weak flesh that fears of death increase
the more that false persuader holds us fast.

40   Ninety times over had the whelming seas
put out the bright torch of the flaming sun
before you rose to reach the heavenly peace.

Now, pitying my living death, look down
from heaven that freed you of our human pain
45   and here, by your means, willed I should be born.

Dying to death, you have become divine,
no longer fearing change of life or will;
not without envy can I write that line.

Fortune and time are baffled, standing still
before your quiet threshold, though they blight   50
our lives with doubtful joy and certain ill.

There is no cloud that can obscure your light,
for you the passing hours have no force,
chance and necessity lose all their might.

Your splendour is not darkened in the course   55
of night, nor ever brightened by the day,
though here below the summer sun burns fierce.

Your death, dear father, teaches me to die,
and in my thought I see you in a place
that's seldom opened to a worldly eye.   60

Death is no evil to the souls who pass
beyond their last to that first endless day,
forever near the heavenly throne by grace,

    where, by the grace of God, I dare to say
I trust and hope to see you, if my mind   65
can draw my cold heart from this earthly clay.

If perfect love of son and father finds
increase in heaven, as all virtues do,
[. . .]

                                        1531 or 1534

87

I wish I willed what I will not, O Lord:
a veil of ice hid between heart and fire
quenches the flame and makes my page a liar;
the pen is fruitless, by the works denied.

With words I love you, and yet then I've sighed   5
that love strikes not my heart; I know not where
to find the gate from which your grace might pour
into the heart to drive out stubborn pride.

You rend the veil, Lord, you break down that wall
whose hardness keeps the light from breaking through,
your sun's light, now extinguished in the world!
    Send down the light that's promised to us all
to your fair bride, so that my heart may burn,
doubts laid to rest, and feeling only you.

                                            1533–4

88

I feel afar a cold face set alight
by fire that burns me, yet itself is ice;
I sense within two lovely arms a force,
itself unmoved, that moves all other weight.
    I alone know a spirit whose sole state
gives others death although it never dies,
that, free itself, still holds me in its ties,
that only heals and yet to me brings hurt.
    How can it be, lord, that from your fair face
such contrary effects are borne in mine?
no one gives others that which he has not.
    Perhaps my loss of joy in life (unless
you save it) means your face is like the sun
which heats the world and is itself not hot.

                                    For TC. 1534

89

With your fair eyes I see a gentle light
that mine alone could never see, being blind;
your feet walk with the burden that is mine,
my lameness could not carry such a weight.
    I have no wings, but yours uplift my flight,
and I am moved to heaven by your mind;
I blanch and blush even as you're inclined,
warm in cold fogs and cold in summer heat.

My will is only there in what you wish,
my thoughts are all created in your heart,   10
my words are spoken by your breath alone.
    Left to myself, I seem the lonely moon,
since here our eyes see nothing but that part
of heaven that is illumined by the sun.

For TC. 1532–4

90

I hold myself more dear than once I did,
and worth more since you came into my heart,
just like a stone wrought by the carver's art,
more precious than when it was rough and rude.
    On written page and painted sheet we set   5
more value than on some mere rag or shred;
so is it with me, since your face has made
me your marked target; I have no regret.
    I can go anywhere, safe with that sign,
like one who has some charm or magic sword   10
with which he comes unscathed through every peril.
    Now I prevail against the fire and flood,
and with your mark bring light back to the blind
and cure for every poison with my spittle.

For TC. c.1532–4

93

When sense diverts its overheated beams
towards some other beauty, not your face,
it loses strength, lord, like the race
of some fierce torrent branched in many streams.
But then the heart that seems   5
to live most fully in the hottest fires
resents the infrequent tear and cooler sigh.
The soul that sees their crime

exults that one of them must die,
10   releasing her for heaven where she aspires.
Reason comes last and shares
the pains out equally; then all four tempers
firmly accord in loving you forever.

                                        1535–7

94

To others kind and to itself unkind
is born a lowly beast who, in great pain,
to dress another's hand sheds its own skin,
only well born if one has death in mind.
5   If only it were destiny that I
should dress my lord's live flesh with my dead skin:
a snake will cast its slough upon a stone,
and for such transformation I would die.
Or if the hairy pelt that I possessed,
10   skilfully woven, might become the gown
that's lucky to enfold that lovely breast,
so he'd be mine by day; or else the slippers
he stands on; with that burden for my own,
I'd carry him around at least two winters.

                            Probably for TC. 1535

95

Give back, O silver streams and fountains bright,
the constant spring you borrowed from my eyes,
the power not yours that makes you swell and rise,
the flow that nature never made so great.
5   And you, dense air, that shade the heavenly light
from these sad orbs and thicken with my sighs,
restore them to the heart that weary lies,
clear your dark face to my new-sharpened sight.
Now let the earth give back my foot's hard print

that grass may grow on what was trodden bare,   10
echo, long deaf, send back my loud lament;
 and may your holy lights at last set free
my longing looks to sometime love another
beauty, since you have no delight in me.

Probably for TC. Date uncertain

97

With flesh of tow and with a sulphur heart,
with brittle bones that kindle like dry wood;
with soul that has no bridle and no guide,
and with desire too quick to seek delight;
 with reason blind, too weak and lame to fight   5
against the snares and birdlime of the world;
no marvel that, there in a flash, one should
be caught in the first fire and set alight.
 The art of beauty which, if man bring it down
with him from heaven, surpasses nature's part,   10
though nature still strives upward everywhere –
 if I was born to that not deaf and blind,
thus framed for one who burns and steals my heart,
the fault is his who made me for the fire.

For TC. 1534

98

Why with my tears and sorrowing words should I
give vent to the desire that I feel,
if heaven that with this fate invests the soul
comes neither soon nor late to set me free?
 Why should my tired heart still work on me   5
to pine, if men must die? My dying will
the less offend these eyes that see too well
how there's no good that's worth my misery.

Thus if the wound is one I cannot shun,
10   a fate I rather seek and steal than fear,
who'll come between the sweetness and the pain?
If only blest when caught and conquered here,
no wonder I remain, naked, alone,
the prisoner of a well-armed cavalier.

For TC. c.1534–5.

101

Since Phoebus does not clasp, does not encase
this cold damp globe with arms that make it bright,
the common people give the name of night
only to that which he does not embrace.
5   So weak is night that in a given place
its life is taken by a man who lights
a little torch – so feeble it takes flight
as soon as flint and tinder rend its space.
And if we say night really is some thing,
10   surely she's daughter of the earth and sun;
one holds the shade, only the other makes it.
Yet be that as it may, they're surely wrong
who praise night's peace, obscure and barely won,
so fragile that a firefly's war can break it.

Date uncertain, probably 1535–41

102

O night, O sweetest time, though black of hue,
with peace you force all restless work to end;
those who exalt you see and understand,
and he is sound of mind who honours you.
5   You cut the thread of tired thoughts, for so
you offer calm in your moist shade; you send
to this low sphere the dreams where we ascend
up to the highest, where I long to go.

Shadow of death that brings to quiet close
all miseries that plague the heart and soul,   10
for those in pain the last and best of cures;
   you heal the flesh of its infirmities,
dry up our tears and shut away our toil,
and free the good from wrath and fretting cares.

Date uncertain

103

All pent-in places, every covered room,
and any space that matter hems around,
preserve the night, even when day comes round,
against the sunshine's light and luminous game.
   Since night is vanquished by mere fire and flame,   5
its heavenly powers are driven out and banned
by what's far baser than the sun; their stand
is broken more or less by a glow-worm.
   What still lies open, naked to the sun,
teeming with myriad seeds and plants, gives way   10
to the fierce peasant and the plough's assault;
   but only darkness serves to plant a man.
Therefore the night is holier than the day,
as man's worth more than any other fruit.

Date uncertain

104

He who created time from nothingness
(but after man's creation, only then)
split time in two: one half held high the sun,
the other had the moon that's near to us.
   From these were born, before the moment passed,   5
the fortune, fate and chance of every man;
I was assigned the dark time for my own,
as what my birth and cradle suited best.

I copy what I think fate says I am,
10   and, as the night grows blacker when it's late,
my growing evil brings more grief and shame.
    Yet there's one consolation; power to turn
into the clearest day my long dark night
is given the sun that's yours since you were born.
                                         Date uncertain

105

My eyes saw nothing mortal when in your
eyes' loveliness I found entire peace,
but deep within, where evil has no place,
one who with love assails a soul like him:
5   not made like God, the soul would seek no more
than outward beauty, pleasing to the eyes;
but, finding that fallacious, it must rise,
transcending to the universal form.
    I say that what must die cannot appease
10   the longing of the living; nor is found
the eternal here in time where flesh decays.
    Uncurbed desire is not love, but sense
that kills the soul; ours makes us perfect friends
on earth and even more, by death, in heaven.
            For TC. Date uncertain, probably after 1534

106

Seeking again the source from which it came,
the immortal form into your earthly jail
came like a pitying angel sent to heal
all minds, and the world's honour to redeem.
5   This alone makes me love, this feeds my flame,
not your serene regard, your outward veil:
love places no firm hope in what must fail,
since in that love virtue has made its home.

And thus it is with all things high and rare
that nature urges forth and heaven so well   10
and generously endows at their creation;
    God, through his grace, is shown to me no more
fully than in some lovely mortal veil;
and that I love only for his reflection.

For TC. c.1536–46

107

My eyes that ever long for lovely things,
my soul that seeks salvation, cannot rise
to heaven unless they fix their gaze
on beauty, for they have no other wings.
Down from the highest stars above   5
there falls a radiance that draws
desire back towards that cause,
and here below men call it Love.
The noble heart has nothing else
to kindle and to guide it but one face,   10
which the eyes find compelling like those stars.

c.1536–44

110

I say to those who to the world have given
the soul, the body and the spirit too:
you have a place reserved in this dark coffin.

Date uncertain: after 1534

III

    Lady, if it be true
that here with us, like any mortal creature,
although divine of feature,
you live and eat and sleep and speak – if then
one chooses not to follow you
(your grace and mercy having banished doubt),
what pain would serve to punish such a sin?
For one who trusts in his own thought,
using the eye that cannot see,
with his unaided strength will love too late.
Impose then from outside a form on me,
as I do here with stone or blank sheet which
within has nothing, and yet all I wish.

For VC. c.1536

115

    Wiles, guiles and smiles, gold, pearls, her festive
        way:
who is it that could say
in actions so divine what's human work,
since gold and silver take
from her their lustre and are doubly bright?
Each gem derives more light
from her eyes than its own intrinsic strength.

Date uncertain

120

    It should be time by now
for me to bid farewell
to love which in old age is seldom kind;
and yet the soul, as you know well,

O Love, is deaf and blind 5
to dying and to time, and still,
though I am facing death, calls her to mind.
I only make this prayer:
you should not think to spare
one single wound inflicted by your bow, 10
even if you break it in a thousand pieces:
he never dies whose suffering never ceases.

Date uncertain

134

— You blessèd who in heaven enjoy the prize
for tears to which the world gives no reward,
can love be even there your lord,
or is the lover set free when he dies?
— Eternal is our peace which lies 5
beyond all time, and thus we love
where no tears fall, no envy tears the mind.
— Then it is my ill fortune that I live,
as you can see, to love and serve
with all too many pains, and to no end. 10
If heaven is the lovers' friend
and if the world puts love to scorn,
then, since I love, why was I born?
For a long life? Why, that's my only terror:
short life is still too long for those who serve and
      suffer.
15
Date uncertain

140

If at the last the soul regains,
as we believe, its long-loved dress,
whether by heaven it be damned or saved,
then hell itself will hold less pain,

5   illumined by your loveliness,
     if you are there for souls to see and gaze at.
     And if, ascending, it returns
     to heaven, as I keenly crave
     and burn with hope to go along with it,
10   there'll be less joy in God above
     if, as on earth, all pleasures give
     place to your countenance, divinely fair.
     Thus I expect to love you better where
     the damned have greater good in suffering less
15   than the saved harm in their diminished bliss.
                For 'the beautiful cruel lady'. Date uncertain

149

     I cannot but fall short in mind and art
     before the one who takes my life from me
     with such excessive ministry
     that with less mercy I would find more grace.
5   And so my soul departs,
     like an eye dazzled by what shines too much,
     transcending to some place
     above my powers. But high enough to touch
     that lady's lowest gift it does not raise me;
10   thus I should learn to see
     that all my works seem thankless in her sight.
     She, full of grace,
     spreads it to others in a flame so great
     that it would burn more with a lesser heat.
                     Probably for VC. Date uncertain

150

Great grace towards a thief being haled to die,
with all hope gone and chilled in every vein,
may kill no less, my lady, than great pain,
if sudden pardon comes to set him free.
Likewise if you should show too suddenly   5
unwonted mercy on this grief of mine,
excess of pity bringing joy again
may take, more than my tears, my life away.
And thus it is with news, bitter or sweet,
contraries linked by the swift death they give,   10
for swollen or contracted hearts must break.
Your beauty here, which Love and heaven support,
should curb my bliss if it would have me live:
a gift's excess undoes a power too weak.

Probably for VC. Date uncertain

151

The best of artists can no concept find
that is not in a single block of stone,
confined by the excess; to that alone
attains the hand obedient to the mind.
Noble and gracious lady, most divine,   5
the evil that I flee and good I crave
thus hide in you; but, that I may not live,
my art proves contrary to my design.
Not love then, nor your beauty or disdain,
your harshness or my fortune or my fate   10
or destiny is guilty of my pain,
if in your heart at once you carry both
mercy and death, and if my lowly wit,
burning, draws from it nothing else but death.

Probably for VC. c.1538–44

152

By what we take away, lady, we give
to rugged mountain stone
a figure that can live
and which grows greater where the stone grows
    less;
5   so, hidden under that excess
which is the flesh, the trembling soul
still contains some good works
that lie beneath its coarse and savage bark.
You only can extract them still
10   and free them from this outer shell
for in myself I find no strength or will.

Probably for VC. c.1538–44

153

It is not just the mould,
empty of art, that waits to be full filled
from the fire with molten silver or gold,
and must be shattered for the work
5   to be brought forth; I also seek
with my love's inner fire
to fill the void of my desire
for infinite beauty by adoring one,
the soul and heart of my frail life.
10   Dear noble lady, she comes down
in me through such small vents that when I strive
to bring her forth I must be split and broken.

Probably for VC. c.1536–42

156

No one, my lady, by the steep long way,
reaches your high bright crown
unless you first send down
your gifts of wisdom and humility:
the climb gets harder and my strength has grown   5
so weak I'm out of breath when halfway there.
Your beauty, set at such a height,
would seem to please the hungry heart
that craves whatever is sublime and rare:
yet to enjoy that loveliness I pray   10
that you descend and stay
within my reach. Comfort lies in one thought:
though you may scorn that I
should love your state as low, hate it sublime,
you must forgive the one who caused my crime.   15

Probably for VC. c.1538–42

158

It seems, Love, that your might
dismisses death clean out of mind,
holding the soul back with the kind
of grace it would be happier without.
The fruit is fallen now and dry the rind,   5
and bitter is the taste that once was sweet;
these last short hours that I live
bring only torment as the fruit
of infinite pleasure in a little room.
Your pity is so fierce, so late,   10
that it's a fearsome gift and gives
pain to delight and to the flesh a tomb;
and yet for such a doom
old age gives thanks: for if I die like this,
you kill me less with anguish than with bliss.   15

For 'the beautiful cruel lady'. Before 1542

159

Lady, that I might less unworthy prove
of the great gift of your vast courtesy,
with all my heart I urged myself to try
what, in exchange, my lowly skill could give.
    But, since my own poor strength could never
5   strive
to rise so high, or open up the way,
pardon I beg for such audacity,
and let my fault teach wisdom to revive.
    And now I see how far they err who hold
10 that my frail fleeting work could hope to climb
to match your outpouring of grace divine.
    Talent and art and memory must yield;
no mortal, though he try a thousand times,
repays with his own store a gift from heaven.

For VC. c.1538–45

161

What biting file wears down
and frets your tired hide, O my sick soul?
when will you cast this slough, this mortal coil,
set free by time to dwell in heaven again
5 as once you were, joyful and pure,
having put off at last this earthly veil?
For though these last short years
have changed the colours that I wear,
I cannot change old habits that still weigh
10 and grow upon me with each passing day.
Love, from you I will not hide
that I grow envious of the dead,
and so bewildered and dismayed
that the soul fears and trembles for itself.

Lord, when my final hour is due, 15
stretch out your arms in mercy; from my self
take me, and make me one who pleases you.

For VC. c.1538–41

162

Now on my right foot, now upon my left
I seek salvation, shifting back and forth.
Torn between vice and virtue's path,
my heart bewildered frets and wearies me,
like one who of the stars bereft 5
is lost on every track and faints away.
A blank white page I lay
out for your sacred ink, that love
may undeceive me, pity write the truth;
and that the soul, of self made free, 10
bend not to error the short stay
that here is left and I may live less blindly.
I ask you, high and holy lady,
whether in heaven a sin that's humble should
hold lower ranking than superfluous good. 15

For VC. c.1538–41

164

As model and as guide to my vocation
beauty alone at birth was given me,
my mirror and my lamp in both the arts.
And to think otherwise is false opinion.
This only lifts the eye to those great heights 5
that here I set myself to carve and paint.
Though foolish and rash judgements may deride
as sensual this beauty that can show
the way to heaven and move each healthy mind,

10   from mortal to divine no eyes proceed
      that are infirm, fixed firmly here below,
      whence without grace we cannot hope to rise.

                              For VC. c.1541–4

166

      Well may these eyes from far or near make bold
      to see your lovely face where it appears;
      these feet, my lady, surely cannot bear
      my arms and hands to hold what eyes behold.
5   The pure and healthy intellect, the soul,
      unbound and free, may through the eyes aspire
      to your high beauty; but my fierce desire
      gives no such privilege to this heavy mould,
          the mortal body, which can hardly follow
10   an angel's track, having no wings to fly;
      to sight alone that pride and praise are due.
          If you have power in heaven as here below,
      of my whole body make a single eye;
      may no part of me not rejoice in you.

                              For VC. c.1541–4

172

          Woman untamed and wild,
          she still insists that I
          should burn for her and die,
          shrivelled to something not an ounce in weight;
5   she bleeds me pint by pint
          and saps my body, for the soul unfit.
          She preens herself and sits
          before the trusty mirror and beholds
          herself reflected like all paradise;
10   then turns, and, in that light,
          my face seems not just old

but fit for mockery as downright ugly,
and hers so much more lovely:
and yet my luck and victory lie there,
surpassing nature's work to make her fair.   15
        For 'the beautiful cruel lady'. c.1536–46

173

A lovely face comes from a happy heart,
ugliness from a sad one; then who's this
woman so fair and fierce
that will not burn for me as I for her?
Since, by the force of my clear star,   5
my eyes received the subtle art
of how to tell one beauty from another,
she is more cruel to herself by far
each time she moves me to complain
'This pallid face comes from a heart cast down'.   10
For if a man who paints a woman
also portrays himself, how then
will she appear who keeps him thus in pain?
So both of us would gain if I
could paint with happy heart and cheeks still
      dry: 15
she'd make herself more fair, and me not ugly.
        For 'the beautiful cruel lady'. c.1536–46

194

Fate wills that here untimely I should sleep.
I am not dead, though newly lodged, but rather,
since lovers are transformed into each other,
live on in you who see me now and weep.
        For Cecchino Bracci. 1544

197

This flesh made earth, and these my bones, that
    now
lie spoiled of their bright eyes and lovely face,
show him to whom I was delight and grace
what prison the soul lives in here below.

1544

198

If others' tears could give new life to me
by changing into flesh and blood to dress
these bones, such pity would be pitiless,
binding to them a soul in heaven made free.

1544

199

They weep me dead within this tomb in vain
who hope that watered thus my bones will be
turned to fruition like some withered tree;
spring doesn't make a dead man rise again.

1544

200

That I once lived only this stone still knows;
if men recall me, it is but a dream;
death is so swift and hungry that it seems
as if what has been truly never was.

1544

217

If, like the phoenix, Braccio were reborn,
his lovely face renewed, admired more;
it's good this good men failed to know before
should first be lost awhile, then found again.

1544

218

The son of Bracci with the sun of nature,
forever spent, I lock away and seal:
death slew him quickly without sword or steel;
the slightest wind bears off the winter flower.

1544

225

Braccio I was: here stripped of soul I lie,
my beauty dust and bones: I pray the stone
that hides me may not open, for in one
who loved me living I would lovely stay.

1544

228

Since for a lifetime earth lends us the body
and heaven the soul, what compensates the loss
of this youth who lies dead and Braccio was,
being owed so many years and so much beauty?

1544

235

It is a man, indeed a god, whose speech
is in the mouth of a woman,
so that because I listen
to her I am at last made such
5   that I can never be my own again.
Now I believe, since she has taken
me from myself, that I can have some pity
on that far self; her lovely face so spurs me
beyond all vain desire
10   that I see death in every other beauty.
Lady, who ferries souls that yearn
to happy days through water and through fire,
grant I may never to myself return.

For VC. 1545–6

236

If man conceives with his diviner part
some face and gesture, then with double strength
he forms a poor small model and from thence
gives life to stone – and this is not mere art.
5   In the same way that faculty will start
with some rough sketch before hand touches brush,
testing, reworking all it best invents
until the figures frame to its conceit.
I too, a model born unprized and vile,
10   was formed, high lady, that through you I might
be reborn to a noble perfect state.
If you, being kind, make good my lack and file
away excess, what penance must await
my passion's flame if thus chastised and taught?

For VC. A much-revised sonnet completed in 1547

237

A whole and healthy taste finds great delight
in work of that first art which shapes a copy
of face and gesture in a human body
where wax, clay, stone give limbs a truer life.
Should then injurious boorish time deface   5
that form, distorted, broken or dismembered,
the beauty that first was is still remembered,
pleasure once vain kept for a better place.

c.1545

238

The soul is not unworthy that intends
to gain eternal life and sweet content
by hoarding the sole coin that heaven mints
and that on earth it's nature's task to spend.

c.1545

239

Lady, how can it be that, as all past
experience proves, a living image known
from carving in the solid mountain stone
outlasts its maker whom years turn to dust?
Cause bows to the effect, and nature must   5
give way to art. I know it, who have shown
in loveliness of sculpture how alone
such works the work of time and death resist.
Thus I can give long life to both of us
in either way, in colour or in stone,   10
with likeness of your face and of mine too;

so that when we are gone a thousand years
your beauty and my sorrow will be seen,
and how I was no fool in loving you.

For VC. c.1538–46

240

Art wills that here alone,
carved in the living stone,
her face should live, outfacing the long years.
What then should heaven do for her
5   since she is heaven's work, as this is mine,
and to all eyes, not only mine, appears
not merely mortal but divine?
And yet she can have no abiding stay.
The nobler part is lamed, for here
10   a rock remains while death hastes her away.
Who can avenge her? Only nature;
if here below her children's works alone
endure, while time will steal away her own.

For VC. c.1544–5

241

Seeking through many years and many trials,
the wise man at the end, when death is near,
attains the true idea
of a live image in hard mountain stone;
5   for we come late to all
high lofty things, and soon our time is done.
Nature works this way too,
going from age to age, from face to face:
once she perfects beauty divine in you,
10   then she is growing old and doomed to perish.
Fear, therefore, closely tied
to beauty, serves to nourish

devouring passion with strange food;
nor can I say whether the sight
of you has brought me greater harm or good,   15
with the world's end or my intense delight.

For VC. c.1542–4

247

Precious is sleep, better to be of stone,
while the oppression and the shame still last;
not seeing and not hearing, I am blest;
so do not wake me, hush! keep your voice down.

c.1545–56

248

From heaven he came down and after sight
of both the hells, the just and merciful,
returned in mortal dress to gaze his fill
on God, then show us all in its true light.
A radiant star, that with his beams made bright   5
my undeserving birthplace; not the whole
bad world would be reward for such a soul;
you only, his creator, could be that.
I speak of Dante, for his works were least
valued by that ungrateful folk who fail   10
to shower favours only on the just.
If I were he! To have such fate at birth,
and, with his virtue, share his harsh exile,
I would exchange the happiest state on earth.

1545–6

249

— For many, for a thousand lovers, lady,
you were created in an angel's shape;
now heaven seems to sleep,
since one has stolen what was given to many.
Restore to us who weep
the sunshine of your eyes, for now you hide
from those poor wretches born without its bounty.
— Let not your holy wishes be disturbed,
for he who seems to tear me from your side
in his great fear enjoys not his great sin:
the state of lovers is less happy when
a great excess curbs great desire's scope
than when in misery they live on hope.

                                        1545–6

250

What should be said of him cannot be said,
his splendour burned too bright for our dim eyes;
to blame his foes is easier than to rise
(even for the best of us) to his least good.
To do us good he went to where the bad
have their reward, and then to God he rose;
the gates that heaven against him did not close
his native land to his just claim kept barred.
Ungrateful land, I say, that feeds on fame
to its own ruin; and the clearest sign
is that it brings its best the worst of harm.
Among a thousand proofs, take this alone:
just as no exile has deserved less blame,
no like or greater man was ever born.

                                        c.1545–6

251

Within the sweetness that vast kindness gives
some lurking insult often lies in wait,
a trap for life and honour; and this threat
weighs on my health and on my will to live.
The man who on another's shoulders grafts   5
the wings to fly, then spreads a hidden net,
there, where it most desires to burn, will dout
the ardent charity that's born of love.
Luigi, then, may your first grace still shine,
to which I owe my life, let not its peace   10
be ever tempested by wind and rain.
All kindly acts offence can undermine
and, if I know what friendship truly is,
a thousand joys count less than one fierce pain.

To Luigi del Riccio. 1545–6

259

Sometimes indeed my hope may be so bold
to rise with my fierce desire and not prove false,
for if heaven looks askance at all we feel,
then for what end would God have made the world?
What better cause to love you can I hold   5
than to give glory to the eternal peace
whence comes your grace divine whose power to
          please
turns noble hearts to holy and pure souls?
The hope is false only of love that dies
with beauty that each passing moment wastes,   10
subjected to some lovely fading face.
Sweet is the love found in a heart that's chaste:
with ageing husk or final hour, its force
fails not, an earthly pledge of paradise.

Probably for TC. c.1546

260

Fierce burning for surpassing loveliness
need not be always harsh and deadly fault,
if with that heat the heart is made to melt
in softness that a dart divine can pierce.
5   Winged by the power of love, man wakes and soars,
nor is vain passion denied a loftier flight
as the first step to the creator's height,
to which the soul, unsated, seeks to rise.
The love of which I speak aspires to climb;
10   women are not like this, and it ill fits
a wise and manly heart to burn for them.
One draws to heaven, the other to earth below,
one in the soul, one in the senses sits
and at things vile and worthless draws his bow.

Probably for TC. c.1546

261

Though long delay brings greater luck and grace
than when swift mercy yields to young desire,
to me this last late joy brings pain and fear,
knowing how brief is aged happiness.
5   Heaven, if it still loves us, sets its face
against those who, when they should freeze, catch fire,
as I for her: hence my sad lonely tears
join with advancing age and weigh no less.
And yet, though this may be my close of day,
10   in cold and deepening dark, with the spent sun
below the far horizon fast descending,
if love inflames the middle of life's way
and nothing more, and I being old still burn,
then she will make a middle of my ending.

c.1546

263

A woman's beauty yet again
unleashes, lashes, spurs me on;
not only am I past my prime,
but nones and vespers too, and night is near.
My lifeline and my luck in love –   5
one sits with death and plays for time,
nor can the other give me peace down here.
I, who had come to terms at last
with my white hair and my advancing years,
held firm that earnest of the other life   10
as promised by a truly contrite heart.
He loses most who fears the least
when death commands him to depart,
trusting himself, his own unaided power,
against that rooted old desire: 15
once he has heard an echo of its voice,
being old won't help him without grace.

                                                    1547

264

Just as within my breast, lady, I've borne
the impress of your face for many a year,
so now that death draws near
may Love with privilege print it on the soul,
that happily it may set down   5
the heavy corpse that was its earthly jail.
Through calm and tempest may it go
safely with such a sign
to serve it as a cross against the foe;
then, homing to the heavenly place   10
whence nature stole you, let the soul return

to be a model where bright angels learn
to flesh another spirit that may grace
the world, when you are gone, with your fair face.

For VC. c.1547

267

I'm locked up here like pulp within the rind
or like a genie trapped inside a bottle;
I live like this, poor, lonely and confined.
    It takes no time to look around my tomb
where thousands of Arachne's workers sit,
each spinning his own bobbin at the loom.
    Around my door I find huge piles of shit
since those who gorge on grapes or take a purge
can find no better place to void their guts.
    I've learned by now to be a proper judge
of piss and of its pipe, seen through the cracks
where dawn's light filters through into my cage.
    Dead cats, full chamberpots, jugs from a jakes –
no guest but leaves such household gifts as these
and then there's one less trip for them to make.
    Within the body soul enjoys such ease
that, if the plug were pulled to free a fart,
it would not stay behind for bread and cheese.
    That blocked back door stops soul from flying out,
and coughs and colds are keeping death at bay
by checking breath escaping through my throat.
    Lumbagoed, ruptured, knackered – that's the way
my toil has left me; death has come to be
the tavern where I live and eat, and pay.
    My happiness consists in melancholy
and these discomforts are my only rest:
just ask for trouble and God grants it free.
    Seeing me, you'd say the hag who haunts the feast
of the Three Kings; my house too fits the part
near palaces put up at such great cost.

No flame of love is left within my heart;
if greater ills drive out a lesser one,
they've clipped the wings my soul had at the start.
My skin's a sack for gristle and old bones,
I've got a hornet buzzing in my head,   35
and in my bladder there are three black stones.
My eyes like blueish powder, ground and
      pounded,
my teeth like keys from some botched instrument –
they move, a sound comes out and then goes dead.
My face is ghastly, but, if I were sent   40
to frighten birds, my clothes alone would scare
crows from dry furrows in a time of want.
I feel a cobweb forming in one ear
a cricket in the other sings all night;
can't sleep for my catarrh, and yet I snore.   45
Love and the muses, bowers of delight,
my scrawls and scribbles, end up as a lot
of tavern-bills, bog-paper, brothel notes.
Making all those big dolls, I wonder what
the point was, if my end is still like one   50
who swims across the sea, then drowns in snot.
The art for which in bygone days I won
golden opinions brings me here at last,
poor, old and servant to another's will,
so that I'm done for, if I don't die first.   55

Date uncertain

270

You give to me from what you have left over
and then you ask things that are not of me.

Date uncertain

271

On you and with you, Love, for many years
I fed my soul and, if not all, in part
my body too; and with its wondrous art,
hope came to make me strong, urged by desire.
5   But, tired now, I wing my thoughts, spur higher
towards a nobler, more secure abode.
For all the empty promises you made
on paper and your faith, my words and tears
[. . .]

c.1546

272

Bring back the days when blind desire would come
and run with loosened bit and slackened rein;
the calm angelic face restore again
that took all virtues with it to the tomb;
5   bring back the restless way I used to roam
with paces now made slow by age and pain;
give fire and water to this breast of mine,
if you would gorge on me for one last time.
But if it's true, Love, that you only feed
10   on tears that mortals bittersweet let fall,
a tired old man will hardly serve your turn;
for now my soul, nearing the other side,
wards off your darts with those more merciful:
and in charred wood there's little left to burn.

c.1547

274

Ah bring me, Lord, to see you everywhere!
So, if I burn for beauty's mortal frame,
that fire will be mere ashes to your flame
where I'll catch fire as I did before.
    On you alone, dear Lord, I call, implore   5
to save me from my torment, blind and vain:
within, without, renew me, you alone
my weakened will and mind and strength restore.
    You woke this sacred soul to time, O Love,
and in this husk, so wearied now and frail,   10
imprisoned it to suffer a harsh fate.
    Have I no other way than thus to live?
My Lord, without you, every good must fail;
power divine alone can change man's state.

1547

276

Whatever object strikes my gazing eyes
as lovely passes through them to the heart
immediately, on such a spacious route
that hundreds, thousands, travel at their ease,
    of every age and sex; hence all my fears,   5
burdened with cares, and jealousy as well;
nor, amid all these faces, can I tell
which, before death, might give me perfect peace.
    If mortal beauty serves to quench its flame,
desire did not come with the soul from heaven;   10
and therefore it is merely human will.
    If it goes further, Love, it scorns your name,
seeking another god – no longer fearing
that you will ambush it for such base spoils.

c.1547–50

277

With pencil or with colours you have set
up art to equal nature, and in part
indeed surpassed her, since for us your art
makes all that she made lovely lovelier yet;
5   but now that to a nobler task you put
your learned hand, by writing to impart
new life to men, you steal the only part
of nature's privilege that you so far lacked.
For though some ages past may well contend
10   with her in making works of beauty, yet
they yield in reaching their foredestined end.
But you, rekindling the spent memory
of other lives, ensure, despite such fate,
that they and you shall live eternally.

For Giorgio Vasari. 1550

278

A man who isn't fond of leaves
shouldn't come round in May.

Date uncertain

279

To what am I spurred onward by a face
so fair? Since elsewhere I find no delight,
to rise among the blest by such a great
grace that it outdoes every other grace.
5   If the Creator to his work has given
a form like his, what blame can I await
from justice if I love – nay, burn, and rate
each gentle person as conceived in heaven?

Date uncertain

280

The restless and bewildered soul can find
within itself no cause but some grave sin
half-recognized, and yet not hid from him
who grants the wretched mercy without end.
    I speak to you, Lord, for no work of mine,   5
without your blood, can make a blessèd man:
seeing that under your law I was born,
have mercy on me – not for the first time.

Date uncertain

282

In such great slavery, such weariness,
and with false concepts and a soul in danger,
to be where I am, carving things divine.

1552

283

Dear Lord, when youth is flowering fresh and
    green
it knows not how taste, love, desires and thoughts
will change as we approach the final step.
    Where the world loses there the soul must gain;
dying and art do not fit well together: 5
where is it then most fit I place my hope?

1552

284

If I conceive some image in your name,
it's never without death appearing too,
dissolving both my art and shaping mind.
   But if we all come back, as some men claim,
5   to life on earth, then truly I will serve you,
provided that my art's not left behind.

                                        1552

285

Through stormy seas and in a fragile bark
my life has reached at last the common port,
where all must come to render their report,
accounting for each good and evil work.
5   So the fond fantasy that used to make
an idol and a tyrant out of art,
I now see as it is, with error fraught,
like what men love despite the harm they take.
   What of those vain and wanton thoughts of love
10   now I approach two deaths? I know that one
is certain, and the other threatens me.
   Painting and sculpture will no longer serve
to calm my soul, turned to that love divine
whose arms were opened for us on the cross.

                                        1554

288

The fables of the world have cancelled out
the time assigned me for the thought of God;
not only I forget what grace I had,
but am more sinful with it than without.

That which makes others wise has made my wit   5
too blind, dull, slow, to see how I have strayed;
my longing grows, although my hope may fade,
to see you loose the bonds of my self-love.
    Shorten by half the climbing road that leads
to heaven, dear Lord; though I shall need still
      more,   10
more of your help only to climb that half.
    Teach me to hate all that the world regards,
the beauties I still honour and revere,
so, before death, I grasp eternal life.

1555

289

There is no viler, baser thing on earth
than what I feel I am, and am without you,
so to the height of all desire I sue
for pardon with my weak and tired breath.
    Stretch down to me, dear Lord, the chain that
      with   5
itself brings linked each heavenly gift: I mean
faith that I catch and course at, while I rue
my sin that checks full grace that comes from faith.
    This gift of gifts will be more dear to me
being so rare; dearer since, lacking that,   10
the world alone has no content or peace.
    You were not sparing of your blood, and yet
how will your gift's great mercy be of use
unless heaven opens to this other key?

1555

290

From worldly ties, O my dear Lord, unbound,
and from an irksome heavy load set free,
to you I turn as, from the storms at sea,
a tired ship hails the sweet calm of land.
    The thorns, the nails, the pierced palms of your
        hands,
your merciful mild face, assure the grant
of grace to make the sinful soul repent,
of hope to reach salvation at the end.
    Let not your holy eyes or your pure ears
bring justice down to bear on my past shame,
nor your stern arm be raised against me here.
    But may your blood alone wash off my fault
and more abound the older I become,
with perfect pardon and with ready help.

c.1555 or later

291

I think some hidden guilt in me must bear
down on my spirit with this suffering;
the senses have deprived, with their rash burning,
the heart of peace, left hopeless all desire.
    Yet one who's with you, Love, what need he fear
could slacken grace's grasp before his passing?

c.1555 or later

292

The prayers I offer would be sweet indeed
if only you would lend me power to pray;
for in my feeble soil there is no way
a fruit born of itself can still be good.

Of pure good works you only are the seed,   5
they spring up where you sow yourself; nor may
a man's unaided strength follow your way,
unless you first point out that holy road.

                                        c.1555 or later

293

Weighed down by years and swollen with my sin,
with evil custom that has taken root,
I see two deaths approach, and yet my heart
still loves the poison that it feeds upon.
    Nor do I have enough strength of my own   5
to change my life and love, my ways, my fate,
without your aid, divinely leading light
that guides and curbs the treacherous course we run.
    To make me yearn for heaven will not suffice,
dear Lord, for you to recreate my soul –   10
not, as the first time, out of nothing born.
    Before you strip it of its mortal dress,
shorten by half, I pray, the high steep road,
and clear and certain shall be my return.

                                        c.1555 or later

294

Painful and sad, yet at the same time dear
to me is every thought that calls to mind
the time gone by, and the account I'm bound
to give for lost days nothing can restore.
    Dear in that, nearing death, I learn before   5
how trustless are the pleasures of mankind;
sad because in one's final years to find
mercy and grace for many sins is rare.

For though we trust the promises you send,
10   perhaps we dare not hope that love will pardon
further delay, Lord, in the time that's left.
Yet with your blood it seems we understand:
since matchless for us is your mighty passion,
measureless too must be your precious gifts.

c.1555 or later

295

Certain of death, yet knowing not the day,
the remnant left to me of life is short;
a longer stay would give the sense delight,
but not the soul which pleads that I should die.
5   The world is blind, good custom conquered by
evil example drowning out the right;
sureness is gone, extinguished is the light,
truth cowers and what triumphs is a lie.
Ah Lord, when shall we see the time which all
10   who trust in you await? for each delay
abridges hope and brings death to the soul.
Why did you promise so much light to men
if death comes first and leaves us without aid,
fixed in the state where we were stricken down?

After 1555

296

Many more years added to many past
are often what my longing promises;
death hourly approaches nonetheless,
though to the unmoved mind he makes less haste.
5   Why seek a longer life for pleasure's sake,
if we adore God only in distress?

Good fortune and protracted happiness
for every joy bring greater harm at last.
   And if at times, dear Lord, the burning zeal
by which, thanks to your grace, my heart is riven,   10
brings solace and assurance to the soul,
   since my own powers have no help to give,
that instant I would choose to rise to heaven:
for our goodwill grows less the more we live.

                                     1555

298

Joyful no less than troubled and dismayed
the blessed were that you, not they, in death
suffered so that to lowly man of earth
heaven's closed gates were opened by your blood.
   Joyful that you redeemed what you had made   5
from the disaster of his primal stain;
dismayed that in such harsh and bitter pain,
servant of servants, you were crucified.
   Heaven showed who you were and whence you came
when its own eyes grew dim and the earth split,   10
the mountains shook, the sea was tempest-torn.
   This freed the patriarchs from the shadowy realm,
plunged the foul angels deeper in the pit;
and only man rejoiced – baptized, reborn.

                              Date uncertain

299

The sugar that you send, the mule, the candles,
a hefty flask thrown in of Malmsey wine,
so far outdo any poor gifts of mine
I leave Saint Michael scales that I can't handle.

Too much fair weather makes the slack sails
5   dangle;
lacking a wind and lost upon the main,
my frail ship makes no headway, seems as vain
as some light straw that rough waves toss and dandle.
   Compared to your great gift, your courtesy,
10   the food, the drink, the means to get around
(this last most welcome and great help to me),
   dear lord, there is no merit I could get
by giving to you everything I am:
it is no gift when one repays a debt.

To Giorgio Vasari. 1555

300

The cross, Monsignor, grace, the pains we suffer
assure me we shall meet in paradise;
yet, before our last breath, I hold it wise
that here on earth we should enjoy each other.
5   If a harsh way with sea and mountain severs
the two of us, our spirit and zeal despise
such petty obstacles as snow and ice;
no nets or chains can stop us flying over.
   With wings of thought I always come to you
10   and weep and speak of my Urbino dead,
who, if alive, would be there with me too,
   as I once meant; but now his death has come
to urge or draw me by another road
to where he waits for me to lodge with him.

To Ludovico Beccadelli. 1556

302

You have no other way, dear Lord, to rid
my soul of love, this mortal vain affection,
than by some adverse chance or strange affliction
by which you set your friends free from the world;
    by you alone the soul is stripped and clad,   5
purified with your precious blood, made whole,
purged of all human urges, sins untold,
[. . .]

1560

FRAGMENTS

Fragment 3

David with the sling and I with the bow.
  Michelangelo

c.1501–2

Fragment 7

A sweet dwelling-place in hell.

1503–4

Fragment 16

Fevers, flanks, pains, plagues, eyes and teeth.

Date unknown

Fragment 18

Therefore love wearies me when victory
turns out no better than an enemy.

c.1520–25

Fragment 26

There's no real loving someone you can't see.

c.1524–6

Fragment 35

Nobody has the whole of it
before he reaches the limit
of his art and his life.

Before 1547

LETTERS

Letter 1

[To Lorenzo di Pier Francesco de' Medici in Florence]
Jesus. On the 2nd day of July, 1496

Magnificent Lorenzo. – Just to let you know that last Saturday
we arrived at Salvamento and went straightaway to call on the
Cardinal of Saint George and present your letter. He seemed
glad to see me and immediately wanted me to go and see some
statues, which took the whole day, so I couldn't give him your
other letters that day. Then, on Sunday, the cardinal went to
his new house and asked for me: I went to him and he asked
me what I thought of the things I had seen. I gave him my
opinion; and indeed I think there are many beautiful things.
Then the cardinal asked whether I had the spirit to make some-
thing beautiful myself. I replied that I might not do anything
quite so fine, but he would see what I could do. We have bought
a block of marble big enough for a life-sized figure, and on
Monday I shall set to work. Last Monday I presented your
other letters to Paolo Rucellai, who offered me the money I
needed, and also the letters for the Cavalcanti. Then I gave
Baldassare his letter and asked him for the Cupid, saying that I
would give him back the money. He answered very sharply that
he'd sooner smash it in a hundred pieces, that he had bought
the Cupid and it was his, that he had letters to prove he had
satisfied those who sent it to him and that he had no idea of
having to give it back. And he complained a lot about you,
saying you had slandered him. Some of our Florentines have
tried to settle matters between us, but it came to nothing. Now
I reckon I shall work through the cardinal, for that's what
Baldassare Balducci advises. You shall hear how it turns out.
That's all for now. I send you my regards. May God keep you
from all harm.

  Michelagniolo in Rome

Letter 2

Domino Lodovico Buonarroti in Florence
In the name of God. On the 1st day of July, 1497

Most revered and dear Father, do not be surprised that I have
not returned because I still haven't been able to settle my affairs
with the cardinal, and I do not want to leave until I am satisfied
and rewarded for my labours: and with these important people
one has to go gently because they can't be forced. But in any
case, I think I shall have everything over and done with this
coming week.

I should let you know that Fra Lionardo came here to Rome
saying that he had had to escape from Viterbo, that he had
been defrocked and that he wanted to go home. So I gave him
a gold ducat that he wanted for the journey, but I expect you
know this since he must have already arrived.

I don't know what else to tell you because I'm kept in sus-
pense and I don't know how things will turn out; but I hope to
be with you soon. I'm well, as I trust you are. Remember me to
my friends.

Michelagniolo, sculptor, in Rome

R2, G2

Letter 3

To Master Giuliano da Sangallo, Florentine, architect to the
pope in Rome

Giuliano – I learned from your letter how the pope took my
departure badly and how His Holiness has made a deposit and
is ready to do what we agreed on, and that I should come back
and not worry about anything.

About my departure, what's true is that on Holy Saturday I
heard the pope, who was talking at table with a jeweller and
with the master of ceremonies, say that he wasn't ready to

spend another penny on stones, big or small; and this really amazed me. Still, before I left I asked him for a part of what I needed to carry on with the work. His Holiness answered that I should come back on Monday: and I came back on Monday, Tuesday, Wednesday and Thursday, as he could see. Finally, on Friday morning, I was sent away, or rather driven out; and the fellow who sent me off said he knew who I was, but those were his orders. So, having heard those words that Saturday and then seen their effect, I grew desperate. But that wasn't the sole cause of my departure: there was something else as well that I don't want to write about. Enough to say that it made me think that if I stayed in Rome, my own tomb would be made before the pope's. And this was why I left so suddenly.

Now you write to me on the pope's behalf, so you can read the pope this: let His Holiness understand that I am more willing than ever to carry on with the work; and if he wants the tomb come what may, he shouldn't be bothered about where I work on it, provided that, at the end of the five years we agreed on, it is set up in St Peter's, wherever he likes; and that it is something beautiful, as I have promised it will be: for I'm sure that if it's completed, there will be nothing like it in the world.

Now if His Holiness wants to go on with it, he should place the deposit for me here in Florence and I'll write to tell him where. And I have many marbles on order in Carrara which I shall have brought here along with those I have in Rome. Even if it meant a serious loss to me, I shouldn't mind so long as I could do the work here; and I would forward the finished pieces one by one so that His Holiness would enjoy them just as much as if I were working in Rome – or even more, because he would just see the finished pieces without having any other bother. For the money and for the work I shall pledge myself as His Holiness desires and give him whatever security he requires here in Florence. Whatever it is, I'll give him that security before all Florence. Enough. One more thing: it would not be possible to do the work for the same price in Rome, because there are so many facilities here that don't exist down there. And I shall do it better and with more love because I won't have so many things to think about. In the meantime, my dear Giuliano, let me have an answer and quickly. There's nothing else.

On the 2nd day of May, 1506

Your Michelagniolo, sculptor, in Florence

R8, G6

Letter 4

To Lodovico di Lionardo di Buonarrota Simoni in Florence
Deliver to the shop of Lorenzo Strozzi, Wool Guild, in Porta Rossa
On the 8th day of February [1507]

Dearest Father – Today I received a letter from you in which I learn that you've been told a long story by Lapo and Lodovico. I'm glad that you reprove me because I deserve to be reproved as a wretched sinner no less than other men, and perhaps more. But let me tell you that I have no sin whatsoever in this affair that you blame me for, neither towards them, nor towards anyone else, unless it's in doing more than I should have done. And all the men I've ever dealt with know what I've given them; and if anyone knows it, Lapo and Lodovico know it better than the rest, for one has had twenty-seven ducats in six weeks and the other eighteen broad ducats as well as expenses: so please don't go out of your way on their account. When they complained about me, you should have asked them how long they were with me and how much they got; and then you could have really asked what they were complaining about! But the great grievance, especially of that poor wretch Lapo, was this: that they let everyone think that they were the ones doing this work, or that they were my associates; and they never realized (especially Lapo) that they weren't the masters until I sent them packing. Only then did Lapo understand that he was working for me. And after all his affairs on the side and his boasting of the pope's favour, he could hardly believe that I had chased him out like a dog. I'm sorry that he got seven ducats out of me, but when I return there he'll have to pay them back anyway;

and if he had any conscience he'd also give back the rest of what he had from me. Enough. I won't go on with this, because I've already written enough about their affairs to Master Agnolo. Please go to him and take Granacci with you if you can, and get Agnolo to read you the letter I wrote him, and you'll understand what scum they are. But please keep secret what I've written about Lodovico, because if I can't find anyone else to come here to do the casting, I'd think about having him back, because in fact I didn't really want to sack him; but Lapo, being too ashamed to turn up alone, led him astray to make things easier for himself. The Herald will tell you all about it and what you should do. Don't speak to Lapo; it would be too shameful, for we can have no dealings with their sort.

As for Giovansimone, I don't think he should come here because the pope is leaving at Carnival and I think he'll go to Florence; and he isn't leaving things in good order here. They say people are afraid of something that it's better not to ask or write about: what matters is that if anything happens (and I don't think it will), I don't want the responsibility of brothers on my back. Don't be alarmed at this and don't talk about it to a living soul, because then, if I needed men, I wouldn't find any who would come; and anyway I still think that things will turn out well. I shall be in Florence soon and I'll do something to satisfy Giovansimone and the others, God willing. Tomorrow I'll write again about some money I want to send down and what you should do with it. I agree about Piero; he will answer for me because he's an honest man and always has been.

Your Michelagniolo in Bologna

Here's some more about the strange things Lapo says I've done to him. I want to write you just one, and it's this: I bought seven hundred and twenty pounds of wax, but before I bought it I told Lapo to see where it could be found and to make the deal and I would give him the money to get it. Lapo went and came back to tell me that it couldn't be had for a penny less than nine broad ducats and twenty *bolognini* per hundred pounds (which means nine ducats and forty pence), and that I should snap it up as a bargain. I answered that he should go and see if he couldn't knock off those forty pence and then I would take it. He replied: it's in their nature, these Bolognese, they won't take a farthing less than they ask. At that point I grew suspicious and let the matter drop. The same day I called Piero aside and told him secretly to go and see for how much he could get a hundred pounds of wax. Piero went to the same man as Lapo and made the deal for eight ducats and a half, and I accepted it and sent Piero for his commission, which he then received. This is one of the strange things I did to Lapo. In fact, I know that what he really found strange was that I saw through the fraud. Not satisfied with eight broad ducats a month and expenses, he had to go about defrauding me, and he may have defrauded me many times for all I know, since I trusted him. Indeed, I never saw a man who looked more honest, so I think that with that honest air he must have fooled others as well. So don't trust him in anything, and pretend not to see him.

R13, G11

Letter 5

To Buonarroto di Lodovico di Buonarrota Simoni in Florence
Deliver to the shop of Lorenzo Strozzi, Wool Guild, in Porta Rossa
[From Bologna]

Buonarroto – Just to let you know that we have cast my statue and that I haven't had much luck with it, because through ignorance or accident Maestro Bernardino did not melt the material properly. It would take too long to write how this happened, but the fact is that my statue came out up to the waist; the rest of the material, that is half the metal, remained in the furnace unmelted, so that to get it out I shall have to dismantle the furnace. That's what I'm doing now and I shall have it reassembled this week; and next week I shall recast the top and finish filling the mould, and I think that, though it started badly, the thing will turn out very well, but not without

a great deal of worry, toil and expense. I had such faith in
Maestro Bernardino that I would have trusted him to cast
without fire, and it's not that he isn't a good craftsman or
that he didn't do it with love. But whoever makes must make
mistakes. And his mistake has damaged both me and him
because he's so disgraced that he can no longer hold up his
head in Bologna.

If you see Baccio d'Agniolo, read him this letter and ask him
to inform Sangallo in Rome and give him my regards; and
regards also to Giovanni da Ricasoli and Granacci. If the thing
goes well, I should be finished with it in two or three weeks,
and then I'll come back home. If it doesn't go well, I might have
to do it again. I shall keep you informed about everything.

Tell me how things are with Giovansimone.

On the 6th day of July [1507].

Enclosed will be a letter for Giuliano da Sangallo in Rome.
Forward it as safely and quickly as you can. If he happens to
be in Florence, give it to him.

[Unsigned]

R28, G26

Letter 6

To Buonarroto di Lodovico di Buonarrota Simoni in Florence
Deliver to the shop of Lorenzo Strozzi, Wool Guild, in Porta
Rossa

Buonarroto – I'm surprised that you write to me so rarely. I
think you have more time for writing to me than I have for
writing to you: so keep me regularly informed about how you
are managing.

You said in your last letter that you had a good reason for
wanting me to return soon, and this left me worried for several
days: so when you write to me, write plainly and make things
clear so that I can understand: that's enough.

Let me tell you that I am far more eager to get back to Florence than you are that I should come, because I live here in the greatest discomfort and with the hardest toil, and do nothing but work day and night. And I have endured and still endure such labour that if I had to do it over again I don't think my whole life would be enough, for it has been a huge task; and in the hands of anyone else it would have turned out badly. But I think somebody's prayers must have helped me and kept me well because in all Bologna nobody believed I would ever finish it when it was cast; and before that nobody believed I could ever cast it.

What counts is that I have brought it to a successful conclusion; but I won't have finished completely before the end of the month as I had hoped. Next month it will be finished at any rate, and then I shall come back. So be of good heart, all of you, because I shall do what I promised, come what may. Cheer up Lodovico and Giovansimone for me and write to say how Giovansimone is managing, and get down to learning how to run the shop so that you'll know how to go about it when you need to, which will be soon.

On the tenth day of November [1507]
Michelagniolo in Bologna

R37, G35

Letter 7

To Lodovico di Buonarrota Simoni in Florence
[June 1509]

Dearest Father – I learned from your last how things are going down there and how Giovansimone is behaving. In ten years I haven't had worse news than the evening I read your letter, because I thought I had settled their affairs so that they had hopes of setting up a good shop with my help, as I promised. And I thought that in that hope they would buckle down to learning the trade, so as to do the job when the time came.

Now I see that they're doing the opposite, and especially Giovansimone; so from this I see that it's no use doing good to him. And if I'd been able to, I would have taken horse the day I got your letter, and by now I would have fixed everything. But since I can't do this, I'm writing him a letter saying exactly what I think. And if he doesn't change his ways from now on, or if he takes as much as a straw from the house or does anything else that upsets you, I ask you to let me know, because I shall see about getting leave from the pope and I shall come down there to show him where he's gone wrong. I want you to realize that all the constant toil I've endured has been for you no less than for myself; and whatever I've bought I've bought so that it will be yours for as long as you live; because if it weren't for you, I wouldn't have bought it. So if you feel like letting the house and leasing the farm, suit yourself. With that income and with what I shall give you, you can live like a gentleman. And if summer were not coming, as it is, I would tell you to do it now and to come and stay with me. I've been thinking of taking away the money he has in the shop and giving it to Gismondo so that he and Buonarroto can team up as best they can. And then you could let those houses and the farm at Pazzolatica, and with that income and with some extra help that I'll give you myself, you could retire somewhere – either inside or outside Florence – where you feel well and where you can have someone to look after you; and leave that wretch with only his arse to hang on to. I beg you to think of your own interest, and in everything you do about what is yours I shall try to help you as much as I can. Keep me informed. About that Cassandra business, I took advice about transferring the case here. I was told that here I would spend three times more than down there in Florence; and that's certain, because what costs a *grosso* down there can't be had for two *carlini* here. Another thing is that here I have no friend I could trust, and I couldn't handle such matters myself. It seems to me that if you want to handle the affair yourself, you should follow the normal course, as reason dictates, and defend yourself as well as you can. And as for the money you need, I won't fail you as long as I have any. And worry about it as little as you can because it's not a matter of life and death. That's all. Keep me informed, as I said above.

Your Michelagniolo in Rome

R48, G48

Letter 8

To Giovansimone di Lodovico Buonarroti in Florence
[June 1509]

Giovansimone – They say that doing good to a good man makes him better, and that it makes a scoundrel worse. I have been trying for years, with words and deeds, to get you to live a decent life, at peace with your father and the rest of us; and you still get worse. I'm not saying you are a scoundrel, but you behave in a way that I don't like, neither me nor other people. I could make a big speech about your affairs, but it would be just words like the others I've already wasted on you. To cut things short, I can tell you for sure that you have nothing left in the world and that I pay your expenses and for the house you live in, and I have done for some time, thinking of you as a brother like the others. Now I am certain you are not my brother, because if you were you wouldn't threaten my father. No, you're a beast, and I shall treat you like a beast. Just know that anyone who sees his father threatened or knocked about is bound to put his life on the line, and that's that. I say you haven't a thing in the world; and if I hear the slightest thing about your affairs, I shall come down there in a hurry to show you where you've gone wrong and teach you to squander your belongings and set fire in the house and the farms that you did nothing to earn. You're not who you think you are. If I come down there, I'll show you something to make you cry your eyes out and then you'll learn what you have to be so proud about.

I have this to say yet again, that if you set about doing good and honouring and respecting your father, then I'll help you as I do the others, and soon I shall set you up with a good shop.

If you don't do this, I shall be down there and I'll settle your affairs so that you'll know who you are better than you ever did before, and you'll see how much you own in the world. That's all. My actions will speak louder than my words.

Michelagniolo in Rome

I can't keep from writing a few more lines, and it's this: that I've dragged myself all over Italy for twelve years, put up with every indignity, suffered every hardship, tortured my body with every kind of toil, taken a thousand risks with my life, and all to help my family. And now that I was beginning to raise it up a bit, you want to be the one who wrecks and ruins in an hour what I've done in so many years and at such a cost. By Christ's body, it won't happen! Because I can smash ten thousand like you if I have to. So pull yourself together, and don't tempt someone who has other things to worry about.

R49, G49

Letter 9

To Buonarroto di Lodovico Simoni in Florence
[5 September 1512]

Buonarroto – I have not written to you for a while because nothing had happened; now, hearing how things are going down there, I think I should tell you my mind, and it's this: since the country is in a bad way, or so they say here, you should see about withdrawing to some place where you'll be safe, and leave the property and everything else, because life's worth much more than property. And if you don't have the money to get out of there, go to the *spedalingo* and have him give it you. And if I were you, I'd take out all the money of mine that's with the *spedalingo* and go to Siena and take a house and stay there until things settle down. I believe the power of attorney that I gave to Lodovico has still not expired, so he can still take out my money. So if the need arises, take it, and spend what you need in emergencies like this, and keep the

rest for me. And don't get involved with affairs of state, either
in words or deeds, but act as you would with the plague: be the
first to run away. That's all. Let me know something as soon
as you can, because I am very worried.

Michelagniolo, sculptor, in Rome

R80, G77

Letter 10

To Buonarroto di Lodovico Simoni in Florence

Buonarroto – In your last letter I heard how the country was in
great danger and I was terribly worried. Now they say that the
Medici are back in Florence and that everything has settled
down; which makes me think that the danger is over, I mean
from the Spaniards, and that there's no longer any need for you
to leave. So live in peace and don't be friendly or familiar with
anyone except God, and say nothing good or bad about anyone,
because you never know how things will turn out: just stick to
your own affairs.

For the forty ducats that Lodovico took out of Santa Maria
Nuova, I wrote you in a letter the other day that, in the case of
mortal danger, you should spend not just forty, but the whole
lot; but, apart from that, I gave you no permission to touch
them. I must warn you that I don't have a penny and that I'm
barefoot and naked, so to speak, and I can't get the balance
owed to me until I've finished the work; and I suffer the worst
of hardships and toil. So, when you have to put up with some
hardship yourself, don't be distressed, and as long as you can
help yourself with your own money, don't take out mine, except
in case of danger, as I said. And even if you have some really
great need, I beg you to write to me first, please. I shall be down
there soon. I won't fail to make it for All Saints, God willing.

On the 18th day of September [1512]
Michelagniolo, sculptor, in Rome

R81, G78

Letter 11

To Lodovico di Buonarrota Simoni in Florence
[October 1512]

Dearest Father – I learned from your last letter that you had taken the forty ducats back to the *spedalingo*. You did well; and if you hear they are not safe, please let me know. I have finished the chapel I was painting: the pope is very happy with it, but other things haven't turned out as well as I hoped. I blame the times, which are so unfavourable to our art. I will not be coming down at All Saints because I don't have what I need in order to do what I want to do, and it's still not the right time. Try and live as well as you can, and don't get involved in anything else. That's all.

Your Michelagniolo, sculptor, in Rome

R83, G79

Letter 12

To Lodovico di Buonarrota Simoni in Florence
[October 1512]

Dearest Father – I learn from your last letter that I shouldn't keep money in the house or carry it around on me. Also that down there it's being said that I spoke against the Medici.

For the money, what I have I keep in Balducci's bank; and at home or on me I keep only what I need from day to day. As for the business of the Medici, I never said a thing against them, except for the general way everybody speaks; about Prato, for example, where the very stones would have spoken if they could. Then they say a lot of things round here and on hearing them I've said: If it's true that they are doing that, then they're doing wrong. Not that I believed them; and, please God, they are not true. A month ago a friend of mine told me some very bad things about their affairs, and I pulled him up short and said that it was very wrong to say such things and that he shouldn't talk to me about it again. So I would like Buonarroto to enquire discreetly where that fellow heard that I had spoken badly of the Medici, so that I can find out where it started and whether it comes from someone who is supposed to be among my friends; so that I can be on my guard. That's all I have to say. I am still not doing anything, but am waiting for the pope to tell me what I have to do.

Your Michelagniolo, sculptor, in Rome

R85, G81

Letter 13

To Lodovico di Buonarrota Simoni in Florence
[October 1512]

Dearest Father – From your last letter I learned how things are going down there [in Florence], though I knew it in part already. We must have patience and commend ourselves to God and repent our sins, for these tribulations come from nothing else, and especially from pride and ingratitude, for I never knew people more ungrateful and more proud than the Florentines. So if justice comes, so it should. As for the sixty ducats you say you have to pay, I find it unfair and very distressing; but we must be patient for as long as God wills. I'll write two lines to Giuliano de' Medici which I shall enclose here. Read them over, and if you feel like it, take them to him and see if they are of any help. If they don't help, think about selling what we've got, and we shall go and live elsewhere. Moreover, if you see that you are being treated worse than others, do your best not to pay and let them rather take everything you've got, and then let me know. But if they treat others of our kind in the same way, then be patient and put your hope in God. You say you have already provided for thirty ducats: take another thirty of mine and send me the balance here. Take them to Bonifazio Fazi and let him have them paid to me here through Giovanni Balducci, and have Bonifazio give you a receipt for the money and send it with your letter next time you write. Get on with your life; and if you can't have the same official honours as other citizens, be satisfied that you have bread to eat and that you live a good life in Christ and poorly – as I do here, for I live in penury and think nothing of life or honours, that is of the world; and I live with immense toil and a thousand cares. And I have been like this for about fifteen years, without an hour of joy; and all this I've done to help you, though you have never recognized or believed it. God forgive us all. I'm ready to do the same again for as long as I live or as long as I can.

Your Michelagniolo, sculptor, in Rome

R82, G82

Letter 14

To Lodovico di Buonarrota Simoni in Florence
[February 1513]

Dearest Father – I answered you about that business of Bernardino, that I wanted to settle the matter of the house that you know about: and so I answer now. I sent for him first because I was promised that in a few days it would be fixed up and I could start to work. Then I saw that it was going to be a long job and now I'm looking round to see if I can't find another house so that I can get out of this one; and I don't want any work done until I'm settled. So let him know how things stand. For the boy who came here, that wretch of a carter cheated me out of a ducat: he swore blind that that was the deal, two broad ducats in gold; but for all the boys who come here with carters it never costs more than ten *carlini*. I was angrier than if I had lost twenty-five ducats because I see that it's all his father's doing who wanted to send him here in style on a mule. Oh, I should have been so lucky! The other thing the father told me, and the boy too, was that he would do everything and look after the mule and sleep on the floor if he had to. And now I'm the one who has to look after him. I needed something like this after all I've been through since I returned! Because the apprentice I left here has been ill on me ever since I came back. It's true that he's better now, but he's been on the brink and had the doctors worried for about a month so that I never got to bed; let alone other problems. Now I have this little shit of a boy who says, who says [sic] that he doesn't want to waste his time and that he wants to learn. And he told me that two or three hours a day would be enough, and now the whole day's not enough, but he wants to draw all night as well. This is the advice of his father. If I said anything, he'd say that I don't want him to learn. But I need someone to look after me; and if he didn't think he could do it, they shouldn't have put me to such expense. But they are frauds, they are frauds and they know just what they're after, and that's all there is to it. Please do me a favour and get him out of here, because he's become such a nuisance that I can't take it any more. And the carter has had so much money that he can just as well take him back again; and he's a friend of the father. Tell the father to send for him; but I won't give him another farthing because I have no money. I'll hang on until he's sent for, and if he's not sent for, I'll get rid of him: though in fact I did send him away the second day and other times as well, and he didn't believe me.

For the shop business I'll send you down a hundred ducats next Saturday. On the one condition, that if you see they are trying to make good use of them, you give them the ducats and make me the creditor as I agreed with Buonarroto when I left. But if they don't try to use them properly, put them in my account in Santa Maria Nuova. It's not yet time to buy.

Your Michelagniolo in Rome

If you speak to the boy's father, put it to him nicely; say that he's a good boy, but too refined and not suited to my service, and that he should send for him.

R90, G88

Letter 15

To Domenico [Buoninsegni in Rome]
[2 May 1517. From Carrara]

Master Domenico – Since I last wrote I have not been able to
work on the model as I said I would: it would take too long to
explain why. I had already roughed out a small one in clay for
my own use here and though it's as crinkled as a fritter I shall
send it to you just the same so that all this doesn't seem like
a hoax.

I have many things to tell you; read patiently for a while
because it's important. It's that I feel I have it in me to do this
work of the façade of San Lorenzo so well that it will be the
mirror of all Italy for both architecture and sculpture. But then
the pope [Leo X] and the cardinal [Giulio de' Medici] should
make up their minds quickly whether they want me to do it or
not. And if they want me to do it they should come to some
decision: either to assign it to me by contract and trust me for
everything or to do it some other way that I don't know, as
they think best; and I shall explain why.

As I wrote you, I have ordered many blocks of marble and
paid out money here and there and started quarrying in a
number of places. And in some places where I spent money the
blocks didn't come out the way I wanted, because they are
treacherous stuff, especially the big blocks that I need if they
are to be as fine as I want them. And in one block that had
already been cut for me certain flaws that couldn't have been
expected showed up near the base, so that I have lost the two
columns that I wanted to make and thrown away half my
investment. And with all these hassles, I shall get so little work
out of so much marble that it won't be worth more than a few
hundred ducats. I'm no good at keeping accounts and in the
end I won't be able to prove what I've spent, apart from the
cost of the actual amount of marble that I deliver. I wish I
could do like the doctor Pier Fantini, but I don't have enough
ointment. What's more, because I'm old I don't feel like losing

so much time to save the pope two or three hundred ducats on this marble; and since down there they keep pressing me about the work, I have to reach a decision somehow.

And my decision is this. If I knew I had the work to do, and if I knew the cost, I wouldn't worry about throwing in four hundred ducats because I wouldn't have to account for them, and I'd get hold of three or four of the best men round here and give them a commission for the marble; and the quality would have to be like the marble I've quarried so far, which is splendid although there's not much of it. And for this and for the money I advanced them I would get insurance in Lucca. As for the marbles I already have, I'd have them transported to Florence and begin work there both for the pope and on my own account. But if the pope doesn't go along with this decision, I can't do anything; and even if I wished, I couldn't first ship the marble for my work to Florence and then ship it on to Rome, but I would have to hurry to Rome to start work because, as I said, they keep pressing me.

The cost of the façade, as I intend to design it and carry it out, with everything included so that the pope wouldn't have to worry about anything, can't be less than thirty-five thousand gold ducats, according to my calculations. And for that sum I would undertake to do it in six years: on this condition, that within six months I must have at least another thousand ducats for the marble. And if the pope doesn't like this idea, then either all the expenditure I've started for this work goes to my profit and loss and I reimburse a thousand ducats to the pope, or else he finds someone else to follow up the project, because I have a number of reasons for wanting to get out of here one way or another.

As for the price I named, once the work is under way, if it turns out that I can do it for less, I'll go to the pope and the cardinal in such good faith that I'll let them know far sooner than if I were the one losing out. But given the way I mean to do things, it's more likely that the price won't be high enough.

Master Domenico, please give me a clear answer about what

the pope and the cardinal are thinking; this would be the greatest of all the favours you have done me.

[Unsigned]

R116, G120

Letter 16

[To Domenico Buoninsegni in Rome]
[March 1518]

Domenico – Since the marbles have come out so splendidly and since what is suitable for St Peter's is easy to quarry and nearer the coast than the others, at a place called Corvara, and from there to the coast there's no need to spend money on a road, except on the patch of marshland near the coast. But to get the kind of marble I need for the statues, one would have to widen the existing road for about two miles from Corvara to up above Seravezza; and for about a mile or so there will have to be a whole new road cut into the mountain with picks to where the marbles can be loaded. So if the pope settles only for the way needed for his own marble (I mean the marshland), then I shall have no way of dealing with the rest, and I won't be able to get the marbles for my own work. And if he doesn't do it, I won't be able to look after the marble for St Peter's, as I promised the cardinal. But if the pope arranges everything, then I can do exactly what I promised.

I've told you all this in other letters. Now you are wise and prudent and I know you wish me well; so I beg you to settle things with the cardinal in your own way and write back quickly so that I can decide what to do. And if nothing happens I can return to Rome and carry on as before. I couldn't go to Carrara because I wouldn't get the marble I need in twenty years. What's more, I've made a lot of enemies over this business and if I go back to Rome I shall be forced to work in bronze, as we said.

Let me tell you that the Board of Works have made great plans about this marble business since I informed them about

it; and I believe they have already settled the prices, tolls and
permits; and I think the notaries and head-notaries and pur-
veyors and assistant-purveyors down there already count on
doubling their share in the pork-barrel. So think about it, and
do what you can to stop this thing getting into their hands,
because then it would be more difficult to deal with them than
with Carrara. Please let me know quickly what you think I
should do, and remember me to the cardinal. I am here as his
man; so I won't do anything unless you say so because I shall
consider what you write as his intention.

When I write to you, if I don't write as correctly as I should,
and if I sometimes miss out the main verb, you must forgive me
because there's a ringing in my ears that won't let me think
straight.

　　Your Michelagniolo in Florence

　　　　　　　　　　　　　　　　　　　　　　　　　　RI19, GI29

Letter 17

To Buonarroto di Lodovico Simoni in Florence
[18 April 1518]

Buonarroto – I learn from your letter that the contract is not
yet made. This worries me a lot, so I'm sending down one of
my men, just for that; he will leave on Friday morning and
come back when he has an answer. And if the contract is settled,
as I asked, I shall carry on with the work. If it isn't settled by
the end of Thursday, when you write, I still shan't assume that
Jacopo Salviati is unwilling to do it, but that he can't; and I
shall take horse and go to the Cardinal de' Medici and the pope
and tell them how I stand, and I shall drop the project here and
return to Carrara where they pray for my coming as if I were
Christ. These stone-cutters I brought from Florence don't know
a thing in the world about quarries or marble. They've already
cost me more than a hundred and thirty ducats and they still
haven't quarried me a sliver of marble that's any good. And
they go around boasting that they've found wonderful stuff and

then they try and work for the Board and for others with the money they've had from me. I don't know who's protecting them, but the pope will hear all about it. Since I've been here, I've wasted about three hundred ducats and I still haven't seen anything for my own use. I might as well try to raise the dead as tame these mountains and bring proper skills to this place. And if the Wool Guild gave me a hundred ducats a month, besides the marbles, to do what I'm doing, they still wouldn't be doing badly – let alone the contract they still won't give me. So remember me to Jacopo Salviati and send a note by my man about how things have gone, so that I can make a decision now, because this is killing me.

    Michelagniolo in Pietrasanta

The barges I hired in Pisa never arrived. I think I've been cheated, and that's how everything goes with me. Oh, a thousand curses on the day and hour I left Carrara! It's been the ruin of me; but I shall be back there soon. Nowadays it's a sin to do good. Remember me to Giovanni da Ricasoli.

R123, G126

Letter 18

To Berto da Filicaia [Overseer at the Board of Works] in Florence
[August 1518. From Seravezza]

Berto – I send you my regards and thank you for all the services and favours; I am always at your command for whatever lies within my power. Things here are going rather well.

    The road is more or less finished, since there is not much left to do: that is, there are a few boulders or rather outcrops to be cut away. One is where the road that leads from the river comes out on the old road to Rimagnio; another is just past Rimagnio on the way to Seravezza, a big boulder across the road; and another is by the last houses of Seravezza towards Corvara. Then there are a few places that need to be levelled with picks.

And all these things, because they don't take long, would be done in a fortnight if the stone-breakers were worth anything. I haven't been to the marsh for about a week. Then they were filling it in as worst they could. If they carried on, it should be finished by now. As for the marbles, I got the quarried column safely down to the riverbed about thirty yards from the road. Slinging it down was a bigger job than I thought. Some work-men got hurt as they slung it and one broke his neck and died on the spot; I nearly lost my own life. The other column was almost blocked out when I found a flaw that left it short; I had to cut back the full width into the hillside to avoid that flaw. That's what I did, and now I think it should be all right and I can block it out. There's nothing else, except that when you speak to His Magnificence Jacopo Salviati, you should give him my apologies for not writing: I don't write because I still have nothing that pleases me to write about. The quarry here is very difficult and the men very inexperienced in this kind of work; so we shall need a lot of patience for a few more months until the mountains are tamed and the men trained. Then we shall work more quickly. What counts is that I shall do what I promised, come what may, and with God's help, I shall create the finest work ever made in Italy.

Since I wrote I have received an answer from those men of Pietrasanta who agreed six months ago to quarry me a certain amount of marble. Now they will neither do the quarrying nor pay back the hundred ducats I gave them. This strikes me as such a daring step that I'm sure they wouldn't have taken it without backing from somebody. So I plan to come to the Tribunal of the Eight in Florence to claim damages for this fraud. I don't know if it will work; I hope His Magnificence Jacopo Salviati will help me to get justice.
[Unsigned]

R129, G139

Letter 19

To my dear friend Lionardo, Saddler, with the Borgherini
[Bank] in Rome
[21 December 1518]

Lionardo – You urge me on in your last letter, and I'm very
glad of it because I see you do it for my good; but I must tell
you that, from another angle, I feel all these urgings as so many
knife-wounds, because I'm worried to death because I can't get
on with what I want to do, given my bad luck. A week ago my
assistant Pietro came back from Porto Venere with Donato,
who has the job of loading the marbles in Carrara; and they
left a loaded barge at Pisa, which has never turned up because
it hasn't rained and the Arno is absolutely dry. And there are
another four barges in Pisa hired for these marbles, and only
when it rains will they come here fully laden and I shall really
settle down to work. All this makes me the most discontented
man in the world. Master Metello Vari is pressing me too about
his figure, which is also down there in Pisa and will come in
one of the first barges. I haven't answered him, and I don't
want to write to you again until I've begun to work; because
I'm dying with the pain of it and I feel as if I'd become a
swindler against my will.

Here I'm setting up a fine workshop where I can stand twenty
figures at a time. I can't roof it over because there's no timber
in Florence and none can arrive unless it rains; and I don't think
it will ever rain again, except when it can do me some mischief.

I'm not asking you to say anything more to the cardinal
because I know he doesn't approve of my behaviour; but soon
he'll have cause to see more clearly. My regards to Sebastiano,
and to you as well.

Your Michelagniolo in Florence

RI34, GI4I

Letter 20

[Addressee unknown]
[March 1520. From Florence]

When I was at Carrara, about my own business, that is for the
marble to be shipped to Rome for the tomb of Pope Julius,
in 1516, Pope Leo sent for me for the façade of San Lorenzo
which he wanted to make in Florence. So on December 5th I
left Carrara and went to Rome, and there I made a design for
this façade, after which Pope Leo commissioned me to quarry
marble for the work at Carrara. Then, when I had returned
from Rome to Carrara on the last day of that December, Pope
Leo sent me a thousand ducats to quarry marble for the work;
these came through Jacopo Salviati and they were brought by
one of his servants called Bentivoglio. I received this money on
the eighth of the next month, January, and duly made out a
receipt. Then, the following August, the pope asked for a model
of that work and I left Carrara to do it in Florence: I made it
to scale in wood, with the figures of wax, and sent it to Rome.
As soon as he saw it, he ordered me to come down there; so I
went and agreed to a commission for that façade, as can be
seen from my copy of the contract with His Holiness. To serve
His Holiness I needed to ship to Florence the marbles for the
tomb of Julius and then, when they were worked, ship them on
to Rome, as I did. And he promised to cover all my expenses,
namely the tolls and the freight, which amounted to about eight
hundred ducats, though the document doesn't say so.

And on February 6th 1517 I returned from Rome to Florence,
having accepted the commission to carry out the work on that
façade of San Lorenzo all at my own expense; and I was to be
paid in Florence by Pope Leo four thousand ducats on account,
as it says in the contract. So, on about the 25th of the month,
I received eight hundred ducats of it from Jacopo Salviati and I
gave him a receipt and went to Carrara. And because the con-
tracts and orders already made for the marble had not been
fulfilled and the Carraresi wanted to gang up on me, I went to

quarry the marble at Serravezza, a mountain near Pietrasanta in Florentine territory. And when I had already blocked out six eighteen-foot columns and many other marbles, and when I had started the new workings that can be seen there today, then, in March 1518, I came to Florence to get the money to begin shipping those marbles. And on the 26th March 1519, the Cardinal de' Medici, through the Gaddi of Florence, paid me five hundred ducats for that work in the name of Pope Leo; and I made out a receipt. Then, at the same time, the cardinal, acting for the pope, ordered me not to continue with the work in hand because they said that they wanted to free me from the bother of shipping marble, for they would supply it themselves in Florence and make a new contract. And that's how things still stand today.

Now at this time the commissioners of Santa Maria del Fiore sent a certain number of stone-cutters to Pietrasanta, or rather to Serravezza, to take over the new workings and seize the marbles I had quarried for the façade of San Lorenzo and use them for the paving of Santa Maria del Fiore. And Pope Leo still wanted to carry on with the façade of San Lorenzo, while Cardinal de' Medici had allocated the marble for that façade to everyone but me, as well as giving my workings at Serravezza to those who were charged with the transport. All without consulting me. I complained bitterly about this because neither the cardinal nor the commissioners had any right to interfere in my business unless I first ditched the contract with the pope. And if I dropped that work of San Lorenzo in agreement with the pope, giving account of all expenses and money received, then the workings and the marbles and all the gear would have to go either to His Holiness or to me; after which both sides would be free to dispose of them as they wished.

Now about all this the cardinal has told me that I should account for all the money received and the expenses incurred and that he would like to free me so that he can take the marble he wants from the workings at Serravezza both for himself and for the Board of Works.

So I've shown that I had received two thousand, three hundred ducats at the times and in the manner stated here; and I've

also shown that I had spent one thousand eight hundred
ducats: of these, two hundred and fifty went for the shipping
up the Arno of the marbles for the tomb of Pope Julius. These
I brought to Florence so that I could work on them here to
serve Pope Leo, and then I transported them to Rome, as I said.
As for the rest of the money, up to that sum of one thousand
eight hundred, as I said, I've proved that it was all spent on the
work of San Lorenzo, not charging Pope Leo for the transport
to Rome of the marble for the tomb of Pope Julius, which
would come to more than five hundred ducats. Nor do I charge
him for the wooden model of the façade that I sent to him in
Rome; nor do I charge him for the three years I have wasted on
this; nor do I charge him for the fact that I've been ruined by
this work of San Lorenzo; nor do I charge him for the great
scandal of bringing me here to do this work and then taking it
away from me, I still don't know why; nor do I charge him for
my house in Rome, which I left to go to rack and ruin, with
marble and gear and finished work, adding up to a loss of over
five hundred ducats. Not charging him for any of these items,
out of two thousand three hundred ducats, all I'm left with is
five hundred.

Now we're agreed. Pope Leo takes over the workings I started
and the marble already quarried; and I keep the money I'm left
with, and I am free. And I've decided to have a brief drawn up
and signed by the pope.

Now you understand how everything stands. Do me the
favour of making a draft of that brief, and settle it so that I can
never be asked to pay back the money received for the work of
San Lorenzo. And also settle it so that, in exchange for the
money I received, Pope Leo takes the workings, the marbles,
the gear [. . .]

[Unsigned, unfinished]

R144, G152

Letter 21

[To Cardinal Bernardo Dovizi da Bibbiena in Rome]
[May–June 1520. From Florence]

Monsignor – I beg your most Reverend Lordship, not as a
friend or servant (for I am not worthy to be one or the other),
but as a poor and foolish nobody, to give Bastiano of Venice,
the painter, some part of the work at the palace, now that
Raphael is dead. But if Your Lordship reckons that the favour
is wasted on a fellow like me, I think one can still occasionally
find pleasure in granting favours to fools, just as a man may
enjoy onions as a change when he is fed up with capons. You
favour worthy men every day: now I ask Your Lordship to give
me a try instead. The favour would be great, and even if it
were wasted on me, it wouldn't be on Bastiano, because he's
a capable man and I'm certain he would do credit to Your
Lordship.
[Unsigned]

RI45, GI53

Letter 22

To Lodovico at Settignano
[September–October 1521]

Dearest Father – I was amazed at your behaviour the other day
when I didn't find you at home; and now, when I hear that
you're complaining about me and saying I turned you out, I am
even more amazed; for I'm certain that never, from the day I
was born till now, have I thought of doing anything, great or
small, to harm you; and always all the toils I've endured, I've
endured them for your sake: and since I came back to Florence
from Rome I've always looked after you, and you know I
confirmed that all I have is yours; and indeed it's only a few
days ago, when you were ill, that I told you and promised that

I would do my best never to fail you as long as I live, and this I confirm. Now I'm amazed that you've forgotten everything so soon. Yet you've tried me out these thirty years, you and your sons, and you know I've always thought about you and helped you whenever I could. How can you go around saying that I turned you out? Don't you see what a reputation you're giving me when they can say I turned you out? That's all I needed, on top of my worries about other things, and all for your sake! A nice way you have of thanking me! Anyhow, be that as it may, I'll try to imagine that I turned you out and that I've always brought you shame and trouble; and just as if I'd really done it, I ask your forgiveness. Just think that you're forgiving a son who has always lived a bad life and done everything possible on this earth to harm you: and so again I beg you to forgive me like the wretch I am, and don't give me the reputation up there of having turned you out, for it matters more to me than you think. After all, I'm still your son!

The bearer of this will be Rafaello da Gagliano. For God's love and not for mine, I beg you to come to Florence because I have to go away and I need to tell you something rather important, and I can't come up there. And because I've heard, from his own lips, things about my assistant Pietro that I don't like, I'm sending him to Pistoia and he won't be coming back to me because I don't want him to be the ruin of our family. All of you, who knew that I knew nothing about his behaviour, should have told me long ago and there wouldn't have been such a scandal.

I'm being urged to go away, but I won't leave without speaking to you first and leaving you here in this house. I beg you to set aside your anger and just come.

Your Michelagniolo in Florence

RI49, GI55

Letter 23

To Lodovico at Settignano
[June 1523. From Florence]

Lodovico – I am not answering your letter except for the things I regard as essential. For the rest I couldn't care less. You say that you can't draw interest on the deposit because I've put it in my name. This is not true, and I must answer to let you know that you could be being cheated by someone you trust who has drawn it out to use for himself, and now he wants to make you think like that for his own ends. I have not put the deposit in my own name, and I couldn't do so even if I wanted to; but it's certainly true that, in the presence of Rafaello da Gagliano, the notary said to me: 'I wouldn't want your brothers to make some arrangement about this deposit, so that when your father dies, you'd find it gone'; and he took me to the bank and made me spend fifteen *grossoni* to put in a clause saying that nobody could use the capital while you are alive: and you are the beneficiary for as long as you live, as it says in the contract that you know.

I have explained the contract to you, that is about cancelling it if you like, since you're not happy with it. I have explained about the account in the bank and you can see it whenever you want. I have always done and undone things to suit you: I don't know what more you want from me. If I annoy you simply by being alive, you've found the way to put that right, and you'll inherit the key to all the treasure you say I have and you'll do well: for all Florence knows what a fine rich chap you were and how I've always robbed you and deserve to be punished: you'll be praised for it! Go shout it out, say what you like about me, but don't write to me any more, because you stop me working: and I need to make up for everything you've had from me over the last twenty-five years. I don't want to say this, but I just can't help telling you. Look after yourself, and watch out for those who need watching; for a man only dies once and there's no coming back to patch up what's been

botched. You have put these things off until the hour of death!
May God help you.
   Michelagniolo

Letter 24

To Ser Giovan Francesco Fattucci in Rome
[December 1523. From Florence]

Master Giovan Francesco – You enquire in your letter how
things stand between me and Pope Julius. I tell you that if I
could claim damages and interest, I reckon I'd have more to
receive than to give. Because when he sent for me to Florence,
I think in the second year of his reign, I had settled to do half
the Council Chamber in Florence, that is, to paint it. I'd been
paid three thousand ducats, and since the cartoon was already
finished, as everybody in Florence knows, I felt the money was
already half-earned. And of the twelve apostles that I still had
to do for Santa Maria del Fiore one was already roughed out,
as can still be seen, and I had already brought in most of the
marble. And when Pope Julius took me away I got nothing for
one or the other. When I was in Rome with Pope Julius, he
commissioned me to make his tomb, which would take a thou-
sand ducats' worth of marble, and he paid me the money and
sent me to get the blocks in Carrara, where I stayed eight
months cutting them and bringing most of them to St Peter's
Square, though some remained in Ripa. Then, when I had
finished paying for the freight of these marbles and when the
money I'd received for the work had run out, I furnished the
house I had in St Peter's Square with my own household stuff
and beds, counting on my hopes of the tomb; and I brought
workmen from Florence, some of whom are still alive, and I
advanced them money of my own. At this point Pope Julius
changed his mind and no longer wanted the tomb. Not knowing
this, I went to ask him for money and was turned out of the
room. Furious at this insult, I left Rome immediately; and what

I had in the house was left to rot; and the marbles that I had
brought to St Peter's remained there until the election of Pope
Leo. So one way or another everything went wrong. Among
other things, I can prove that two nine-foot blocks were stolen
from me at Ripa by Agostino Chigi [a Sienese banker]; they
had cost me over fifty gold ducats. And I could claim compen-
sation for this, because there were witnesses. But to come back
to the marbles; from the time I went to get them and stayed in
Carrara until the day I was turned out of the palace, more than
a year went by – during which I never received a thing but paid
out tens of ducats.

Then, the first time that Pope Julius went to Bologna, I was
forced to go there with a rope round my neck to ask his pardon.
At which he set me to make his statue in bronze, seated and
about fourteen feet high: and when he asked me how much it
would cost, I answered that I thought I could cast it for about
a thousand ducats, but that casting wasn't my art and I didn't
want to commit myself. He answered: 'Get to work, and keep
on casting until it comes; and we'll give you enough to make
you happy.' To cut things short, I cast it twice, and after the
two years I spent there I found myself four and a half ducats to
the good. And I got nothing else in all that time; and all my
expenses for those two years were included in the thousand
ducats that I had said the casting would cost; these were paid
me in instalments by Master Antonio Maria da Legnano of
Bologna.

The statue was erected on the façade of San Petronio and I
returned to Rome. But Pope Julius still didn't want me to make
the tomb and instead set me to paint the vault of the Sistine,
and we settled for three thousand ducats. The first design for
this work was for the twelve Apostles in the lunettes, with the
usual ornamentation in the remaining space.

When the work was under way, I thought it was turning out
a rather poor thing, and I told the pope that I thought just
doing the Apostles would be a poor thing. He asked me why
and I said: 'Because the Apostles were poor themselves.' Then
he gave me a new commission to do what I liked, and said that
he would content me and that I should paint down to the scenes

below. Meanwhile, when the vault was almost finished, the pope returned to Bologna. I went twice for the money that I was supposed to have, and I got nothing and wasted all that time until he returned to Rome. Back in Rome I started to make cartoons for that work, that is for the heads and faces around the Sistine Chapel; and though I hoped to receive some money and finish the work, I never managed to get anything. But one day when I was complaining to Master Bernardo da Bibbiena and to Attalante [a superintendent of the construction of St Peter's] that I could no longer stay in Rome and would have to go with God, Master Bernardo told Attalante to remind him of it, for he wanted some money given to me no matter what. And he had me given two thousand Camera ducats; and these are what they are putting on my account together with the first thousand that I received for the marbles. But I reckoned I was owed more for the time I had lost and the works I had created. And out of that money, since Master Bernardo and Attalante had saved me, I gave one a hundred ducats and the other fifty.

Then came the death of Pope Julius; and at the beginning of Leo's reign a new contract was drawn up because Cardinal Aginensis wanted to have the tomb enlarged, making a greater work than my first design. And because I did not want the three thousand ducats that I had received put on the account of the tomb, Aginensis called me a swindler.
[Unsigned]

R I 57, G I 66

Letter 25

To Pope Clement VII in Rome
[January 1524]

Since intermediaries often cause serious misunderstandings, I make bold to write directly to Your Holiness about the tombs here in San Lorenzo. I must say I do not know which is better, the ill that helps or the good that harms. Witless and unworthy I may be, but I am certain that if I had been allowed to carry on as I started, all the marbles for these works would be in Florence today, blocked out as I need them and costing much less than they have so far; and they would be of admirable quality like the others I brought here.

Now I see that it is set to be a long business and I do not know how it will go on. If, therefore, something happens that displeases Your Holiness, I beg pardon, for I do not feel that I can be guilty where I have no authority. And if Your Holiness wants me to achieve something, I beg that you should not set other men over me in my own art, but have faith in me and give me a free hand; then Your Holiness will see what I can do and what account of myself I shall render.

Stefano has finished and unveiled the lantern of San Lorenzo: everyone admires it, and so, I hope, will Your Holiness when you see it. The ball that goes on top will be about two feet wide, and I thought it should be faceted to distinguish it from the others, and that is being done.

The servant of Your Holiness,
Michelagniolo, sculptor, in Florence

R160, G181

Letter 26

To my dear friend, Master Giovan Francesco, priest of Santa Maria del Fiore of Florence, in Rome
[December 1525]

Master Giovan Francesco – If your last letter had given me as much strength as it did amusement, I think I could accomplish all the things you write to me about, and quickly too; but since I don't have that much, I shall have to do what I can.

About that eighty-foot colossus which you tell me is to go, or to be placed, at the corner of the loggia of the Medici Garden and opposite the corner of Master Luigi della Stufa, I have been thinking of it quite a lot, as you told me; and I think that it wouldn't be right in that corner because it would take up too much of the road. But in the other corner, where there is the

barber's shop, I reckon it would turn out much better, because
the square is in front and it wouldn't block so much of the
street. And since perhaps they might object to removing the
barber's shop because of the income it provides, I think
the figure could be made sitting down; and then, with a proper
use of blocks, the seat could be hollow and so high that the
barber's shop would go underneath, and the rent wouldn't be
lost. And to give the shop a vent for the smoke, as it has now,
I think of putting a horn of plenty in the statue's hand and that
would serve as a chimney. Then I'd have the statue's head
hollow like the limbs and I think we could profit from that too,
for there's a huckster in the square, a good friend of mine, who
told me in private that he'd like to make a fine dovecot inside.
I'm struck by yet another notion, which would be much better;
but then the statue would have to be made much bigger – yet
it could be done, given that towers are built of blocks. I mean
that the head should serve as the bell-tower of San Lorenzo,
which really needs one: and with the bells inside and the sound
coming out of the mouth, it would seem as if the colossus were
crying for mercy, especially on feast days when they ring more
often and with bigger bells.

Now to getting in the marbles for this statue, so that nobody
knows anything about it: I think they should be brought in at
night and well wrapped up, so as not to be seen. There'll be a
bit of a risk at the gate, but we'll see to that as well. At the
worst, there's always the San Gallo gate, where the postern
stays open all night.

As for doing or not doing the things that have to be done
and that you say should be postponed, it's better to let them be
done by those who have to do them, because I'll have so much
to do that I don't care for doing any more. That's enough for
me, so long as it's honourable work.

I'm not replying to everything you wrote because Spina will
soon be going to Rome and he'll do it better and in more detail
by word of mouth than I can with the pen.

Your Michelagniolo, sculptor, in Florence

R176, G189

Letter 27

[To Master Giovan Francesco Fattucci in Rome]
[17 June 1526. From Florence]

Master Giovan Francesco – In this coming week I shall cover
the figures in the sacristy that are already roughed out, because
I want to leave the sacristy free of those marble-cutters, and I
want them to start installing the tomb facing the one that is
already there and fully built in, or almost. And while they are
installing the tomb, I thought we could do the vault, and I
believe that with enough men it could be done in two or three
months, but I don't know. After next week, if he wants it done
now, the Lord our Master can send in Master Giovanni da
Udine whenever it suits him, because I shall be ready.

For the vestibule four columns have been built and one was
built earlier. The tabernacles will be a bit behind, but still I
think they'll be finished four months from now. The floor could
be started now, but the linden wood is not yet ready. We'll
speed up the seasoning as much as we can.

I'm working as hard as I can, and in a fortnight's time I'll
start on the other captain: then the only important things left
will be the four rivers. The four figures on the sarcophagi, the
four figures on the ground which are the rivers, the two cap-
tains, and Our Lady who goes in the tomb at the head of the
chapel – these are the figures I want to make with my own hands,
and six of them are already started. And I have energy enough
to do them in good time, and meanwhile have the other less
important ones done as well. There's nothing else. Remember
me to Giovanni Spina and ask him to write a line to Figiovanni
asking him not to call off the carters and send them to Pescia,
because then we shall be left without stone. And what's more,
he should stop charming the stone-cutters on to his side by
saying: 'These people don't care about you, making you work
till sundown now that the nights are so short.'

We would need a hundred eyes to keep one of them at work,
and even that one is spoiled by someone who gets sentimental.

Patience! God forbid that I should be upset by what doesn't
upset him.
[Unsigned]

R177, G190

Letter 28

To my dear friend Battista della Palla in Florence
[September 1529. From Venice]

Battista, dearest friend – I left Florence, as I think you know,
to go to France, and when I reached Venice, I asked about the
route and was told that from here I would have to pass through
German territory which is difficult and dangerous. Therefore, I
thought I should first learn from you, if you please, whether
you still feel like going yourself; and I decided to ask you, as I
now do, to let me know and tell me where you want me to wait
for you: and so we shall go together. I left without saying a
thing to any of my friends and in a chaotic way: and although,
as you know, I had wanted to go to France in any case and I
had asked permission and been refused many times: yet this
was not because I wasn't fully and fearlessly determined first to
see the war through to the end. But on Tuesday morning,
20 September, someone came out from the San Niccolò gate
where I was at the bastions and whispered that I should stay
there no longer if I wanted to save my life: and he came home
with me and ate something and brought me some horses and
didn't leave me until he had got me out of Florence, with the
assurance that this was for my good. Whether he was God or
the Devil I can't say.

Please answer what I wrote above and as soon as you can,
because I'm dying to be on my way. And even if you no longer
feel like coming, I still beg you to let me know so that I can
decide whether to go by myself as best I can.

Your Michelagniolo

R184, G197

Letter 29

[To Master Tommaso de' Cavalieri in Rome]
[From Rome]

Most inadvisedly I began to write to your lordship, and I had
the presumption to make the first move, as if I were obliged to
do so in reply to something from you: later I recognized my
error all the more when, by your grace, I read and savoured
your answer. And it seems to me that, far from being only just
born, as you write of yourself, you have been in this world a
thousand times before: and myself I would consider as not
born, or rather born dead, as it were in disgrace with heaven
and earth, if your letter had not given me to see and believe
that your lordship would willingly accept some of my work.
This has caused me great wonder and no less pleasure. And if
you truly feel within what you say in writing, that you esteem
my work, then if I make something that pleases you, as I hope
to do, then I shall consider it as having been far more fortunate
than good in itself. I shall say no more. Many things that could
be said in this reply remain unpenned so as not to weary you,
and because I know that Pierantonio, the bearer of this letter,
will be willing and able to supply what I leave out.

On the first, for me happy, day of January [1533]

It would normally be right for the giver to tell the recipient
what gifts he is sending, but there is good reason for not doing
this here.
[Unsigned]

R191, G205

Letter 30

[To Master Tommaso de' Cavalieri in Rome]
[28 July 1533. From Florence]

My dear lord – If I did not believe that I had convinced you of
the immense, indeed boundless love I bear you, then I would
not find strange or surprising the fear expressed in your letter
that, because I did not write, I might have forgotten you. But
since so many other things end up the wrong way round, it is
hardly unusual or surprising that this does too; for what your
lordship says to me, I would have said to you. But perhaps you
did this to test me or to kindle a new and greater flame, if
greater it could be. But be that as it may, I well know that I can
only forget your name when I forget the food by which I live;
indeed, I could sooner forget the food which unhappily feeds
this body than your name which feeds both body and soul,
filling both with such sweetness that I can feel neither pain nor
fear of death while the memory of you endures. Think in what
a state I should be if the eye could also play its part . . .
[Unsigned, unfinished]

                                                    R193, G207

Letter 31

[To Frate Sebastiano del Piombo in Rome]
[August 1533. From Florence]

Dear friend – I received the two madrigals and Ser Giovan
Francesco has had them sung several times, and he tells me that
they are thought admirable as music: the words did not deserve
so much. That's what you wanted, and it gave me great plea-
sure, and I beg you to advise me how I should acknowledge the
composer so that I may not seem more ignorant and ungrateful
than I have to.

I won't write about the work I'm doing here because I think

I've written enough about it already, and I've done my best to imitate the manner and style of Figiovanni in every detail because I think that's the way to handle someone who wants a say in everything. Don't show this letter.

You say you have given a copy of the madrigals to Master Tommaso; I am very grateful, and I beg you to commend me to him a thousand times. And when you write, tell me something about him so that I can keep him ever in mind; for if he faded from my memory, I think I should drop down dead.
[Unsigned]

R194, G206

Letter 32

To Febo [di Poggio]
[September 1534. From Florence]

Febo – Although you hate me so much, I don't know why. I don't believe it's because of the love I bear you, but because of what others say, which you should not believe since you have already tried me. But I can't help writing you this. I am leaving tomorrow morning and going to Pescia to see Cardinal Cesis and Master Baldassare: I shall go with them to Pisa, and then to Rome: and I shall not come back here. And I want you to understand that as long as I live, wherever I am, I shall always be at your service with faith and love like no other friend you have in the world.

I pray that God will open your eyes to see things another way so that you will realize that the man who desires your good more than his own wellbeing knows how to love and not to hate like an enemy.
[Unsigned]

R198, G211

Letter 33

[To Master Pietro Aretino in Venice]
[September 1537. From Rome]

Magnificent Master Pietro, my lord and brother – On receiving
your letter I felt both joy and sorrow: great joy because it came
from you who are sole in this world for talent; but considerable
sorrow too because, having already completed a large part of
the design, I cannot put into effect your concept which is so
convincing that, if the Day of Judgement had already taken
place and you had been there yourself to see it, your words
could not have described it better. As for your writing about
me, I say not only that it would please me, but that I beg you
to do so, since kings and emperors count it a great favour to be
named by your pen. In the meantime, if I have anything that
you happen to like, I offer it to you with all my heart. Finally,
don't let your desire to see my painting change your resolution
not to come to Rome, for that would be too much. I commend
myself to you.

   Michelagniolo Buonarroti

R199, G214

Letter 34

[To Master Niccolò Martelli in Florence]

Master Niccolò – Through Master Vincenzo Perini I have
received your letter, together with two sonnets and a madrigal.
The letter and the sonnets addressed to me are such a marvellous
thing that only someone blameworthy could find something
there to blame. The truth is that they give me such praises that,
even if I held paradise in my breast, they would still be more
than enough. I see that you imagine me to be what God wanted
me to be. I am a poor man of little worth, labouring on in the
art that God gave me to prolong my life as much as I can. Such

as I am, I am your servant and the servant of the whole house
of Martelli. And for the letters and sonnets I thank you, but
not as much as I should, for I cannot rise to such high courtesy.

From Rome on the 20th day of January, 1542

Michelagniolo Buonarroti

R212, G225

Letter 35

To Master Luigi del Riccio at the Bank
[May–June 1542. From Rome]

Master Luigi, my dear lord – Arcadente's air is held to be a
beautiful thing, and since he says he intended to please me no
less than you who asked him for it, I would not like to appear
ungrateful. So please think of some present I could make him,
of silks or money, and let me know and I shall do it without a
second thought. That's all I have to say. I commend myself to
you, to Master Donato, and to heaven and earth.

Your Michelagniolo yet again

R217, G232

Letter 36

To Master Luigi del Riccio
[October–November 1542. From Rome]

Master Luigi, dear friend – Master Pier Giovanni keeps urging
me to start painting. For another four or six days I don't think
I can, because, as anyone can see, the plaster is not dry enough
for me to start. But there's something else that worries me
more than the plaster and that keeps me from living, let alone
painting; and that's the ratification that still hasn't come; and I
know I'm being fobbed off with words, so that I'm truly des-
perate. I coughed up one thousand, four hundred *scudi* which
would have allowed me to work for seven years, enough to

make two tombs instead of one: and I did this so that I could be left in peace and serve the pope with all my heart. Now I find myself without the money and with more trouble and strife than ever. What I did about that money I did with the agreement of the duke and with a contract that would leave me free; and now that I've paid it out, the ratification doesn't come: so you can see what this means without my writing it down. Enough, it's no more than I deserve for thirty-six years of trust and for giving myself up freely to others: painting and sculpture, toil and trust have been my ruin and still it goes from bad to worse. I would have done better to spend my youth making matches, for I wouldn't be suffering so much now. I write this to your lordship so that, as one who wishes me well and has dealt with the affair and knows the truth of it, you can inform the pope and let him know that I can't live like this, let alone paint. And if I raised hopes that I would start, I did it in the hope of the ratification that should have come a month ago. I won't bear this burden any longer nor be insulted every day as a cheat by those who have robbed me of my life and honour. Only death or the pope can rid me of it.

Your Michelagniolo Buonarroti

R226, G238

Letter 37

[Addressee uncertain]
[October–November 1542. From Rome]

Monsignor – Your Lordship sends word that I should just paint and stop worrying. I answer that one paints with the head and not with the hands; and if he can't keep his head, a man's disgraced: so until this business [of the tomb] is settled, I can do nothing good. The ratification of the last contract has not arrived, and because the other, made in the presence of Clement, is still valid, I get stoned every day as if I'd crucified Christ. I say the aforesaid contract was not the one read over in the presence of Clement as the copy said it was. It happened like this: Clement sent me to Florence the same day and the ambassador Gianmaria was with the notary and made him put in whatever he liked; so when I returned and examined it, I found it specified a thousand more ducats than had been fixed, that the house where I lived was included, and a thousand other traps to ruin me; which Clement would not have allowed: and Fra Sebastiano can bear witness since he wanted me to let the pope know everything and have the notary hanged. I decided not to do this, because the contract didn't oblige me to do anything that I wouldn't have done if I'd been left free. I swear I know nothing about receiving the money that the contract mentions and that Gianmaria claims I had. But let's say that I did have the money since I've acknowledged it and since I can't get out of the contract, and let's add any other sums if they can be found, and heap the whole lot into one big lump sum. Then see what I did for Pope Julius in Bologna, in Florence, in Rome, in bronze or marble or in painting, and all the time I was with him, which was all the time he was pope; and then see what I deserve. In good conscience and taking account of what I get from Pope Paul, I say that the heirs of Pope Julius owe me five thousand *scudi*. And I say this as well: the reward for my pains that I received from Pope Julius was my own fault for not knowing how to handle my affairs; but if it weren't for what I've been given by Pope Paul, I'd be dying of hunger today. And according to these ambassadors, it seems I've been enriching myself and stealing from the altar: and they are making a big fuss about it: and I should know how to silence them, but I'm not up to it. Gianmaria, who was ambassador at the time of the old duke, after the said contract had been drawn up in the presence of Clement and when I had got back from Florence and started work on the tomb of Julius, said that if I really wanted to do the duke a favour, I should just clear off in God's name, because the duke wasn't interested in the tomb, though he took it very badly that I was working for Pope Paul. Then I understood why he had put the house into the contract: to get rid of me and then grab it on the strength of that text: so it's clear what they are up to, and they bring shame on our enemies, their masters. This fellow who has just arrived wanted first to know what I have in Florence, and then how the tomb is coming on. I find that I've lost all my youth tied to this tomb, defending it as best I could against Popes Leo and Clement. Too much unrewarded loyalty has been my ruin. That's my fate! I see plenty of people snug in bed with an income of two or three thousand *scudi* while I tire myself out with working to grow poor.

But to return to painting, I can't refuse anything to Pope Paul: I shall paint unhappily and produce unhappy things. I have written this to Your Lordship so that you will be better placed to tell the pope the truth when the time comes; and I would like the pope to hear it and to know what's involved in this war being waged against me. Let them understand who can.

Your Lordship's servant, Michelagniolo

There is something else I should say: and it's this, that the ambassador says that I lent Pope Julius' money at interest and got rich with it: as if Pope Julius had counted me out eight thousand ducats in advance. The money I received for the tomb was meant for the expenses I incurred for it at the time, and it seems to add up to roughly the sum that should be stated in the contract made in Clement's time; because in the first year of Julius, when he commissioned the tomb, I spent eight months in Carrara quarrying marble and having it transported to St Peter's Square, where I had my workshop behind Santa Caterina. Then Pope Julius decided not to have the tomb made in his lifetime and put me on to painting instead; then he kept me in Bologna for two years doing the bronze pope that was later destroyed; then I returned to Rome and stayed with him until his death, always keeping open house, with no grant or salary, always living on the money of the tomb because I had no other income. Then, after the death of Julius, Aginensis wanted to proceed with the tomb, but on a bigger scale. So I brought the marble to Macello de' Corvi, where I finished the part that is now erected in San Pietro in Vincoli and made the figures that I have at home. At that time Pope Leo, who did not want me to make the tomb, pretended that he wanted to do the façade of San

Lorenzo in Florence and asked Aginensis for me; so he was obliged to give me leave, but on condition that while in Florence I would finish the tomb of Pope Julius. When I was in Florence for the façade of San Lorenzo, not having any marble for the tomb of Julius, I went back to Carrara and stayed there thirteen months, and brought all the marble to Florence and built a place to house it and began to work. At this time Aginensis sent Master Francesco Palavicini, now Bishop of Aleria, to urge me on, and he saw the workshop and all the marble and the roughed-out figures for the tomb, which are still there. Seeing this, namely that I was working on the tomb, Medici, who was then in Florence and who was later to be Pope Clement, would not let me continue. And so I was blocked until Medici became Clement. And then the last contract for the tomb before this new one was drawn up in his presence, and there it stated that I had received the eight thousand ducats which they now say I lent out at interest. And now I must confess a sin to Your Lordship because, when I spent thirteen months at Carrara for the tomb, I ran out of money and spent on the marble for that work a thousand *scudi* that Pope Leo had sent me for the façade of San Lorenzo, or just to keep me busy; and I sent him a few words to plead that there were problems; and this I did because of my love for the work. Now I'm paid for it by being told that I'm a thief and usurer by ignoramuses who weren't even born at the time.

I am writing this down for Your Lordship because I dearly want to justify myself to you as well as to the pope who hears such evil things of me that Master Piergiovanni says he has to speak up in my defence; and also so that Your Lordship can say a word in my defence if you get the chance, because I'm writing the truth. Among men, if not before God, I regard myself as an honest man, because I've never cheated anyone, and also because having to defend oneself against scoundrels is enough to drive a man mad sometimes, as you can see.

I beg Your Lordship to read this account when you have time, and keep it for me, and you can be sure that for most of what I've written there are still witnesses. I'd be glad, too, if the pope could see it, and the whole world, because I'm writing

the truth, and much less than I could say. And I am not a
thieving usurer, but a citizen of Florence, of gentle birth, the
son of an honest man, and not some nobody from Cagli.

Since writing this, I have received a message from the
ambassador of Urbino that if I want to have the ratification, I
should settle with my conscience first. I say that he has fabri-
cated his own Michelangelo out of the same stuff as himself.

To continue with this affair of the tomb of Pope Julius, I say
that when he had changed his mind about having it made in his
lifetime, as I said, some boats came to Ripa carrying marble
that I had ordered from Carrara. Since there was no money
from the pope because of his second thoughts about the work,
I had to pay shipping charges of a hundred and fifty, or rather
two hundred ducats, which I borrowed from Baldassare Bal-
ducci (that is, from the bank of Iacopo Galli). At the same time
some stone-cutters that I'd hired to work on the tomb came
from Florence (some of them are still alive) and when I had
fixed up the house behind Santa Caterina with beds and other
furniture for the men who were going to do the frame and other
things for the tomb, I found myself blocked for lack of money.
I was doing my best to persuade the pope to keep things going,
and one morning, when I went to talk to him about it, he had
me turned away by a groom. A bishop from Lucca who saw
this said to the groom: 'Don't you know who this man is?' And
the groom said to me: 'Forgive me, sir, these were my orders.'
I went back home and wrote to the pope: 'Most Blessed Father,
I was turned out of the palace this morning by order of Your
Holiness; I therefore inform you that from now on, if you need
me, you must seek me elsewhere than in Rome.' And I sent this
letter to Master Agostino, a steward, to give to the pope; and I
called into the house a carpenter, Cosimo, who was working
for me to fit up the house, and a stone-cutter, who is still alive,
and who was also with me, and I told them: 'Go and find a
Jew and sell everything in this house and then come back to
Florence.' Then I went and took a post horse and set off for
Florence. The pope, when he received my letter, sent five horse-
men after me, who caught up with me at Poggibonsi about
three hours after sunset and gave me a letter from the pope

that said: 'As soon as you have seen this, return to Rome immediately, under pain of our displeasure.' The horsemen insisted that I send an answer so that they could prove they had found me. I answered the pope that whenever he fulfilled his obligations towards me, I would return, but that otherwise he could never hope to have me. And while I was in Florence Julius sent three briefs to the Signoria. At the last the Signoria sent for me and said: 'We don't want to get caught up in a war against Pope Julius for you: you must leave; and if you decide to go back to him, we shall give you letters of such authority that if he does you any harm, it will be done against this Signoria.' And that's what they did, and I returned to the pope; and what followed would take a long time to tell. Enough to say that this business cost me more than a thousand ducats, because after I had left Rome there was a great row about it, to the shame of the pope; and almost all the marble I had in St Peter's Square was looted, especially the smaller pieces which I had to do all over again; so I say and affirm that, with the damage and the interest, the heirs of Pope Julius owe me five thousand ducats. And now those who robbed me of my youth, my honour and my goods call me a thief! And again, as I already wrote, the ambassador of Urbino informs me that I should settle with my conscience first, and then I shall see the ratification from the duke. That's not what he said before he made me deposit fourteen hundred ducats. In these things that I write I may make some mistakes about the dates between then and now, but everything else is true, truer than I can write.

I beg Your Lordship, for the love of God and the truth, to read these things when you have time so that when the occasion arises you can defend me before the pope against those who speak ill of me, though they know nothing, and whose false reports have put it into the duke's head that I am a great scoundrel. All the discords that arose between Pope Julius and me came from the envy of Bramante and Raphael of Urbino: and that is why he did not go ahead with the tomb in his lifetime, and it was meant to ruin me. And Raphael was right to be envious, because whatever art he had, he had it from me.

R227, G239

Letter 38

[To Lionardo di Buonarroto Simoni]
[11 July 1544. From Rome]

Lionardo – I've been ill: and you came here instead of Giovan
Francesco to kill me off and to see whether I'd left anything.
Don't you already have enough of mine in Florence? You can't
deny that you're just like your father who turned me out of my
own house in Florence. Learn that I've made my will in such a
way that you can stop thinking about anything I've got in
Rome. So go with God and don't let me see your face, and
never write to me again, and do what the priest says.

   Michelagniolo

                                            R238, G250

Letter 39

[To Master Luigi del Riccio]
[February–March 1546. From Rome]

Master Luigi – Please send back the last madrigal which you
don't understand so that I can revise it, because that snapper-up
of rough drafts, Urbino, was so quick that he didn't give me
time to look it over.

   As for meeting tomorrow, you must excuse me, because the
weather is bad and I have things to do at home. But what we
had counted on doing tomorrow we shall do this Lent instead
at Lunghezza with a nice fat tench.

[Unsigned]

                                            R250, G269

Letter 40

[To Vittoria Colonna, Marchesa di Pescara]
[Date uncertain. From Rome]

Before taking the things that Your Ladyship has so often wanted
to give me, I wanted to make you something of my own hand,
so that I could receive them as little unworthily as possible: but
having since seen and acknowledged that the grace of God
cannot be bought and that to keep you waiting is a great sin, I
admit my fault and accept those things most willingly: and
when I have them, I shall feel as if I am in paradise, not so
much because I have them in my house, but because I am in
theirs. For which, if it were possible, I would be even more
obliged to Your Ladyship than I am already.

The bearer of this letter will be my servant Urbino, to whom
Your Ladyship may say when you want me to come and see the
head of Christ that you promised to show me. I commend
myself to you.

Michelagniolo Buonarroti

R201, G274

Letter 41

[To Vittoria Colonna, Marchesa di Pescara]
[Date uncertain]

Signora Marchesa – Since I am here in Rome, I did not think
there was any need to leave the crucifix with Master Tommaso
and make him the intermediary between Your Ladyship and
myself, your servant, so that I might serve you; especially
because I wanted to do more for you than for anyone I have
ever known on earth. But the great task that I had and still
have on hand prevented me from letting Your Ladyship
know this: and since I know that you know that love needs no
master and that the lover sleeps not, there was even less need

of intermediaries: and, although it seemed I had forgotten, I
was doing something I did not talk about so that I could come
up with something unexpected. Now my plan has been spoilt:
'He sins who can forget such faith so soon.'
    Your Ladyship's servant,
    Michelagniolo Buonarroti in Rome

                                                    R202, G275

Letter 42

To the Most Christian King of France

Sacred Majesty – I do not know which is greater, the favour
that I receive or the wonder that Your Majesty has deigned to
write to one of my rank, and even more to ask him for some
of his works, although they are in no way worthy of Your
Majesty's name. But such as they are, let it be known to Your
Majesty that I have long desired to serve you, but have been
unable to do so because even in Italy I have not had enough
occasion to practise my art. Now I am old and am engaged for
some months on work for Pope Paul; but if, after this task,
some life is still left to me, I shall endeavour to carry out the
long-held desire of which I have already spoken: that is, to
make for Your Majesty something in marble, something in
bronze and something in painting. And even if death should
frustrate this desire of mine, if there is sculpture and painting
in the next life, I shall not fail you there, where there is no more
growing old. And I pray that God may give Your Majesty a
long and happy life.
    From Rome, day XXVI April MDXLVI
    Most humble servant, Michelagniolo Buonarroti

                                                    R266, G285

Letter 43

[To Master Luigi del Riccio]
[Date uncertain, 1544–6. From Rome]

Master Luigi – You think that I am answering as you desire I should, when in fact it's the opposite. You give me what I refused, and you refuse me what I asked. And you do not sin unwittingly, for you sent it to me by Ercole, being ashamed to give it me yourself.

A man who has saved me from death may well insult me; but I hardly know which weighs more heavily, death or the insult. So I beg and beseech you, by the true friendship between us, to have that plate I dislike destroyed and to burn the prints already made: and if you want to trade in me, don't let others do so as well. And if you break me into a thousand pieces, I shall do the same – not with you, but with what is yours.

Michelagniolo Buonarroti

Neither painter nor sculptor nor architect, but whatever you wish; but not a drunkard as I told you when I stayed with you.

R244, G294

Letter 44

[To Master Bartolomeo Ferratini in Rome]
[1547. From Rome]

Master Bartolomeo, dear friend – It cannot be denied that Bramante was as skilled in architecture as anyone since the ancients. He made the first plan for St Peter's, not full of confusion, but clear and unencumbered, luminous and detached, so that it did not interfere with the palace; and it was thought beautiful, and obviously still is; so that anyone who strays from Bramante's design, as Sangallo has done, strays from the truth; and that this is so any impartial eye can see from his model.

With that outer ambulatory, the first thing he does is take all
the light from Bramante's plan; and not just this, but it lacks
any light of its own: and there are so many hiding-places above
and below, dark enough to favour every kind of dirty work –
hiding outlaws, forging false coin, getting nuns pregnant and
other dirty deeds – so that in the evening, when they close the
church, it would take twenty-five men to look for those who
might be hidden, and they would still have a job finding them.
There would be this other drawback as well: in surrounding
Bramante's composition with the addition shown in the model,
they would have to pull down the Pauline Chapel, the offices
of the Piombo, the Rota and many other buildings: nor, I
believe, would the Sistine Chapel survive intact. As for the part
of the ambulatory that has been built, they say it cost a hundred
thousand *scudi*, but this isn't true because it could be done with
sixteen thousand. And not much would be lost by pulling it
down because the dressed stones and the foundations could
hardly be more useful and the construction would save two
hundred thousand *scudi* in cost and three hundred years in
time. This is how I see it, and without any personal interest,
because I would lose a lot by winning the argument. And if you
could get the pope to understand this you would do me a great
favour, for I don't feel very well.

    Your Michelagniolo

Following the Sangallo model would also produce this result:
that everything done in my time might be pulled down, which
would be a very great loss.

                                         R274, G414

Letter 45

To Benedetto Varchi
[March 1547]

Master Benedetto – To show that I have received your book (as
I have), I shall give some answer to what you ask, though I

don't know much about it. I say that painting seems to me better the more it approaches relief, and relief the worse the more it approaches painting. And that's why I used to think that sculpture was the light of painting and that the difference between them was like the sun and the moon. Now that I've read your book where you say that, philosophically speaking, things that have the same purpose are one and the same, I have changed my mind. And, unless greater need for judgement, greater difficulty, obstacles and toil, make for greater nobility, then painting and sculpture are the same thing. And to show that this is the case every painter should do no less sculpture than painting; and likewise every sculptor as much painting as sculpture. By sculpture I mean what is made by taking something away: what is done by adding something is like painting. It is enough that since both of them, sculpture and painting, come from the same intelligence, we can make peace between them and drop all these disputes; for we spend more time on that than on making the figures themselves. As for the man who said painting was more noble than sculpture, if that's how well he understands the other things he writes about, then my servant-girl would have written them better. There would be countless things, still unspoken, to be said about this kind of knowledge; but, as I said, it would take too much time, and I have little because I'm not just old but almost numbered with the dead. So I beg you to excuse me. And I commend myself to you and thank you to the best of my ability for the honour you do me, which is too great and which I don't deserve.

Your Michelagniolo in Rome

R280, G355

Letter 46

To Master Luca Martini [of the Florentine Academy] in
Florence
[March 1547]

Magnificent Master Luca – Master Bartolommeo has passed
on a letter of yours together with a little book – a commentary
on one of my sonnets. The sonnet does come from me, but the
commentary comes from heaven; and it really is a wonderful
thing, not just in my opinion, but in that of learned men and
especially of Master Donato Giannotti who never tires of read-
ing it: and he sends you his regards. As for the sonnet itself, I
know what it amounts to, but even so I still can't help feeling
a touch of vanity at having been the cause of such a lovely
learned commentary. And since I feel that the author's words
and praises make me something that I'm not, I beg you to speak
to him for me in terms that befit so much love, affection and
courtesy. I beg you to do this, because I feel of little worth; and
a man who enjoys a good reputation should not tempt fortune;
and it is better to keep silent than to fall from on high. I am
old, and death has taken from me the thoughts of youth; and
let those who don't know what old age is like just have patience
until it comes, because they can't know it in advance. Give my
regards, as I said, to Varchi, as one devoted to him and to his
virtues and at his service wherever I may be.

Yours and at your service in all that is in my power.
Michelagniolo Buonarroti in Rome

R279, G356

Letter 47

To Lionardo di Buonarroto Simoni in Florence
[3 September 1547]

Lionardo – With your letter I got the receipt for the five hundred and fifty gold *scudi* which I paid out here to Bettino. You write that you will give four to that woman for the love of God, which pleases me. I want the balance of fifty also spent for the love of God, partly for the soul of Buonarroto your father and partly for my own. So look out for some needy citizen who has daughters to marry or to place in a convent and give him the money, and make sure you're not cheated and get a receipt made out and send it to me. But do all this secretly because I'm talking about the kind of needy citizens who would be ashamed to beg.

As for your taking a wife, I must say that I can't recommend one more than another because it's so long since I was down there in Florence that I can't know the real standing of people. So you had better think about it yourself; and when you've found what suits you, I'd like to be told.

You sent me a brass rule as if I were a mason or a carpenter to carry it around with me. I was ashamed to have it in the house, and I gave it away.

Francesca [Lionardo's sister] writes me that she is not well and that she has four children and that she has many troubles because of her ill-health. I'm very sorry to hear it: otherwise, I don't think she lacks for anything. As for troubles, I think I have more than she does, with old age to boot, and I have no time to entertain relatives. So comfort her for me and remember me to Guicciardino [Francesca's husband].

I advise you to spend the money I sent you on something solid, property or something else, because it's dangerous to keep it around, especially these days. So be sure to sleep with your eyes open.

Michelagniolo Buonarroti in Rome

Letter 48

To Lionardo di Buonarroto Simoni in Florence
[22 October 1547]

Lionardo – I'm glad you informed me about the proclamation because if so far I have been careful not to talk or mix with exiles, from now on I shall be even more careful. As for my being in the house of the Strozzi when I was ill, what matters to me is not that I was in their house, but that I was in the room of Master Luigi del Riccio, who was my great friend; and since Bartolomeo Angelini died, I have found nobody better or more faithful about my business. And since Master del Riccio died, I no longer frequent that house. Of this all Rome can testify and of the kind of life I lead, for I am always alone, rarely go out and speak with nobody and especially not with Florentines. And if somebody greets me in the street, I can't do less than give a courteous answer, but then I go my way. And if I knew in advance who the exiles were, I wouldn't answer at all. So, as I say, from now on I shall be very careful – especially because I have so much else to think about that life is very wearisome.

As for setting up a shop, do what you think is likely to work, because it's not my profession and I can't give you good advice. I only tell you this: if you waste the money you have, you won't see it again.

Michelagniolo in Rome

R291, G318

Letter 49

To Lionardo di Buonarroto Simoni in Florence
[16 January 1548]

Lionardo – I learned from your last letter of the death of Giovansimone. It distressed me greatly because, although I am old, I had hoped to see him before he died and before I die. We must resign ourselves to the will of God. I would especially like to know the manner of his death, and whether he died with confession and communion and all the rites of the Church; for if I knew he had all these, I would be less distressed.

I wrote to you about the documents and book of contracts and asked you to send a muleteer to collect them: I gave them to the man who came with your letter, and it was on the day of the Epiphany, if I remember well, about ten days ago, I think; and I gave them to him in a big box wrapped in waxed cloth, corded and properly packed: so make sure you get it and let me know when it arrives because it's very important. I can't say any more in this letter because I received yours too late and I have no time to write. Remember me to Guicciardino and Francesca and to Master Giovan Francesco.

Michelagniolo Buonarroti in Rome

R299, G314

Letter 50

To Lionardo di Buonarroto Simoni in Florence
[2 May 1548]

Lionardo – I received the barrel of pears which came to eighty-six. I sent thirty-three to the pope who thought they were fine and was delighted with them. About the cheese, the Customs say the carter is a scoundrel and never took it to the customs-house; so when I find that he's in Rome, I'll give him what he deserves, not because of the cheese, but to teach him to show such little respect for people. I've been very ill these days through not being able to urinate, because that's my great weakness, but now I feel better. I'm writing this before some loudmouth sets you off by writing a pack of lies. Tell the priest [Giovan Francesco Fattucci] that he should not write any more 'to Michelagniolo sculptor', because here I'm known only as Michelagniolo Buonarroti; and that if a Florentine citizen wants an altarpiece painted he should go and find a painter: because I have never been the kind of painter or sculptor who sets up a

shop. I have always avoided that for the honour of my father
and brothers, although I have served three popes, which I was
obliged to do. There's nothing else. My last letter gave my
opinion about you taking a wife. As for what I've written about
the priest, don't tell him anything because I want it to look as
if I didn't get his letter.

    Michelagniolo Buonarroti in Rome

                                      R306, G322

Letter 51

To Lionardo di Buonarroto Simoni in Florence
[March 1549]

Lionardo – Your last letter was unreadable and I couldn't make
it out, so I threw it on the fire: that's why I can't reply to
anything that was in it. I've written often enough to say that
every time I get a letter from you, I get feverish before I manage
to read it. So I'm telling you, from now on don't write to me
again, and if there's anything you have to let me know, find
someone who can write, because I've got other things on my
mind than agonizing over your letters. Master Giovan Fran-
cesco writes that you would like to come to Rome for a few
days: I'm very surprised you are able to leave since you told me
you had just gone into partnership. So take care not to throw
away the money I sent you; and Gismondo should take care as
well, because nobody understands money who hasn't earned it
himself; and this we learn from experience, for most of those
who are born to wealth throw it away and die ruined. So open
your eyes and think and remember in what toil and misery I
live, old as I am. The other day a Florentine citizen came to
talk to me about one of the Ginori daughters who has been
suggested for you and whom, he says, you like. I don't believe
it's true, and again I can't give you any advice because I have
no information. But I don't like the idea of you taking a wife
whose father wouldn't give you a decent dowry if he had one

to give. To my mind, if anyone wants to give you a wife, he should think of giving her to you yourself and not to your property. It seems to me that, since you're not looking for a large dowry, you should take the first step in seeking a wife; not that others should try to give you a wife because she has no dowry. So all you should be looking for is soundness of mind and body, and noble blood; and the upbringing and relatives she has, these are important.

I have nothing else to say. Remember me to Giovan Francesco.

Michelagniolo Buonarroti in Rome

R322, G327

Letter 52

To Giovan Francesco Fattucci, Priest of Santa Maria del Fiore, dearest friend, in Florence
[February 1550]

Master Giovan Francesco, dear friend – Although we haven't written anything to each other for months, I have not forgotten our long good friendship, nor that I want what's good for you, as I always have, and that I love you with all my heart, and more for all the kindnesses received. As for the old age that we both share, I would like to know how yours is treating you, because mine doesn't make me very happy: so please write me something. You know we have a new pope [Julius III] and who he is: for which all Rome rejoices, thanks be to God, and we expect nothing but great good of him, especially for the poor, given his generosity. As for my affairs, I'd be grateful and you'd do me a great favour if you let me know how things are going with Lionardo – and the plain honest truth, because he's young and I'm worried about him, especially because he's alone and has nobody to advise him. There's nothing else, except that the other day Master Tommaso de' Cavalieri asked me to give his thanks to Varchi for a wonderful little book that's now in print, where, he says, he speaks very honourably of him, and no less of me. And he's given me a sonnet that I did for him about the same time, asking me to send it to him [Varchi] to expound; which I send you with this. If you like it, give it to him; if not, throw it in the fire, and remember that I'm fighting with death and that my thoughts are somewhere else: yet sometimes this is what one has to do. For doing me so much honour in his sonnets, as I said, please thank Master Benedetto, offering him the little that I am.

Your Michelagniolo in Rome

                                                    R343, G360

Letter 53

To Master Giovan Francesco Fattucci in Florence
[From Rome]

Master Giovan Francesco, dear friend – Since I happen to be writing to the painter Giorgio [Vasari] in Florence, I take the liberty of troubling you to give him the enclosed letter, assuming that he's a friend of yours. And not to make this letter too brief and having nothing else to say, I am sending you some of the poems I wrote for the Marchesa di Pescara, who was devoted to me, and I no less to her. Death robbed me of a great friend. There's nothing else. I'm the same as usual, bearing with patience the ills of old age. As I suppose you do.

On the first day of August 1550
[Unsigned]

                                                    R347, G363

Letter 54

To Lionardo di Buonarroto Simoni in Florence

Lionardo – I received the pears, that is ninety-seven of the *bronche* kind, since that's what you call them. There's nothing else to say about that. About your taking a wife, I sent you my opinion last Saturday, that you should not think about the dowry, but only about finding someone of good stock, noble, well brought-up and healthy: I can't be more particular than that because I know as little of Florence as someone who's never been there. I was told about one of the Alessandri girls, but heard nothing particular. If I do hear something I shall let you know next time.

Master Giovan Francesco asked me about a month ago for something by the Marchesa di Pescara, if I had anything. I have a little book in parchment, which she gave me about ten years ago, and which contains a hundred and three sonnets, not counting those on paper that she sent me from Viterbo, forty of them: these I had bound in the same book and at the time I lent them to many people so that now they are all in print. Then I have many letters that she wrote me from Orvieto and Viterbo. That's what I have by the Marchesa. So show this letter to the priest, and let me know what he says.

As for the money that I already wrote to you about, saying it should be given for alms, as I think I wrote on Saturday, I shall have to exchange it for bread because, with the famine that's here, I'm afraid they will all die of hunger if no other help arrives.

On the 7th day of March, 1551
Michelagniolo Buonarroti in Rome

R360, G376

Letter 55

To Lionardo di Buonarroto Simoni in Florence

Lionardo – I learn from your last letter that you have brought your wife [Cassandra Ridolfi] home and that you are very happy with her, and that you send me her greetings, and also that you have still not given security for the dowry. I'm delighted that you are pleased with her and I think that we should thank God unceasingly with heart and mind. As for giving security, if you don't have the dowry, don't give security, but keep your eyes open because there's always some disagreement over these money matters. I don't understand about these things, but I reckon you should have had everything fixed before you brought your wife home. Anyway, thank her for her greetings and pay her those compliments for me that you can express better by word of mouth than I can by writing. I want it to be seen that she's the wife of a nephew of mine, but I haven't been able to demonstrate this because Urbino has been away. He came back two days ago, so now I intend to make some kind of gesture. I'm told that a fine necklace of precious pearls would be a fitting gift. I've asked a jeweller, a friend of Urbino, to look for one, and I hope to find it; but don't tell her anything about it. And if there's anything else you think I should do, let me know. There's nothing else. Look after yourself, be wary, think what you're doing, because there are always far more widows than widowers.

On the twentieth day of May, 1553
Michelagniolo Buonarroti in Rome

R381, G397

Letter 56

To Giorgio Vasari

Master Giorgio, dear friend – Your last letter gave me great plea-
sure, because I see that you still remember a poor old man, and
even more because you were present at the triumph you write
about and saw the arrival of another Buonarroto [Lionardo's
first son]. For this I thank you with all my heart; but yet I'm not
happy about such display, for a man shouldn't laugh while the
whole world weeps. So I think Lionardo doesn't show much
judgement in celebrating a birth with that joy we should reserve
for the death of someone who has lived well. There's nothing
else. I thank you profoundly for the love you bear me, although
I'm unworthy of it. Things here are much as usual.

On I don't know what day of April, 1554
Your Michelagniolo Buonarroti in Rome

R389, G405

Letter 57

To Giorgio Vasari, most excellent painter, in Florence

Master Giorgio, dear friend – You will surely say that I must
be old and mad for wanting to write sonnets: but since so many
people say I'm in my second childhood, I wanted to act the
part. I see from your letter how much you love me, and believe
me that I would dearly like to lay my frail bones beside those
of my father, as you beg me. But if I left here now, I would be the
cause of the total ruin of the construction of St Peter's, which
would be a great shame and a very great sin. But when the whole
structure is so fixed that it can no longer be altered, I hope to do
everything you have written – if indeed it isn't already a sin to be
frustrating the vultures who can't wait to see me leave.

On the 19th day of September 1554
Michelagniolo Buonarroti in Rome

R390, G406

Letter 58

To Lionardo di Buonnaroto Simoni in Florence

Lionardo – I see from your letter that you have received the hundred *scudi* that I sent you and that you understand what to do with them, that is to send me ten feet of dark violet cloth and to use the rest for charity where and how you think fit, and then let me know.

As for the child you are expecting, you write me that you're thinking of naming him Michelagniolo. I say that if it pleases you, it pleases me too; but if it's a girl I don't know what to say. Please yourselves, especially Cassandra to whom I send my regards. There's nothing else. About that charity, do it without much fuss.

On the 9th day of February 1555
Michelagniolo Buonarroti in Rome

R393, G409

Letter 59

To Lionardo di Buonarroto Simoni in Florence
[March 1555]

Lionardo – From your last I learned the death of Michelagniolo [Lionardo's second son], and now I am as grieved as I was first overjoyed – indeed, much more. We must bear it patiently and think that it is better than if he had died in old age. But you should do your best to stay alive so as not to leave our hard-earned property without men to run it.

Cepperello has told Urbino that he's going to Florence and that the woman we talked about, who had a lifelong lease of the farm, is dead. I think he will make a deal with you. If he's ready to offer it at a fair price with good security, take it and let me know, and I shall send you the money.

Michelagniolo Buonarroti in Rome

R395, G411

Letter 60

To my dear Master Giorgio Vasari in Florence

Master Giorgio, dear friend – Quite recently one evening I had a visit at home from a very discreet and proper young man, namely Master Lionardo, the duke's chamberlain; and, with great love and affection, he made me the same offers on behalf of His Lordship that you did in your last letter. I answered exactly as I had answered you, that is, that he should thank the duke most heartily on my behalf for such generous offers, but that he should beg His Lordship that I might, with his permission, continue to work on the construction of St Peter's until it had reached that stage of completion where it could not be changed and given another form; because for me to leave earlier would be the cause of great ruin, a great shame and great sin. And I pray you, for the love of God and St Peter, to beg this of the duke and to commend me to His Lordship. My dear Master Giorgio, I know that you can see in what I write that I am now at the eleventh hour and that no thought is born in me that does not have death carved within. God grant that I may put it off for a few more years.

On the 22nd day of June 1555
Your Michelagniolo Buonarroti in Rome

R402, G418

Letter 61

To Lionardo di Buonarroto Simoni in Florence

Not without the greatest sorrow did I learn from your letter the death of my brother Gismondo. We must bear it patiently; and since he died conscious to the end and with all the sacraments ordained by the Church, we should thank God.

I have many worries here. Urbino is still very sick in bed and I don't know how it will turn out. I am as distressed as if he were my son because he has served me faithfully for twenty-five years. And now that I'm old I don't have time to train someone else to suit me. So it upsets me a lot. So if you know some devout people down there, I beg you to get them to pray God for his recovery.

On the 30th day of November 1555
Michelagniolo Buonarroti in Rome

R407, G422

Letter 62

To Giorgio Vasari, dear friend, in Florence

Master Giorgio, dear friend – I can hardly write, but I shall still say something in reply to your last letter. You know that Urbino is dead: which has been a great grace of God to me, but great harm and infinite sorrow too. The grace was that just as he kept me alive during his life, so now by dying he has taught me how to die, not with regret, but with desire of death. He was with me for twenty-six years and I found him most loyal and faithful; and now that I had made him rich and expected him to be the staff and comfort of my old age, he has left me. The only hope left me is to see him again in Paradise. And of this God has given me a sign in the happy way he died; for, more than dying, he regretted leaving me in this treacherous world with all its troubles – though the greater part of me has gone with him and I am left with nothing but infinite misery. And I commend and beg you, if it is no trouble, to give my apologies to Master Benvenuto for not answering his letter, because I am so distressed by thoughts like these that I cannot write; and commend me to him as I commend myself to you.

On the 23rd day of February, 1556
Your Michelagniolo Buonarroti in Rome

R410, G425

Letter 63

[To Cornelia, widow of Urbino]
[28 April 1557]

I had realized that you were angry with me, but I could not find the reason. Now, from your last letter, I think I understand why. When you sent me the cheeses, you wrote that you wanted to send me other things as well, but that the handkerchiefs weren't finished yet; and because I didn't want you to go to any more expense for me, I wrote that you shouldn't send me anything more, but that if you should ask me for something it would give me the greatest pleasure, since you know (indeed you know for sure) the love I still bear to Urbino, dead as he is, and to all that was his. As for me coming down to see the children or you sending Michelagniolo [Urbino's son] here, I must tell you about the conditions I live in. Sending Michelagniolo here is not a good idea, because I have no women and there's nobody to look after the place, and the child is still too delicate, and something might happen that I would really regret. And then there's the fact that for the past month the Duke of Florence, in his kindness, has been making great efforts and generous offers to persuade me back to Florence. I have asked him for enough time to settle my things here and leave the construction of St Peter's in a decent state: so that I reckon I shall stay here all summer. And when my affairs and yours are settled at the Monte della Fede, this winter I shall move to Florence for good, because I am an old man and there will be no time for me to return to Rome; and I shall come by and see you; and if you want to give me Michelagniolo, I shall keep him in Florence with more love than my own nephews, the sons of Lionardo, teaching him what I know and what his father wanted him to learn. Yesterday, the twenty-seventh of March [a mistake for April] I received your last letter.

Your Michelagniolo in Rome

R431, G445

Letter 64

To the Most Illustrious Cosimo, Duke of Florence
[May 1557]

My Lord Duke – About three months ago, or a little less, I informed Your Lordship that I still could not leave the construction of St Peter's without great damage to it and very great shame to me; and that in order to leave it as I would like, with nothing necessary left undone, I would need not less than another year. And I understood that Your Lordship was ready to give me this time. Now I have a new letter from Your Lordship urging me to return more strongly than I expected: this causes me no little anxiety because I am now in more toil and trouble over the things of the construction than I ever was before; and the reason is that, because I am old and cannot go there often, a mistake has been made in the vault of the chapel of the King of France, which is a complex and unusual work: so I shall have to undo a large part of what was done.

And Bastiano di San Gimignano, who was an overseer there, can testify which chapel this is and how important for the rest of the building. Once the chapel has been set right, I think everything will be finished by the end of the summer. After which all I shall have to do is leave the model of the whole thing, as everybody asks (especially Carpi), and then return to Florence to lie down with Death, whom I seek night and day to befriend so that he may treat me no worse than other old men.

Now, to return to the subject, I beg Your Lordship to grant me the time I ask of one more year for the construction, as I thought you were ready to do when I last wrote.

The least of Your Lordship's servants,
Michelagniolo Buonarroti in Rome

R433, G447

Letter 65

To Master Giorgio Vasari, dearest friend
[22 May 1557. From Rome]

Master Giorgio, dear friend – I call God to witness that it was against my will and under intense pressure that I was set by Pope Paul to work on the construction of St Peter's in Rome ten years ago. And if the work had been continued the way it started back then, I would already have brought it to the state I wanted so that I could return to Florence. But it has been greatly slowed down by lack of money, and it is still being slowed down at the hardest and most difficult stage, so that to abandon it now would mean nothing but the huge disgrace of losing all the reward for the toils I have endured over the last ten years for the love of God.

I have given this explanation in reply to your letter, and also because I received a letter from the duke that has left me marvelling that His Lordship should deign to write with such kindness. For this I thank God and His Lordship with all my heart. I am wandering off the point because I'm losing my memory and my mind; and writing is a great trouble to me for it is not my art. The point is this: I want you to understand what would follow if I abandoned the construction and left Rome. The first thing is that I would delight a bunch of thieves and bring about its ruin and perhaps even cause it to be closed up forever. Another is that here I have certain obligations and a house and other things worth a few thousand *scudi*, and if I left without permission I don't know what would happen to them. Yet another thing is that I am constantly ailing, what with gravel and the stone and a pain in my side, like all old men; and Master Eraldo can testify to this because he keeps me alive. So I don't have the heart to go to Florence only to come back here; and if I go back there for good, I shall need time to settle things here so that I no longer have to worry about them. The fact is that I left Florence so long ago that when I came here Pope Clement was still alive, who died two days later.

Master Giorgio, I send you my regards and I ask you to remember me to the duke; and do something for me because I no longer have my mind on anything but dying; and what I write you about my health is no less than than the truth. I replied to the duke the way I did because I was told I should reply, though I had no mind to write to His Lordship, especially so soon. And if I had been able to ride, I would have gone straight to Florence and back before anyone here knew about it.

Michelagniolo Buonarroti

R434, G448

Letter 66

To Lionardo di Buonarroto Simoni in Florence

Lionardo – I've received the wool and the shot silk: as soon as I find someone to take it, I'll send it to Urbino's widow and she'll send me the money at once. For the balance of the money, you'll let me know when you've spent it in the way I wrote you.

As for how I am, I am ill in body with all the ills that usually plague old men – the stone so that I can't urinate, pains in my side, pains in my back, so that often I can't climb the stairs. And the worst is that I'm full of anxiety because if I left the comforts for my ailments that I have here, I wouldn't last three days; but I don't want to lose the duke's favour on that account; nor do I want to fail in my task at the construction of St Peter's, nor fail myself. I pray that God may help and enlighten me; and if I should fall ill, I mean in danger of death, I'll send for you immediately. But don't think of it and don't set about coming if you don't get my letter telling you to come.

Remember me to Master Giorgio who can help me a great deal if he wants to, because I know the duke is fond of him.

On the 16th day of June, 1557

Michelagniolo Buonarroti in Rome

R435, G449

Letter 67

To Lionardo di Buonarroto Simoni in Florence

Lionardo – I have received the shirts and all the other things you mentioned in your letter. You will know best how to thank Cassandra for me.

I've had two letters from you begging me very warmly to return to Florence. I think you don't know that about four months ago, through Cardinal di Carpi, who is one of the deputies for its construction, I had permission from the Duke of Florence to carry on with the building of St Peter's in Rome. I thanked God for this and I was delighted by it. Now I don't know whether you write so warmly, as I said, from your desire that I should come back, or whether there's something else. So be a bit clearer, because everything brings me bother and trouble.

I really should tell you that the Florentines intend to erect a great building here, namely their own church, and of one accord they have all tried and are still trying to make me look to it.

I've replied that I am here at the duke's request for the work on St Peter's and that without his permission they won't get anything out of me.

On the 15th day of June 1559
Michelagniolo Buonarroti in Rome

Writing is very hard on my hand, my eyesight and my memory. That's what old age does!

R449, G463

Letter 68

To the Most Illustrious and Reverend Lord and Honourable
Patron, Lord Cardinal Carpi

Most Illustrious and Reverend Lord and Honourable Patron –
Master Francesco Bandini told me yesterday that your Most
Illustrious and Reverend Lordship had told him that the con-
struction of St Peter's could not be going worse than it is. This
really distressed me a great deal both because you have not
been truly informed and because, as indeed I should, I, more
than anyone, wish things to go well. And, if I am not mistaken,
I can truly affirm that, as regards the current work, it could
not go better. But since perhaps I can be easily deceived by
self-interest and old age and thus, against my will, do some
harm or damage to the building, I intend, as soon as I can, to
ask His Holiness Our Lord for my release. Indeed, to save
time, I would implore, as I now do, Your Most Illustrious and
Reverend Lordship to be pleased to free me of this burden,
which, as you know, at the pope's command, I have borne
voluntarily and without salary for seventeen years. What my
efforts have done for the building in that time is clear to see.
Once again I earnestly beg you to release me, since for this once
you could not do me a greater favour. And with all reverence I
humbly kiss the hand of your Most Illustrious and Reverend
Lordship.

From my house in Rome, the 13th day of September, 1560
Your Most Illustrious and Reverend Lordship's humble
servant
[Unsigned]

R462, G478

Letter 69

[Addressee uncertain]
[Date uncertain. From Rome]

Most Reverend Monsignor – When a plan has many parts all those that are of the same kind and size should be ornamented in the same way and the same manner, and likewise their counterparts. But when the plan changes form entirely, it is not only permissible but necessary to change the ornaments, and their counterparts as well. And the central parts can be as free as they like; just as the nose, being in the middle of the face, is not related to one eye or the other, whereas one hand must be like the other and one eye like the other because they are lateral and corresponding. And therefore one thing is certain: the parts of architecture are derived from the parts of man. Nobody who has not been or is not a good master of the human figure, and especially of anatomy, can hope to understand this.
    Michelagniolo Buonarroti

                                                            R358, G480

Letter 70

To Lionardo di Buonarroto Simoni in Florence

Lionardo – I see from your letter that you are putting your trust in certain envious scoundrels who write you a heap of lies because they can't cheat or rob me. They are a bunch of vultures, and you are so silly that you trust what they say about my affairs, as if I were a child. Get rid of them as envious, scandal-mongering, low-lived scoundrels. You write about me suffering because of the way I'm looked after, and other things – as for being looked after, I tell you I couldn't be better off, nor more faithfully looked after and treated in everything: about being robbed, which is what I think you mean, I tell you that in this house I have people I can trust and be sure of. So look after yourself and don't bother about my affairs, because I know how to look out for myself if I have to, and I'm not a child. Keep well.

From Rome, on the 21st day of August, 1563
Michelagniolo

R479, G497

Letter 71

To Lionardo di Buonarroto Simoni in Florence

Lionardo – I received your last letter with the twelve splendid *marzolino* cheeses; I thank you for them. Delighted to hear that you're in good health, as I am too. If I've had several letters from you and not replied, this is because I can't use my hand to write; so from now on I shall get someone else to write and sign it myself. There's nothing else.

From Rome, on the 28th day of December, 1563
I, Michelagniolo Buonarroti

R480, G498

GIORGIO VASARI,
'LIFE OF MICHELANGELO'
(1550)

The most industrious and distinguished spirits, enlightened by the celebrated Giotto and his followers, had been striving to give the world some proof of those powers that the benevolence of the stars and their own temperament had given to their minds; but though they longed to imitate the greatness of nature with the excellence of art, they struggled in vain to approach that supreme knowledge that many call understanding. Then the most benign Ruler of Heaven kindly turned his regard towards the earth, where, seeing the vain multiplication of so much labour and the most assiduous studies still without any fruit, and the presumptuous opinion of men even further from the truth than darkness is from light, he decided to free us from so many errors by sending down a spirit who would be so universally skilful in every craft and art that his work alone would demonstrate how to solve the real difficulties in the sciences of drawing and painting, how to work with judgement in sculpture and how to create truly pleasing architecture. And he chose also to grant him true moral philosophy, with the ornament of sweet poetry, so that the world might choose and look up to him as a singular model in life, in works, in holiness of conduct, and in all human actions, and that we might acclaim him as being of heaven rather than of earth. And since he saw that in the practice of these disciplines and noble arts of painting, sculpture and architecture the Tuscans have always been pre-eminent, being more devoted than any other Italians to the labour and study of all the arts, he chose Florence, most worthy of cities, as this man's native land. Thus, in one of her citizens, he duly brought to perfection all those gifts that in Cimabue, in Giotto, in Donatello, in Filippo Brunelleschi and in Leonardo da Vinci[1] had made such a marvellous beginning that one could hardly doubt that time would reveal a genius to show us, in his goodness, the perfection of their ultimate end.

In Florence then, in the year 1474,[2] there was born to Lodovico Simon Buonarroti a son whom he christened Michelangelo as if to suggest that he might be more heavenly and divine than mortal. And he was of noble birth, for the Simoni have always been noble[3] and honourable citizens. A poor man, with a large family and a small income, Lodovico set his many sons to various trades; at home he kept only Michelangelo who, already as a child, spent much of his time drawing upon paper and on walls.

So Lodovico, being a friend of the painter Domenico Ghirlandaio, went to his workshop and spoke to him at length about Michelangelo; and when Domenico had seen some of the papers that the child had daubed, he judged him talented enough to succeed in that admirable and worthy art. Then Lodovico, reminding Domenico of the burden of having a large family that brought him no income, decided to entrust Michelangelo to him; and together they agreed upon fair and honest wages as was the custom at that time. Domenico took the boy for three years and they drew up a contract that can still be seen in the record book of Ghirlandaio, written in his own hand: and in the hand of Lodovico there are the regular receipts. All these things are now with Ridolfo Ghirlandaio, son of Domenico.[4]

The character and powers of Michelangelo developed in a way that amazed Domenico who saw him doing things that were quite extraordinary for one so young; for not only did Michelangelo surpass the many other pupils, but he even seemed to equal the things done by his master. For it so happened that one day, while Domenico was away from his work on the main chapel of Santa Maria Novella, Michelangelo set about drawing the scaffolding, with the benches and all the tools and some of the young men who were busy there. When Domenico returned and saw Michelangelo's sketch, he said: 'This fellow knows more than I do'; and he was dumbfounded by the heaven-sent freshness and skill of imitation at such a tender age; for in truth it was no less than would be expected of an artist with many years' experience.

This came about because the natural power and knowledge with which he had been graced was developed by study and practice, and brought forth every day fruits more divine than human. And this began to be evident in the copy he made of a print by Albert Durer which brought him great fame.[5] For, shortly after it came to Florence, Michelangelo made a new kind of pen-and-ink drawing of the copper engraving which showed the devils beating St Antony. He also did it in colours, and when it came to copying some strange forms of devils he went and bought fish with weirdly-coloured scales; and in all this he showed a skill that gained him a reputation and a name.

At that time Lorenzo the Magnificent had a garden on the Piazza di San Marco where he kept many fine antiques that he had collected at great expense; and he employed the sculptor Bertoldo not so much as custodian or keeper, but rather because it was his great wish to create a school of excellence for painters and sculptors, and he wanted them to find a guide and a leader in Bertoldo, who had been a pupil of Donatello. Though Bertoldo was too old to work, he was nonetheless an experienced and highly regarded master, not only because he had carefully polished the bronze pulpits of Donatello,[6] but for many other works that he had cast in bronze, battles and other small things, with a mastery beyond anyone else in Florence.

Lorenzo, with his great love for painting and sculpture, regretting that in his time there were no famous and noble sculptors to rival the many celebrated and skilful living painters, decided, as I have said, to found a school. With this in mind he told Domenico Ghirlandaio that if he had in his workshop any pupils who showed the right inclination, he should send them to his garden where they would be taught and trained in a way that would do honour both to himself and to his city.

So, along with some of his best pupils, Domenico sent him Michelangelo and Francesco Granacci. When they came to the garden they found Torrigiano (a young man of the Torrigiani family),[7] working on certain clay figures in the round that

Bertoldo had given him to do. Seeing this, Michelangelo set out to rival him and made some himself; and Lorenzo took note of this high spirit and began to have high hopes for him. Thus emboldened, Michelangelo set to work on a marble copy of an ancient head that was there in the garden. Lorenzo was delighted, celebrated the event, and, as an encouragement and to help out his father, arranged to pay him five ducats a month. Also, to make him happy, he gave him a purple cloak and found a post for his father in the Customs. It is true, indeed, that all those young men received a stipend, great or small, through the generosity of that noble and magnificent citizen; and by him, as long as he lived, they were rewarded.

The garden was full of antiquities and furnished with many fine things collected there for their beauty and for study and pleasure. Michelangelo always had the keys of the place, as he was far more assiduous than the others and always alert and resolute in whatever he undertook.

For many months he made drawings in the Church of the Carmine after the paintings of Masaccio,[8] copying with a judgement that astonished the craftsmen and others who saw them, with the result that envy began to grow with his fame. It is said that Torrigiano, who had become his friend, was moved by such envy at seeing Michelangelo more skilful at his art and more honoured than himself that he began to mock him; and then he gave him such a friendly punch on the nose that it was broken and crushed in a way that marked Michelangelo for life. Michelangelo worked on a marble Cupid (later bought by Baldassare del Milanese) where he imitated the ancient manner. It was then taken to Rome, buried in a vineyard, dug up again, regarded as a genuine antique and sold at a very high price. When he went to Rome, Michelangelo admitted that it was his work, though everyone else found this difficult to believe.[9]

He made the wooden crucifix which is now in the church of Santo Spirito in Florence above the lunette of the high altar.[10] Also in Florence, in the Palazzo Strozzi, he made a marble Hercules which was much admired and later taken to France by Giovan Battista della Palla. In the old manner he made a tempera painting of St Francis with the stigmata, which is in the first chapel on the left of San Pietro in Montorio in Rome.[11] Angelo Doni, a Florentine citizen who loved to collect fine things by both ancient and modern artists, wanted to have something by his friend Michelangelo. So Michelangelo started on a *tondo* in tempera showing a kneeling Our Lady lifting up the child and handing him to Joseph. Here, in the way Christ's mother turns her head and gazes on the perfect beauty of the Son, Michelangelo conveys her wonderful happiness and her joy in sharing it with that holy old man, who takes the child with no less love, tenderness and reverence, as can easily be seen in his face. Nor was this enough, for, to make an even greater display of his art, in the background of the painting Michelangelo placed many nude figures leaning, standing and sitting; and he gave this work such meticulous attention that of all his easel paintings, few as they are, this is certainly the most finished and the most beautiful.[12] When it was finished, he sent it to the house of Angelo Doni along with a messenger who carried a note asking seventy ducats in payment. Doni, who was a prudent man, found it strange to pay so much for a painting, even though he knew it was worth more; so he told the messenger that forty would be enough and gave them to him. But Michelangelo returned them with a message saying that now he wanted a hundred ducats or the painting back. So Doni, who really liked the work, said: 'I'll give him the seventy.' But Michelangelo was not satisfied, and to punish Doni's bad faith he demanded double what he had first asked, so that to get the painting Doni was forced to send him a hundred and forty ducats.[13]

The wonderful things he had heard about the ancients convinced Michelangelo to move to Rome. When he got there, in the house of the Galli, facing the Palazzo San Giorgio, he made a larger-than-life Bacchus with a satyr.[14] It is clear that here Michelangelo wanted a striking combination in the limbs, and especially the male slenderness of a youth together with a female fleshiness and rotundity – a splendid thing that showed how he surpassed all previous modern sculptors. During his stay in Rome, he made such progress in the study of his art that it was incredible to see the ease with which he conveyed lofty thoughts and mastered difficult techniques, astonishing the experts who were used to good work, no less than the simple who had little experience in such matters; for indeed everything else seemed worthless compared to what he produced. As a result, when the French Cardinal of Rouen wanted to leave a fitting memorial of himself in that famous city, he was eager to employ such a rare artist; and he commissioned a marble *pietà* in the round, which, when finished, was placed in St Peter's in the Chapel of the Madonna della Febbre on the site of the Temple of Mars.[15]

No artist or sculptor, however gifted, could hope to surpass the design and grace of that figure; nor, however hard he toiled, could he cut and polish the marble with the skill of Michelangelo, for the work displays all the worth and power of sculpture. Among its many beauties (apart from the wonderful drapery) is the figure of Christ where the beauty of the limbs and the moulding of the body are such that no one could hope to see such a marvellous nude figure, or a dead man that looked so dead. The lovely expression of the head, the harmony of the muscles in arms, legs and body, and the delicate tracing of veins and arteries leave one astounded that an artist's hand could make something so admirable and inspired in such a short time; for it is certainly a miracle that what was once a formless stone should ever be brought to that perfection which Nature can hardly attain in the flesh.

Michelangelo put so much love and effort into this work that he did something he never did again: he left his name inscribed on the sash that crosses Our Lady's breast, as if to show his complete satisfaction with what he had done. And that it really is like a true living figure has been attested by a man of great talent:

> All beauty and all goodness too,
> Grief, pity, here in living stone lie dead,
> Ah, cease to mourn the way you do,
> Nor let your weeping be so loud,
> Lest you untimely wake from death,
> Against his will, our living Lord,
> Who is the spouse and son and father,
> Of you, his only spouse, daughter and mother.[16]

This statue gave him a great reputation. And if some more or less stupid people say that he made Our Lady too young, they seem not to know that those who remain virgins unspotted preserve their untainted youthful aspect for a long time, while it is the contrary for those who suffer as Christ did. At all events, this work brought more fame and glory to the genius of Michelangelo than anything he had done before.

Some friends wrote from Florence urging him to come back because there was a good chance that he might be able to make a statue out of a block of marble that was standing spoiled in the Office of Works – something he had already thought of doing. Pier Soderini, then *gonfaloniere* of the city,[17] had considered giving the block to Leonardo da Vinci. It was eighteen feet high, but unfortunately a certain Simone da Fiesole had already made a start on a giant figure.[18] The work was so bungled that there was a great gap between the legs and everything else was botched and twisted. So the wardens of Santa Maria del Fiore, who were in charge, left it unfinished; and it had lain abandoned for many years and looked like staying that way. Michelangelo measured it again to see whether he could get a reasonable figure out of that stone by adapting his work to what had been left botched by Simone. He then decided to ask the wardens; and they let him have it as something quite worthless, thinking that whatever he did with it would be better than leaving it the way it was, for neither in that state nor broken in pieces could it be of any use in the building. So Michelangelo made a wax model of the young David holding a sling; this was intended as an appropriate symbol for the Palace, signifying that just as David had defended his people and governed them with justice, so whoever governed Florence should defend the city bravely and rule it justly. Then, in the Office of Works of Santa Maria del Fiore, he set up a partition of planks and trestles around the marble and worked on it constantly without anyone seeing it before its final perfection. And because the marble had already been botched and bungled by Simone, there were places where Michelangelo could not shape it as he would have wished; so he left some of Simone's old chisel-marks at the edges of the block where they can still be seen. And indeed it seemed as miraculous as if Michelangelo had raised someone given up for dead.

When the statue was finished its sheer size gave rise to disputes about how it should be transported to the Piazza della Signoria. But Giuliano da Sangallo and his brother Antonio[19] made a strong wooden frame and suspended the statue from it with ropes so that when it was moved it would sway without being broken, and they pulled it with winches over beams laid on the ground until they put it in place. When the work was finally complete and erected, Michelangelo unveiled it; and truly it has eclipsed all other statues, modern or ancient, Greek or Roman; for such were the measure and beauty that his skill brought to the finished form that neither the Marforio in Rome nor the Tiber and Nile of the Belvedere nor the giants of Monte Cavallo[20] can stand the comparison. The legs are beautifully shaped, the flanks slender and the joints perfect; nobody has ever seen a pose so sweet and graceful, nor any work where feet, hands and head are in such harmony with everything else in the design. Indeed, whoever sees this need no longer bother to see the work of any other sculptor living or dead. Piero Soderini paid Michelangelo eight hundred *scudi* and the statue was erected in the year 1504.[21] Since it had made him famous as a sculptor, he then made for the *gonfaloniere* a lovely bronze David which Soderini later sent to France. At the same time he also roughed out (but did not complete) a marble *tondo* for Taddeo Taddei which is still in the latter's house; and for Bartolomeo Pitti he began another which Fra Miniato Pitti of Monte Oliveto, a man knowledgeable in many fields and especially in painting, later gave to his friend Luigi Guicciardini.[22] Both these works were greatly appreciated and admired. Yet again at that time he roughed out a statue of St Matthew in the Office of Works of Santa Maria del Fiore.[23]

It so happened that while that rare painter, Leonardo da Vinci, was working in the council chamber (as we saw in his Life), Piero Soderini, then *gonfaloniere*, seeing Michelangelo's great talent, assigned another part of the chamber to him; and that is how, in competition with Leonardo, he came to do the other wall, choosing as his subject the Pisan War.[24] For this task Michelangelo had a room in the Dyers' Hospital of Sant'Onofrio, and there he began a huge cartoon which he would not let anyone see. He filled it with naked men, who are bathing in the Arno because of the heat, when suddenly the alarm is sounded in the camp for an enemy attack. As the soldiers get out of the water and run to dress themselves, the inspired hand of Michelangelo depicts one man hauling out another, some pulling on clothes as they hurry to take arms and help their comrades, others buckling breastplates and various types of armour, and countless more fighting on horseback as they enter the fray. Among the other figures there is an old man wearing a garland of ivy to shade his head: he is sitting down to put on his hose but cannot do so because his legs are still wet; and, hearing the noise of the soldiers and the shouting and the roll of the drums, he is trying to force a stocking on to his foot: besides all the muscles and nerves of the body, one can see clearly from the way he twists his mouth how much he suffers and strives right down to his toes. There are drummers too and naked figures with their clothes bundled up running towards the fight: and one can see men in extraordinary postures: some upright, some kneeling or bending over or suspended in motion in mid-air – all done with the most difficult foreshortenings. There are many other groups of figures sketched in various ways, some outlined with charcoal, some drawn with a few strokes, some shaded in and heightened with lead-white – all this to show how well he knew his craft. At this the other artists were struck dumb with wonder and admiration, seeing in that cartoon by Michelangelo the perfection to which art could be brought. Thus some who saw those inspired figures say that they can never be surpassed in sublimity either by Michelangelo himself or by anyone else.

And this can surely be believed because once it was finished and carried to the pope's chamber, with acclamation from the artists and glory to Michelangelo, all those who studied and drew from it (as both Florentines and foreigners continued to do for many years) achieved excellence in the art, as we have seen: for that cartoon was studied by Aristotile da San Gallo (Michelangelo's friend), Ridolfo Ghirlandaio, Francesco

Granaccio, Baccio Bandinello and the Spaniard Alonso Beruguete; these were followed by Andrea del Sarto, Francia Bigio, Iacopo Sansovino, Rosso, Maturino, Lorenzetto, Tribolo in his boyhood, Iacopo da Pontormo and Perin del Vaga, all of whom were and are excellent Florentine artists. Having thus become the study of artists, the cartoon was taken to the great upper chamber of the Medici house, and this was how it was too easily entrusted to the hands of artists; for during the illness of Duke Giuliano, while nobody cared about such things, they cut it into pieces so that it was scattered over a number of places, as can be proved by a few fragments still to be seen in the house of Uberto Strozzi, a gentleman of Mantua, who preserves them with great reverence. And surely they appear more divine than human.

The *pietà*, the giant statue of David and the cartoon had made Michelangelo so famous that Pope Julius II decided to have him build his tomb.[25] Michelangelo was summoned from Florence and, after talking the matter over, they agreed on a work that would serve both as a memorial to the pope and as a witness to the genius of Michelangelo, a work which in its beauty, sublimity and invention should surpass every ancient imperial tomb. So Michelangelo set boldly to work and went to Carrara to excavate blocks of marble which he then transported to Florence and Rome; and he made a model for the project, full of figures and adorned with the most difficult kinds of work. He decided initially to make it free-standing so that it could be seen from every side, and he carefully finished one side of the quadrangle, complete with the architectural elements and ornaments, cornices and suchlike. At the same time he began work on some naked figures of Victory standing above captives and figures representing a vast number of provinces bound to marble plinths in a regular succession; and he roughed out a part featuring captives in postures different from those that are bound; and four finished figures of these captives are still in his house in Rome.[26]

He also completed a ten-foot marble Moses, a statue whose beauty can never be equalled by any modern work, nor by any ancient either.[27] Sitting in a highly dignified attitude, he lays one arm on the tablets that he grasps with his hand, while with the other he holds his beard that hangs down in long marble curls, wrought in such a way that the hairs (which are so difficult for sculpture) are finely feathery, soft and so precisely drawn out that the chisel seems impossibly to have become a brush. Not only is the face beautiful with its truly saintly and regal expression, but it also makes one wish for a veil to cover it, so radiant and dazzling is it to the sight and so well has Michelangelo conveyed the divinity that God gave to that most sacred countenance. And then the drapery is carved and finished with a lovely turning of the hem, and the arm muscles and the bones and nerves of the hands are finely wrought, and the legs, knees and feet are perfectly clothed and shod. Indeed, every part of the work is completed in such a way that now more than ever Moses may be called the friend of God, since, before all others, by the hand of Michelangelo, God has restored and prepared that body for the Resurrection. Long may the Jews continue to visit and adore it, as they do in crowds every Sabbath, both men and women, like flocks of starlings; for they will be adoring what is not human but divine. This tomb was later unveiled in the time of Pope Paul III and completed thanks to the liberality of Francesco Maria, Duke of Urbino.[28]

In the meantime the pope, who had recaptured Bologna and chased out the Bentivogli, decided to commemorate the event with a bronze statue: and Michelangelo was ordered to suspend work on the tomb and go to Bologna where he made a ten-foot bronze in the likeness of Pope Julius. There was great art in the posture, for everything conveyed majesty and grandeur; there was richness and magnificence in the draperies, and in the face courage, strength, resolution and awesome severity. It was placed in a niche over the door of San Petronio.[29] They say that while Michelangelo was working on it a painter and goldsmith called Francia turned up to see it because he had heard the fame and praises of Michelangelo and his works, but had never seen anything by him. So arrangements were made and finally he obtained permission. He was amazed at the artistry of the statue; but when Michelangelo asked what he thought of the figure, he answered that it was beautifully cast. Michelangelo was indignant at the thought that he was praising the bronze rather than the workmanship and replied angrily: 'Get off to a whorehouse, you and Cossa; a fine pair of ignorant botchers!'[30] Poor Francia felt that he had been deeply insulted in the presence of all those standing by. It is said that the gentry of Bologna went to see that statue and, finding it very stern and awesome, they turned to Michelangelo saying that the posture was so threatening that the pope seemed to be giving them a curse rather than a blessing. To which Michelangelo replied with a laugh: 'That curse has already fallen.' Those gentlemen took it badly, but the pope, who understood what Michelangelo meant, gave him an extra three hundred *scudi*. This statue was later destroyed by the Bentivogli and the bronze was sold to Duke Alfonso of Ferrara who used it to make a cannon called *La Giulia*. Only the head was saved and is still in the duke's wardrobe.[31]

The pope had already returned to Rome where, moved by the love he bore to the memory of his uncle, he ordered that the ceiling of the Sistine Chapel (still bare at that time) should now be painted.[32] It seems that Bramante, as a friend and relative of Raphael, had tried to prevent the project being assigned to Michelangelo;[33] but by the pope's commission and the order of Giuliano da Sangallo, Michelangelo was summoned from Bologna and when he arrived the pope commanded that the whole chapel should be redone, not only the ceiling but the walls as well. And the price of it all was to be fifteen thousand ducats. So Michelangelo, obliged by the sheer size of the task, decided to seek help and sent for assistants. He was determined to prove that he could surpass those who had worked there before him and he also wanted to show modern artists how to draw and paint. Indeed, the very nature of the work spurred him to aim so high both for his own fame and for the good of the art itself, and thus he set to work on the cartoons. Then, ready to colour them, but lacking all experience of fresco, he sent to Florence for some of his painter friends, many of them highly skilled in that kind of work, so that they could help him out and he could see their technique. Among those who came to Rome were Granacci, Giuliano Bugiardini,

Iacopo di Sandro, the elder Indaco, Angelo di Donnino and Aristotile. With the project already underway, Michelangelo got them to start on a few things as samples of their work; but when he saw that their efforts were unsatisfactory and nowhere near what he intended, he decided one morning to pull down everything they had done. Then he locked himself in the chapel and refused to open up. Even when he was at home he refused to see them, until at last they thought the joke had lasted long enough and went shamefaced back to Florence. So Michelangelo arranged to do the whole thing by himself and brought it close to conclusion through his unstinting effort and study: nor would he ever see anyone lest he might have to show his work. Thus, with every day that passed, people became more and more impatient to see it.

Pope Julius was very keen to see what Michelangelo was doing and the fact that it was hidden stimulated his curiosity. So one day he went to see it, but was not allowed in, because Michelangelo did not want to show his work. This made him even more eager and he tried so many ways of getting in that Michelangelo was very worried, suspecting that some of his workmen or assistants might be bribed to betray him, as indeed they were. So to find out whether he could trust them, he gave orders that nobody should be allowed in, not even the pope. Then he pretended that he was going to leave Rome for a few days and, after repeating his orders, left them the key. But, in fact, after leaving them, he locked himself in the chapel to work. Immediately the workers, expecting a hefty tip, informed the pope that, with Michelangelo out of town, he could come whenever he pleased. Coming down to the chapel, the pope was the first to poke his head inside, but he had hardly taken one step before Michelangelo starting throwing planks from the top platform of the scaffolding; at which the pope, knowing his character, retreated with no less anger than fear and uttering violent threats. Michelangelo got out through a window of the chapel, left the key with Bramante da Urbino and hurried back to Florence, hoping that Bramante would make his peace with the pope, whom he really thought he had injured.[34]

Back in Florence then, and having heard those threats of the pope, he decided never to return to Rome. But the pope's anger had been appeased by the entreaties of Bramante and other friends and, not wanting such a great work to remain unfinished, he wrote to Piero Soderini, then *gonfaloniere* in Florence, that Michelangelo should be sent back to kneel at his feet because he had forgiven him. Piero informed Michelangelo, but he was still determined not to return, for he did not trust the pope. So for his greater safety Piero decided to send him with the status of an ambassador, and with this good security Michelangelo finally went back. Piero Soderini also wrote to his brother, the Reverend Cardinal of Volterra, with instructions to present Michelangelo to the pope. When Michelangelo arrived, however, the cardinal was feeling unwell and sent one of his assistant bishops to make the presentation. Coming before the pope, who was walking up and down with a mace in his hand, the bishop presented Michelangelo on behalf of the cardinal and his brother Piero, saying that he should be forgiven, for these artist fellows are always ignorant. At this the pope flew into a rage and struck him with the mace, saying, 'You're the one who's ignorant.' And turning to Michelangelo, he blessed him and laughed it off. From then on Michelangelo was maintained by the pope with many gifts and favours, and he strove so hard to amend for his fault that he finally brought the work to a perfect completion.[35]

This work has truly proved the beacon that so improved and enlightened the art of painting as to illumine a world that for centuries had lain in darkness. And indeed painters no longer need to seek out new inventions or original postures, special clothing for figures or unusual expressions or painterly devices for conveying sublimity and awe, because every perfection that could belong to the art has already been given to this work by Michelangelo. Now everyone is amazed to see the excellence of the figures, the perfection of the foreshortenings, the wonderful contours of the curves, slim and graceful, rounded with the fair proportion that is seen in the beautiful nudes. To show the scope and perfection of his art he made them all of different ages, different in expression and form, both of face and figure, some slender and some more full-bodied; and the same skill can be seen in the variety of lovely postures, some sitting, some moving about, others holding up festoons of oak and acorns to indicate the arms and device of Pope Julius and to suggest that his time, his reign, was the Golden Age when Italy was free of its present strife and misery;[36] while the figures down the middle of the ceiling hold relief medallions painted like bronze and gold with episodes from the Book of Kings.

Furthermore, to reveal the perfection of art and the greatness of God, in one scene Michelangelo portrayed the division of light from darkness, in which is seen the majesty of God, sustaining himself alone, with arms wide open, to show both love and creative power. In the second scene, with fine judgement and skill, he showed the creation of the sun and the moon, where God, supported by many *putti*, is in an attitude made awesome by the foreshortening of the arms and legs. In the same scene he showed God after the blessing of the earth and the creation of the animals, flying on the vaulting as a foreshortened figure who always seems to turn and change direction wherever you walk in the chapel. So also in the next scene where he divides the water from the earth – beautiful figures and inventions of genius that could only have come from the inspired hands of Michelangelo! He went on to the creation of Adam where he depicts God as borne by a group of naked infant angels who seem to be supporting not only a figure but the whole weight of the world, an effect produced by the figure's venerable majesty and by the movement that embraces some of the *putti* with one arm, as if to hold himself up, while with the other he stretches out his right hand towards Adam, who is given such a beauty, attitude and outline that he seems indeed newly made by the supreme first Creator rather than by the brush and drawing of a mere man. A little further on, in another scene, he depicts our mother Eve being taken from Adam's rib, where one of the two naked figures is so enslaved by sleep that he seems almost dead, while the other has become alive and awake through the blessing of God. So from the brush of this most gifted artist we see the whole difference between sleep and waking, and how firm and stable, humanly speaking, may appear the Divine Majesty.

Next comes the scene where Adam, persuaded by a figure who is half serpent and half woman, partakes of his death and ours in the apple; and there also we see both Adam and Eve driven out of Paradise by the angel, who comes in sublime grandeur to carry out the sentence of a wrathful Lord. In the attitude of Adam we see remorse for his sin together with fear of death; likewise in the woman may be seen shame, abasement and the desire to seek pardon, as she folds her arms over her breast, clasps her hands together and bows her head on her bosom, turning towards the angel with more fear of God's justice than hope in his mercy. Equally beautiful is Noah's sacrifice, with those who carry wood, those who blow upon the fire and those who cut the victim's throat, a scene certainly not executed with less care and precision than the others. He used the same skill and judgement in the scene of the Flood, which shows many men dying, fearful in the terror of those days and striving in various ways to save their lives; for in the heads of those figures one may see how life falls a prey to death in fear, dismay and despair. In many figures one can also see compassion as they help each other to climb on the top of a rock in search of safety. Among them there is a man who is clasping someone already half-dead and struggling to save him – a thing that Nature herself could not have done better. Nor can one say how well expressed is the story of Noah when, drunk with wine, he sleeps exposed, in the presence of one son who laughs at him and two others who are covering him up, a scene demonstrating such incomparable skill that it could not be surpassed except by the artist himself. Then, as if emboldened by what had been done so far, his genius soared higher and proved even greater in the five sibyls and the seven prophets, each ten-foot high or more, all in different attitudes and with beautiful draperies and all, in short, showing such marvellous invention and judgement that they must appear inspired to anyone who studies the emotions they express.

There can be seen Jeremiah with his legs crossed, holding his beard in one hand and with his elbow on his knee, while the other hand rests in his lap. His head is bowed in a way that clearly shows the melancholy, anxiety, concern and bitterness brought on by his people. Equally fine are the two *putti* behind him and the first sibyl [the Persian sibyl] beyond him towards the door. Since in this figure Michelangelo wished to give the idea of old age, she is not only enveloped in draperies to show that her blood has been chilled by time, but she is also reading a book that she holds very close to her eyes because her sight is already failing. This figure is followed by an aged prophet [Ezekiel] who has ample garments and a most graceful movement; in one hand he holds a scroll of prophecies while he raises the other hand and turns his head as if about to speak of great and lofty things; and behind him there are two *putti* holding his books. Next comes a sibyl [the Erythrean sibyl] who, unlike the one we have just described, holds the book away from her and is turning a page while, with one knee over the other, sunk in thought, she ponders what she should write; and behind her stands a *putto* blowing on a burning brand to light her lamp. This is a figure of extraordinary beauty in the expression of the face, the head-dress and the disposition of the draperies; and the bared arms are as lovely as all the rest. Beyond her, withdrawn into himself, there is another prophet [Joel] who has taken up a scroll that he reads with great attention and emotion. He seems like a living man who is concentrating deeply and his expression shows that he is content with what he reads. In the same vein, over the door of the chapel Michelangelo placed an old man [Zachariah] who is looking in a book for something that he cannot find; he has one leg on the ground and the other awkwardly lifted behind him, but the sheer intensity of his search makes him forget the discomfort of his position. Wonderful in its representation of old age, this figure is rather full in form and wears lovely draperies with few folds. Next towards the altar on the other side, together with her *putti* and no less to be praised, there is another sibyl [the Delphic sibyl] who displays certain writings. But what of the prophet [Isaiah] who comes next? Lost in thought and sitting with his legs crossed, he keeps his hand inside a book to mark the place while he rests the elbow of the other arm beside the book and leans his cheek upon his hand; and called by one of the *putti* behind him, he remains immobile, merely turning his head.

Whoever examines this figure will see touches taken from
Nature herself, the true mother of the art; and studied properly,
it will amply teach all the precepts required to make a good
painter. Beyond this prophet is an aged woman of great beauty
[the Cumaean sibyl] who sits and studies a book in a most
graceful way, accompanied by two lovely *putti*. Nor could one
imagine adding anything to the excellence of the youthful figure
that Michelangelo has made for the prophet Daniel who is seen
with a great book, copying down certain passages from other
writings with incredible eagerness. And to help him with that
weight there is a *putto* between his legs, who holds up the book
while Daniel writes. No brush in any other hand could ever
equal either this or the splendid Libyan sibyl who, having writ-
ten a great volume derived from many books, is shown in an
attitude of womanly grace, about to rise to her feet while at the
same time she prepares to close her book, a posture that anyone
but the Master would find difficult, if not impossible, to depict.

What can be said of the four scenes at the corners, on the
spandrels of the ceiling? In one of them David, using all his
youthful strength, defeats Goliath and cuts off his head, to
the amazement of some soldiers who are there in the camp.
Marvellous too are the attitudes Michelangelo depicts in the
story of Judith at the opposite corner where one sees the head-
less trunk of Holofernes, still writhing, while Judith puts the
lifeless head in a basket carried by her old serving-woman who
is so tall that she has to bend down so that Judith can settle the
burden on her head. As she raises her hands to support the
burden and to cover it up, the old woman turns her head
towards the body, which, though lifeless, makes a noise in the
tent by raising an arm and a leg. Her expression conveys fear
at being in that camp and terror at the sight of the dead man –
truly a picture where everything has been thought out.

But more beautiful and inspired than these or than all the
other scenes is the story of the serpents of Moses on the left
above the altar. Here one sees the massacre caused by the
stinging, biting rain of serpents, and there also is the bronze
serpent that Moses raised upon a pole. The scene shows vividly
the various kinds of death suffered by those who are doomed

by the serpent bites, how the deadly poison kills countless numbers in terror and convulsions, not to speak of the splendid heads upturned and screaming, or the rigid legs and twisted arms of those who remain fixed in the posture where they were stricken down. No less finely depicted are those who feel their pains diminish and life return as they gaze on the uplifted serpent with intense emotion: among them is a woman who is being supported by someone in a way that shows not only the help she receives but also her need of it in the sudden terror of being stung. In the other scene, where Ahasuerus lies in bed reading his chronicles, there are also many beautiful figures; among them, eating at a table, there are three men who represent the council that decided to free the Hebrew people by hanging Haman. Haman himself is done with exceptional foreshortening, since the trunk of the body and the arm stretching forward seem real and in relief rather than painted, just like the leg that he thrusts out and the other parts of his body that turn inward. Of all Michelangelo's difficult and beautiful figures, this is surely the most beautiful and the most difficult. One simply cannot describe all the details of this work, such as the draperies and the facial expressions and the vast number of new extraordinary and wonderfully ingenious inventions. There is nothing that is not the work of genius; all the figures are done with beautiful and brilliant foreshortening and everything one sees is most praiseworthy and inspired. But finally who will not be lost in admiration and amazement at the awesome sight of Jonah, the last figure in the chapel? The inward curve of the vaulting, which naturally follows the masonry, is artfully countered by the figure who bends the other way, so that, conquered by the art of design and the play of light and shade, the vault really seems to curve backwards.

Oh, truly happy age of ours, and truly blessed artists! For well may you be called blessed who in your time could clear the dimness of your vision at the source of so much light and have all that was once difficult made easy by such a wonderful and peerless artist. Surely the glory of his labours will bring fame and honour to you, for he has stripped the veil from your darkened mental eyes and shown you how to distinguish the truth from the falsehood that clouded your minds. For this, therefore, thank heaven; and strive to imitate Michelangelo in all things.

When the work was revealed, the whole world came hurrying to see it, and certainly it was enough to strike men dumb with wonder; and the pope, feeling exalted by that work and emboldened to attempt even greater things, rewarded Michelangelo with money and rich gifts. So Michelangelo returned to the tomb and continued to work on it, while also preparing designs for the façades of the chapel. But envious Fortune decreed that the memorial which had begun so perfectly should not be brought to such a perfect end. For in that time Pope Julius died, and the work was abandoned on the election of Pope Leo X. No less spirited and high-minded than Julius, Leo (as the first Florentine pope) desired to leave to his native city, in memory of himself and of the inspired artist who was his fellow citizen, such wonders as only a great prince like himself could undertake. Thus he gave orders that the façade of San Lorenzo, a church built by the Medici family in Florence, should be completed for him; and this is why the tomb of Julius was left unfinished.

Endless discussions followed this decision, for the idea was to divide the work among several artists, and many of them came hurrying down to the pope in Rome in the hope of being commissioned for the building. Designs were proposed by Baccio d'Agnolo, Antonio da Sangallo, Andrea Sansovino and the gracious Raphael of Urbino who was later called to Florence for that purpose during the pope's visit there. At this Michelangelo resolved to make a model himself and to refuse any supervisor or guide for the architecture.[37] But this rejection of assistance was the reason why neither he nor anyone else got to work on the project, and all those masters returned in despair to their usual occupations.

Michelangelo, who was on his way to Carrara, stopped in Florence with an order for Jacopo Salviati[38] to pay him a thousand *scudi*. But finding Jacopo closeted in a business meeting with some citizens, he refused to wait for an interview, and immediately left for Carrara without a word. Then Jacopo, hearing of Michelangelo's visit, but no longer finding him in Florence, sent the thousand *scudi* after him to Carrara. The messenger wanted a receipt, but Michelangelo objected that the money was to cover the pope's expenses not his own and that the messenger could take the money back for he was not in the habit of giving receipts for other people. So the frightened messenger returned to Jacopo without a receipt.

For the Medici Palace Michelangelo made a model of the corbelled windows for the apartments that are at the corner of the building. Giovanni da Udine did the stucco work and painting which have been much admired; and the goldsmith Piloto, on Michelangelo's orders, made the admirable perforated copper shutters.[39]

Michelangelo devoted four years to quarrying marble for the façade of San Lorenzo, though it is true that at the same time he made wax models and other things for the project. But the work dragged on so long that the money the pope had set aside for it was spent on the war in Lombardy, and when Leo died the façade remained unfinished, with nothing done except for the laying of a foundation in front and the shipment of a huge marble column from Carrara to Piazza San Lorenzo. The death of Leo was a fearful blow to art and artists both in Rome and Florence, and as long as Adrian VI lived, Michelangelo stuck to his work on the tomb of Julius. But then came the death of Adrian and the election of Clement VII who was no less eager than Leo and his predecessors to leave a name famous for works of architecture, sculpture and painting. Clement summoned Michelangelo, and, after discussing many things together, they resolved to start work on the new sacristy of San Lorenzo in Florence. So Michelangelo left Rome again and raised the cupola that can be seen today, designed in a composite style and with a beautiful ball of seventy-two facets made by the goldsmith Piloto. It happened that while he was raising the cupola some friends asked: 'Michelangelo, shouldn't you make your lantern very different from that of Filippo Brunelleschi?' And he replied: 'Different it can be made, but not better.'[40]

Inside the sacristy, adorning the walls, Michelangelo built four tombs to hold the bodies of the elder Lorenzo and his brother Giuliano (both fathers of popes), and also those of Giuliano, the brother of Pope Leo, and Duke Lorenzo, his nephew.[41] And, since he wanted to imitate the old sacristy of Filippo Brunelleschi but with a different kind of ornamentation, he created a composite order, in a style more varied and original than any of the ancient or modern masters had been able to achieve. For the beautiful cornices, capitals, bases, doors, tabernacles and tombs were highly innovative, departing considerably from the measure, order and rule that architects usually observed by following Vitruvius[42] and the works of antiquity; for these he did not wish to repeat. This licence has encouraged those who have seen how he worked to follow his example, and their decorative style has since been marked by new fantasies and by the grotesque rather than by reason and rule. Thus all artists owe a vast and eternal debt to Michelangelo because he has broken the chains and bonds that kept them working in an old habitual way. Michelangelo later demonstrated this new style even more effectively, at that same place, in the library of San Lorenzo with its lovely distribution of windows, the pattern of its ceiling and the wonderful entrance hall. Never has been seen such a resolute grace as here in the corbels, the tabernacles and the cornices; nor a more commodious staircase, where he created such unusual intervals in the design of the steps and departed so much from common practice that everybody was astonished.

At that time Michelangelo sent his pupil, Pietro Urbano of Pistoia, to Rome to complete a naked figure of Christ holding the cross, a marvellous thing for Master Antonio Metelli, who had it placed in Santa Maria sopra Minerva beside the main chapel.[43] Meanwhile he continued his work in the sacristy, in which seven statues were left partly finished and partly not; and if they are considered together with his architectural inventions for the tombs, then it must be confessed that he surpassed everybody else in all three arts; and to this bear witness the marble statues that he blocked out or finished and that can still be seen there. One of these is of Our Lady who sits with her right leg crossed over her left, resting one knee on the other, while the child, straddling the uppermost leg, turns towards his mother with a lovely gesture to ask for milk; and she holds him with one hand and supports herself with the other as she leans forward to give it to him. Some parts of the statue are unfinished, but even in the imperfection of what is only roughed out and full of chisel-marks one still sees the perfection of the whole.[44] Yet Michelangelo caused even more wonder by the way he made the tombs of Duke Giuliano and Duke Lorenzo de' Medici, where, to convey the idea that the earth alone was not enough to give honourable burial to their greatness, he decided to include all aspects of the world by placing four statues above and around their tombs. Thus to one tomb he gave Night and Day and to the other Dawn and Dusk, statues wrought with such beautiful postures and such masterly treatment of the muscles that, if the art of sculpture were lost, they would suffice to restore it to its original lustre. There, among the other statues, are those two captains in armour: one is the pensive Duke Lorenzo, the very image of wisdom, with legs so splendidly done that one could not see better; the other is the proud figure of Duke Giuliano, with the inspired head and throat, setting of eyes, outline of nose and mouth, hair, hands, arms, knees and feet – in short, everything here is so well done that the eyes can never be tired or sated at the sight. And truly to study the beauty of the buskins and breastplate is to believe it a heavenly not a mortal creation.

But what shall I say of the Dawn, a nude female figure that seems designed to arouse melancholy in the soul and confound all styles of sculpture? In her posture, still heavy with sleep as she rises from her downy bed, may be seen her foreboding, for on her awakening she has found the eyes of the great duke closed forever. And what shall I say of the Night, a statue not so much rare as unique? Who at any time, ancient or modern, has ever seen a statue made like this? For in her may be seen not only the stillness of one who sleeps, but the sorrow and melancholy of one who has lost something great and worthy. Indeed, she might well be the night that obscures all those who have ever hoped, I will not say to surpass, but even to equal Michelangelo in sculpture and design. In the slumber of this figure may be seen the living image of sleep; and, therefore,

many learned persons have praised it in Latin verse or vernacu-
lar rhymes such as these by an unknown author:[45]

> The sweetly sleeping Night on which you look
> has all the life an angel's hand could give
> to stone; and thus, because she sleeps, she lives:
> wake her, if you still doubt it; she will speak.

To which, in the person of Night, Michelangelo replied:

> Precious is sleep, better to be of stone,
> while the oppression and the shame still last;
> not seeing and not hearing, I am blest;
> so do not wake me, hush! keep your voice down.

But the work was denied completion by the enmity that exists
between Fortune and Genius, for the former will always envy
the excellence of the latter. Had this not been the case, Nature
would have seen that all her ideas are surpassed by those of
Art. While Michelangelo was giving all his love and care to
these great works, he was interrupted by the siege of Florence
in the year 1530. This meant that he did little or no more work
on the statues, for he was now given the task of fortifying the
territory. And thus, after lending a thousand *scudi* to the repub-
lic and becoming a member of the Nine [a military council
appointed for the war], he put his heart and mind into fortifying
the hill of San Miniato, where he built walls that could not have
been better if they had been meant to outlast eternity. It is true,
however, that, as the siege gradually closed in, he thought of
his own personal safety and decided to leave Florence for
Venice. His preparations were made in secret so that nobody
should know, and he took with him his pupil, Antonio Mini,
and his faithful friend, the goldsmith Piloto, with *scudi* sewn
into their doublets. On their way, they rested at Ferrara where
the Duke Alfonso d'Este was keeping a strict watch, being
alarmed by the war and by the league between the pope and
the emperor who were besieging Florence. He had given secret
orders that all those who gave lodgings to travellers should

send him the names of their guests, and every day he received
a list with the details of all foreign visitors and their origin. So
no sooner had Michelangelo and his companions dismounted
than the news came to the duke who, as a magnanimous prince
and a lifelong admirer of genius, immediately sent some of the
leading courtiers to escort him to the palace in the name of His
Excellency; they were to take along the horses and baggage;
and to give the guest the most comfortable quarters. Finding
himself in the power of another, Michelangelo could only sub-
mit with a good grace and go along with them to the duke,
though without taking his belongings from the inn. The duke
gave him a splendid welcome with costly and honourable gifts
and tried to keep him in Ferrara with the promise of a good
stipend; but Michelangelo had other intentions and refused to
stay. Once again the duke offered everything in his power and
urged him to stay at least until the war was over. At which, not
wishing to be outdone in courtesy, Michelangelo thanked him
profusely and, turning to his two companions, said that he had
brought to Ferrara twelve thousand *scudi* and that, if they could
be of use, both the *scudi* and himself were at the duke's disposal.
The duke then took him round the palace, showing him all the
fine art that he possessed, including a portrait of himself by
Titian which was much praised by Michelangelo. But there
was no way of keeping Michelangelo in the palace; instead he
insisted on going back to the inn. There the host received
countless things from the duke so he could pay due but discreet
honour to the guest who was to be charged nothing when he
left. Michelangelo went on to Venice where many gentlemen
were eager to meet him; but he had a low opinion of their
knowledge of art and left the city to live on the island of
Giudecca.[46]

He had not been there long, however, when the war came to
an end and he went back to Florence by order of Baccio Valori.
On his return he completed in tempera on wood a wonderful
painting of Leda and the Swan which, through his pupil
Antonio Mini, he later sent to France. For Baccio Valori he
then began a small marble figure of Apollo drawing an arrow
from the quiver – this in the hope that Baccio would intercede

to make his peace with the pope and the House of Medici whom he had greatly offended.[47] And his genius was such that he deserved to be forgiven, although he had lowered himself to some nasty things and had promised to make insulting drawings and statues to denigrate those who had first sustained him in his poverty.[48] It is said that at the time of the siege he had the chance to acquire a long-desired eighteen-foot-high block of Carrara marble that Pope Clement, after rivalry between the two artists, had finally awarded to Baccio Bandinelli.[49] Now that it was public property Michelangelo asked the *gonfaloniere* for it, and so he also was given his chance, although Baccio had already made a model and cut away much of the stone as he blocked it out. Michelangelo in his turn made a model which was thought wonderfully beautiful; but when the Medici were restored it was given back to Baccio because Michelangelo had to go to Rome to see Pope Clement. Although he had been deeply offended, the pope, as a friend to genius, forgave him everything and ordered him to return to Florence and finally complete the sacristy and library of San Lorenzo. And to hasten on the work, many of the projected statues were allocated to other masters. Two Michelangelo assigned to Tribolo, one to Raffaello da Monte Lupo and one to Giovanni Angelo of the Servite order; and he helped all these sculptors by making the clay models for them. Thus they all set to work with a will, while he saw to the library, where, working from his designs, the ceiling was finished with woodcarving by Carota and Tasso, expert Florentine carvers and master-carpenters. The book-shelves too were completed by Battista del Cinque and his friend Ciappino, both fine craftsmen. And the marvellous Giovanni da Udine was brought to Florence to give the work the finishing touch by doing the stucco work on the tribune, assisted by his own men and various Florentine craftsmen. Thus everyone was working hard to complete that great project.

Michelangelo was about to have the statues finally carved when the pope took it into his head to have him on hand in Rome, being eager to have the walls of the Sistine Chapel done by the man who had already painted the ceiling for Julius II. Michelangelo had already started on the drawings when

Clement VII died; and this was why the Florentine project, which he had striven so hard to complete, was left unfinished; for the craftsmen working on it were laid off by those who had nothing left to spend.

Then came the happy election of the Farnese Pope Paul III, an old friend who, knowing that Michelangelo had a mind to finish the work he had already started in Rome as his own and last memorial, had the scaffolding raised and gave orders that the project should proceed. And he arranged for Michelangelo to have a monthly stipend and means to carry out the work.

For the wall of the chapel Michelangelo took good care to build something that had not been there before, a projection of bricks overhanging about a foot from above, so that no harm could come from dust or dirt settling on the work. One day, when the pope had decided to see the chapel, the Master of Ceremonies came haughtily in and condemned the painting for its many nude figures. Then Michelangelo, in revenge, portrayed him to the life as Minos in hell amid a heap of other devils.

About this time it happened that Michelangelo fell from not very high on the scaffolding and hurt his leg; and in his pain and anger he refused to be treated by anyone. Now still alive in those days was Master Baccio Rontini, a clever Florentine physician, a friend of Michelangelo and an admirer of his genius. Moved by compassion, he went one day to knock on Michelangelo's door; and, receiving no reply even from the neighbours, he managed to get into the house and climb stealthily up from room to room until he reached Michelangelo, who was in a desperate state. Then Baccio refused to go away or even leave the bedside until he was cured. Once he was better, Michelangelo returned to the chapel and worked on it constantly so that in a few months he completed it, giving the painting such force as to justify Dante's words, 'The dead seemed dead, the living seemed alive.'[50] Here one sees the misery of the damned and the joy of the blessed. Indeed, when this Last Judgement was revealed, it showed that Michelangelo had not only surpassed the other artists who had worked there before him, but had even striven to outdo his own celebrated ceiling so that, by making something far better, he surpassed himself. For he imagined to himself the terror of those days and represented, for the greater punishment of those who have not lived well, the whole Passion of Christ, with various naked figures in the sky carrying the cross, the column, the spear, the sponge, the nails and the crown of thorns in a variety of postures where the ease of movement is very difficult to convey. There is Christ, seated with a stern and terrible face and turning to curse the damned; not without great fear on the part of Our Lady who gathers her cloak around her at the sight and sound of so much desolation. In a circle around him are countless figures of apostles and prophets, and notably Adam and St Peter who are thought to have been placed there because one was the first parent of those who are being brought to judgement and the other was the first foundation stone of the Christian religion. At the feet of Christ is a wonderful St Bartholomew displaying his flayed skin; there is also a nude St Lawrence and all around a countless number of saints and other figures, male and female, near and far, who embrace and rejoice at having obtained everlasting blessedness by the grace of God and as a reward for their own good works. Below the feet of Christ there are the seven angels described by St John the Evangelist with the seven trumpets that sound the call to Judgement; and in their faces is such terrible wrath that one's hair stands on end at the sight. Among others there are two angels, each holding the Book of Life, while nearby can be seen the Seven Deadly Sins, masterfully depicted as a band of devils pulling down to hell the souls that are flying to heaven, all in admirable postures and with wonderful foreshortening. Nor did Michelangelo hesitate to show how, at the Resurrection of the Dead, they recover flesh and bone from the earth itself; and how, helped by others of the living, they take wing to heaven, where they are again assisted by souls already blessed – none of this without proper attention to every detail that belongs to such a work. That manifold study and effort appears throughout the work, and especially clearly in Charon who, with a frenzied expression, uses his oar to beat the souls whom the devils drag down into his boat. Here Michelangelo recalls how his beloved Dante describes the scene:

> Charon, his eyes red like a burning brand,
> Thumps with his oar the lingerers that delay,
> And rounds them up, and beckons with his hand.[51]

One cannot imagine how much variety there is in the heads of those devils who are truly monsters from hell. In the sinners may be seen both their sin and their fear of eternal damnation. And besides the beauty of the details, it is extraordinary to see how the whole work is so harmoniously painted and carried through that it seems to have been done in a single day, with a finish that no miniaturist could ever achieve. In truth, the multitude of figures and the grandeur and sublimity of the work defy description, for it gives wonderful expression to all possible human emotions. Thus the proud, the envious, the avaricious, the lustful and other sinners can easily be recognized by any perceptive man, for Michelangelo has observed every rule of decorum in depicting them with all the appropriate postures, expressions and natural details. Wonderful and great though this is, it was not impossible to Michelangelo because he had always been a wise and acute observer of men, and had gained by experience that knowledge of the world that philosophers acquire through speculation and books. Thus any discerning man who understands painting will see the sublimity of art and in those figures will perceive thoughts and emotions that have never been depicted by anybody else. He will also see how Michelangelo has created an immense variety of attitudes in the strange and diverse gestures of young and old, men and women. And in these who sees not the awesome power of art together with the grace that the artist had from nature, for they move the hearts of ignorant and expert alike? There are foreshortenings that look like relief, and with the harmony, smoothness and refinement that give grace to the details, they show indeed what the work of good true painters should be. And in the contours that he shapes by a method nobody else could imitate one sees the true Judgement, the true Damnation and Resurrection.

In our art this is the great example of painting sent down by God to mortal men that they may see how destiny works when supreme minds descend to earth, infused with the grace and divinity of knowledge. Behind it, as prisoners in chains, follow all those who think they know the art of painting; and, seeing the outlines of any of its forms, even the boldest spirits and most skilful in drawing are seized with fear and trembling. And to gaze on these labours is to have the senses stunned at the mere thought of how other paintings, past and future, will seem when compared to this perfection. Ours may truly be called a happy age, and happy is the memory of those who have truly seen this stupendous wonder of our century. Most blessed and most fortunate Paul III, for God has granted that your protection of Michelangelo should ensure the glory that the pens of writers will accord to his memory and your own! How much fame will your merits acquire through his genius! Certainly the artists of this age have been favoured by Fortune in his birth, for they have seen the veil of difficulty stripped away from all that can be done or imagined in painting, sculpture and architecture.

Let those who wish to see the sum of wonders think also how many of its great gifts heaven has instilled into his happy genius: let them not only contemplate those things that belong to the difficulties of his chosen art, but, beyond these, read the lovely *canzoni* and the magnificent sonnets, written with the greatest of care, made into songs by famous poets and musicians, read and commentated by learned men in the most celebrated academies throughout Italy. Moreover, Michelangelo's merit was such that the divine Marchesa of Pescara wrote to him and composed works that sing his praise; and he in turn sent her a beautiful drawing of a *pietà* at her request.[52] Nobody could put a pen to better use, either in writing or in drawing; and the same is true for the pencil or any other instrument of drawing.

Michelangelo has often produced beautiful drawings, like those he sent in the past to his friend Gherardo Perini or those sent more recently to Master Tommaso de' Cavalieri, a Roman gentleman who has some stupendous examples such as a Rape of Ganymede, a Tityos and a bacchanal that could not be more harmonious.[53] Also to be seen are his cartoons, which are quite without equal as attested by the fragments scattered here and there, especially the following: one that is in the house of Bindo Altoviti in Florence, drawn by his hand for the chapel; all those that were seen in possession of his pupil Antonio Mini who took them to France along with the painting of Leda; a very finished *Venus* in charcoal which he gave to Bartolomeo Bettini; and a *Noli me tangere* which he did for the Marchese del Vasto and which was finished in colour by Jacopo da Pontormo.[54] But why do I keep wandering on from one thing to another? It is enough to say simply this: that he revived whatever he touched with his inspired hand and gave it eternal life.

But to return to the work in the chapel: when he had finished The Last Judgement, the pope granted him the revenues from the ferry across the Po at Piacenza, which gave him six hundred *scudi* a year in addition to his regular stipend. His next assignment was another chapel known as the Pauline Chapel where the sacrament was to be kept. Here he painted two scenes, one with St Peter where Christ gives him the keys[55] and the other the terrible conversion of St Paul. At the same time he was trying to complete the part of the tomb of Julius II that was still to be done; and he had it erected in San Pietro in Vincoli in Rome, spending no time on anything but the practice of his art, day and night; for he gave himself to unceasing study, and his love of solitude showed how his soul was overburdened with cares. Thus in a short time he finished two marble statues which he set up in the tomb, with the statue of Moses between them;[56] and in his house, blocked out in a single piece of marble, there are still four figures, including a Deposition of Christ.[57] One may suppose that if this had been finished it would have surpassed every other work of Michelangelo, given the sheer difficulty of extracting so many perfect figures from that stone.

Michelangelo's religious sense has always been evident in his way of life; and, as an admirable example of this, he has avoided court society as much as possible, and frequented only those

who have needed him for professional reasons or those whom
he has been induced to love for the qualities seen in them. He
has always given proper help to his relatives, but has not cared
to have them around him. Nor has he cared much to open his
house to other artists in his field, although he has done what
he could for all of them. He has never condemned the work of
others unless he himself has first been attacked or denigrated.
He has made many architectural designs for princes and for
private people as well. These include one for the Church of
Santa Apollonia in Florence because he had a niece who was a
nun there, the design for the Capitol, the tomb of Cecchino
Bracci for his friend Luigi del Riccio,[58] and the tomb of Zanobi
Montaguto which he designed for Urbino to make.[59] He kept
very few assistants in his art, maintaining only Pietro Urbano
of Pistoia and Antonio Mini, a Florentine, who grieved him
considerably when he took it into his head to go off to France:
and yet Michelangelo amply rewarded his services, giving him
the drawings that I spoke of above, the painting of Leda that
is now with the King of France, and two chests full of models
in clay and wax, which were lost when Mini died in France.
Finally, he engaged Urbino who has served him and looked
after him ever since; and indeed Michelangelo was so heartily
satisfied with his service that when Urbino fell ill a short time
ago, he looked after him day and night, never leaving his side,
saying that he himself was the one to suffer for, being an old
man, he was likely to die of sorrow. This was the result of
sincere affection and of respect for the obligations he felt
towards him.

Certainly one may judge that he has never been surpassed
for benevolence, prudence and wisdom in the practice of his
art. And all those who have attributed his departures from
convention to mere caprice or oddity should forgive him
because in truth one may say that whoever wishes to reach
perfection in art is obliged to flee conventions; because, instead
of having the mind distracted by such things, genius requires
thought, solitude and time for reflection. Thus he has never
been less than himself and his labours have been of great benefit
to all other artists; and he has always given his genius an

appropriate outward dignity, delighting in fine horses, maintaining his rank as a man born of noble stock and demonstrating the wisdom of a wonderful artist.

After so many labours, he has reached the age of seventy-three and in all this time his shrewd and witty remarks have made him known as a prudent man whose speech is habitually veiled and ambiguous, for his words often have two meanings; and he always says that a man who wants to live in peace should not have too many irons in the fire. But this is a precept that in recent times he has not been able to observe, for with the death of Antonio da Sangallo he has had to take over projects for the Farnese Palace in Campo di Fiore and for the construction of St Peter's. On one occasion, when a friend remarked that the thought of death must grieve him since he was constantly labouring at his art without any respite, he replied that it was no matter, for if life were pleasing then death could hardly be less so, being given by the hand of the same master. A fellow citizen, who found him at Orsanmichele in Florence where he had stopped to look at Donatello's statue of St Mark, asked what he thought of it: Michelangelo answered that he had never seen a statue that seemed so much like an honest man and that if St Mark really looked like that then one could believe what he had written. He was shown a drawing by a beginner who had been recommended to him; and when some people started making excuses for the lad on the grounds that he had only just started studying the art, Michelangelo simply said: 'That's obvious.' He said something similar to an artist who had painted a *pietà*, remarking that it was well done because it really was pitiful to see.[60] Hearing that Sebastiano Veneziano [del Piombo] had to paint a friar in the chapel of San Pietro in Montorio, he said that it would ruin the place: when asked why, he answered that since friars had ruined the whole wide world, it wouldn't take them much to ruin a small chapel. He was asked what he thought of a painter who was well paid on the unveiling of a work that had taken him considerable time and immense effort: he replied: 'As long as he wants to be rich, he'll always be poor.' A friend, who had already taken holy orders and said mass, arrived in Rome all dressed up in silver points and silks and greeted Michelangelo, who at first pretended not to recognize him; then, when the friend was finally forced to say his name, he feigned amazement at seeing him in such clothes, saying, as if in congratulation: 'O how handsome you look! If you were as fine inside as you are outside, it would be good for your soul.'

While he was finishing the tomb of Julius in San Pietro in Vincoli, Michelangelo got a stone-cutter to make a terminal figure for it. He said things like 'Cut away here; level there; polish here' until finally the man had carved a statue without realizing it. As the man looked in amazement at the finished work, Michelangelo asked: 'What do you think of it?'. 'I think it's fine,' said the man, 'and I'm much obliged to you.' 'Why?' asked Michelangelo. 'Because, thanks to you, I've discovered a talent I never knew I had.' A friend came along to recommend someone who had already done a statue for Michelangelo, asking whether he could not be given something more to do; and Michelangelo very kindly obliged. But the friend was, in fact, consumed with envy and had only asked Michelangelo that favour because he was convinced it would be refused; and when he saw that it had after all been granted, he went around complaining. News of this came back to Michelangelo who remarked that he did not like sewer men, thus using an architectural metaphor to mean that one should have little to do with men who have two mouths. He was asked what he thought of someone who had made marble copies of some famous antique statues and then boasted that he had far surpassed the ancient masters: he answered: 'A man who follows another can't overtake him.' Some painter or other had produced a picture where the best thing was an ox: asked why the painter had made the ox more lifelike than anything else, Michelangelo replied: 'All painters are good at self-portraits.' Passing by San Giovanni in Florence, he was asked his opinion of Ghiberti's doors, and he answered: 'They are so beautiful that they could serve as the gates of Paradise.'

As I said at the beginning, heaven sent Michelangelo down to earth as an example in his life, conduct and works, so that those who admire and imitate him might approach the fame of an eternal name, honouring nature by their works and studies and heaven by their virtue, in the very way that Michelangelo has always honoured both nature and heaven. And let no man marvel that I have here written the life of Michelangelo while he is still alive; for since we cannot expect that he should never die, it seemed fitting that I should do this small thing in his honour, so that when, as all men must, he leaves the body behind, no mortality will touch his immortal works, whose glorious fame will live as long as the world lasts, both in the mouths of men and in the pens of writers, in spite of envy and in defiance of death.

Appendix 1:
The Buonarroti Family

Lodovico di Lionardo di Buonarroti Simoni (1444–1531)
First marriage (1472) Francesca (d. 1481)
Second marriage (1485) Lucrezia da Gagliano (d. 1497)

Children of Lodovico and Francesca

Lionardo (b. 1473), friar
Michelangelo (1475–1564), sculptor, painter, architect
Cassandra (dates unknown)
Buonarroto (1477–1528), wool merchant, married Bartolomea della
    Casa (1516)
Giovansimone (1479–1548)
Gismondo (1481–1555)

Son of Buonarroto and Bartolomea

Lionardo (1519–99), married Cassandra Ridolfi (1553)

Children of Lionardo and Cassandra

Buonarroto (1554–1628)
Michelangelo (b. & d.1555)
Michelangelo the Younger (1568–1647), minor poet, playwright, first
editor of the poems of Michelangelo (1623)

Appendix 2:
The Popes, the della Rovere and the Medici

Reigns of Popes

Sixtus IV (Francesco della Rovere)	1471–84
Innocent VIII (Giovanni Battista Cibo)	1484–92
Alexander VI (Roderigo de Borgia)	1492–1503
Pius III (Francesco Todeschini)	Sept–Oct 1503
Julius II (Giuliano della Rovere)	1503–13
Leo X (Giovanni de' Medici)	1513–21
Adrian VI (Adrian Dedel)	1522–3
Clement VII (Giulio de' Medici)	1523–34
Paul III (Alessandro Farnese)	1534–49
Julius III (Giovanni del Monte)	1550–55
Marcellus II (Marcello Cervini)	April–May 1555
Paul IV (Giovanni Pietro Caraffa)	1555–9
Pius IV (Giovanni Angelo Medici)	1559–65

The della Rovere

Francesco (Pope Sixtus IV, 1471–84)	1414–84
Giuliano (Pope Julius II, 1503–13), nephew of Sixtus IV	1443–1513
Francesco Maria, Duke of Urbino, nephew of Julius II	1490–1538
Leonardo Grosso, Cardinal Aginensis, nephew of Julius II	d.1520

The Medici

Lorenzo the Magnificent	1449–92
Giuliano (1), brother of Lorenzo	1453–78
Pietro the Unfortunate, first son of Lorenzo	1471–1503

Giovanni (Pope Leo X), second son of
   Lorenzo   1476–1521
Giuliano (2), Duke of Nemours, third son
   of Lorenzo   1479–1516
Giulio (Pope Clement VII), illegitimate
   son of Giuliano (1)   1478–1534
Lorenzo, Duke of Urbino, son of Pietro   1492–1519
Alessandro, Duke of Florence, illegitimate
   son of Clement VII   1511–37
Cosimo I, Duke of Florence, son of
   Giovanni delle Bande Nere (from the
   younger branch of the Medici family)
   and of Maria Salviati, grand-daughter
   of Lorenzo the Magnificent   1519–74

Notes

POEMS

Abbreviations:
M = Michelangelo
TC = Tommaso de' Cavalieri
VC = Vittoria Colonna

4

The tradition of envying clothes their contact with the beloved goes back at least as far as Ovid. M will apply it to TC in 94.

5

Written while M was working on the Sistine Chapel (1508–12) and addressed to Giovanni di Benedetto da Pistoia, poet and later chancellor of the Florentine Academy. The caudate sonnet adds one or more three-line tails to the standard fourteen lines and is frequently a vehicle for satire. For an even more grotesque self-portrait, see 267. In the manuscript the poem is illustrated by a small sketch of himself in the awkward posture described.

1. *I've got a goitre from this job I'm in:* A goitre is an enlargement of the thyroid gland of the neck, a disease traditionally associated with the alpine regions of Italy.
20. *This is no place for me ... no painter:* M frequently insists that he is a sculptor by profession and a painter only by necessity.

6

The poem probably reflects M's difficult relations with Pope Julius II during the painting of the Sistine Chapel.

10. *potent sword:* Julius II was a notoriously military pope.

14. *withered tree*: Possibly a play on the pope's family name, della Rovere (*rovere* = oak). For the della Rovere family see Appendix 2.

10

Denunciation of Rome in the tradition of Petrarch's three anti-papal sonnets (*Canzoniere* 136–8). Written from Rome, the poem is signed by 'Your Michelangelo in Turkey' as a way of pressing home the point that he does not consider Rome a Christian city.

1–3. *From chalices . . . the shield and spear*: Condemning the military ambitions of the papacy.

5–7. *But let him come . . . they sell his skin so dear*: An attack on simony, the sin of trafficking in sacred things.

9–11. *If ever I sought ruin . . . petrifying game*: Probably referring to the withdrawal of some commission by the pope, whose indifference makes his gaze like that of the Medusa which was reputed to turn men to stone – an ironic fate for a sculptor.

12–14. *but if high heaven . . . the life to be*: Deliberately cryptic lines. The 'great restoration' may be the renewal of Rome's spiritual mission, which will not be possible as long as the city follows the sign of simoniacal riches or military might rather than the sign of the cross.

14

Written on a sketch for the Medici Chapel and referring specifically to the figures of *Day* and *Night* that flank the figure of Giuliano de' Medici, Duke of Nemours (see Appendix 2). The status of the text is not clear. It may have been intended as an epitaph or it may be the prose paraphrase of a projected or lost poem. The hyperbolic compliment is far from original. *Night* speaks in a very different vein in 247.

18

Probably the beginning of an unfinished allegorical poem.

4–5. *The sea, the mountain . . . I live on*: The mountain suggests some kind of arduous spiritual ascent and the fiery sword recalls that of Genesis 3:24, which bars Adam and Eve from Eden.

21

The kind of song associated with carnival processions and possibly sung by young men in skeleton costumes following the Chariot of Death. Though the sentiments are perfectly traditional, M may be remembering the grim sermons of Savonarola. Condivi's Life confirms M's admiration for the apocalyptic Florentine reformer who was burned at the stake in 1498. (See also Introduction, p. xiii.)

25

A caudate sonnet. One of many poems dealing with the problems of love in old age.

9-11. *But fire knows no such law ... warms his chill*: The imagery of dry wood is frequent in M, though elsewhere it is used to suggest that old men are more easily destroyed by the fire of love.

15-20. *And should someone in mirth ... due restraint and measure*: Refuting the view often expressed elsewhere by M himself that love and old age are incompatible. The argument seems to be that the love of a thing divine may be continuous with the love for things of nature, provided the latter are seen without illusions.

32

Fragment of a sonnet.

1. *I live to sin, dying to myself I live*: The phrase 'dying to myself' would normally have positive spiritual implications, but is here used ironically to suggest that his life serves only to kill the soul. The Pauline echoes (Romans 6:11 and Galatians 2:20) are indicative of M's theological orientation.

34

A Neoplatonic exaltation of human love as a way to the divine.

5-6. *When both our souls left God ... a perfect eye*: The 'perfect eye' of the lover perceives the presence of God in transitory human beauty.

9-11. *Heat cannot be divided ... whence it came*: The capacity to perceive beauty is given by heaven and therefore cannot be divided from whatever has the same origin.

12-14. *Since in your glance ... before your eyes*: Suggesting the Neoplatonic idea that the soul has a prior existence in heaven.

37

Probably the tercets of a sonnet. Addressed to the beloved, whose beauty forms the poet's soul for the contemplation of God.

41

Exploiting the Petrarchan motif of the beloved as a perfect work of heaven and nature which are respectively the ultimate and proximate causes of beauty.

12–14. *What custom ... be spared by death*: The complex litotes underlines the speaker's difficulty in coming to terms with the inevitable death of beauty.

42

A dialogue sonnet in which Love responds to the lover's questions by asserting that the beloved becomes more truly beautiful when her beauty is transmitted by the 'mortal eye' to the lover's 'immortal part', the soul.

14. *this and not that now comes before your eyes*: What the lover now sees is *this* immortal beauty shaped within the soul and not *that* external beauty.

46

The poem probably refers to the death of M's brother Buonarroto. Buonarroto's influence in moving M to virtue was like that of the hammer that shapes a hammer. Just as the blow is stronger if the hammer is lifted higher, so Buonarroto's influence will be greater now that he has risen to heaven, where, moreover, he will find other virtuous souls to help him at the smithy. The poem only makes sense if we assume that the 'this' of line 11 refers to the symbolic hammer of Buonarroto. The irritating vagueness of pronominal reference is not entirely dissipated by M's own prose explication:

> He was alone in the world to exalt virtue with his own great virtues; he had nobody to work the bellows. Now in heaven he will have many companions because nobody is there who does not love virtue; so I hope that from up there he will complete my [hammer?] down here. At least in heaven he will now have someone to work the bellows; for on earth he had no companion at the forge where virtues are exalted.

54

Thirteen (incomplete) stanzas of *ottava rima*. An unfinished mock love-poem in the burlesque tradition of Lorenzo de' Medici's *Nencia da Barberino*.

The lacunae and the switching from second to third person and back indicate a project that M abandoned.

39–40. *like emptied bowels ... because the pain was great*: The scatological imagery anticipates 267.

69–70. *did I think then ... take my leave*: Parodying the convention of the lover who seeks solitude.

73–76. *You entered me ... because the belly's wide*: A comic version of the idea that love enters through the eyes. The metaphor is taken from the practice of ripening fruit in bottles.

81–83. *Think about air ... closes it again*: The same air that opens the valve of a ball by pressure from outside then keeps it closed by pressure from inside.

58

1.   *immortal wish*: Desire for what is immortal.

3–4. *pitiless / lord*: The beloved.

9–14. *Alas, how therefore shall the chaste desire ... still won't believe*: The sestet seems to allude to a separation provoked by slanderous rumours that M's love is of a carnal nature.

59

The sequence of conditional clauses starting with 'if' is a popular device that sixteenth-century sonneteers inherited from Petrarch.

7–8. *if love's gold dart ... strikes them with its flame*: A biblical metaphor (Revelation 2:23).

14.   *that only scorn can still untie or break*: The overall optimism of the sonnet is slightly undermined by the lingering fear that TC might still be influenced by slanderous gossip.

60

Like 58, the sonnet suggests that TC may have been reticent about acknowledging the strength of M's affection.

1–4. *You know, my lord ... from exchanging greetings then*: The tortuous repetition of 'know' conveys the sense of implicitly recognized emotions that fail to find direct expression.

10. *what in yourself you love*: The spiritual dimension.

14. *whoever would know this must know death first*: Either a metaphorical death to the world or a literal death followed by eternal life.

61

Less troubled than the previous sonnets. Though old age may seem to make M's love less passionate and immediate than it would have been when he was young, this turns out to be an advantage since he is now more ready for an uplifting spiritual relationship.

1-4. *If I had thought ... to be reborn*: The phoenix is TC who transmits his powers of self-renewal to M.

62

1-4. *Only with forging fire ... its purest state refined*: The refining of metal as a metaphor for spiritual purification may reflect M's own experience as an artist, but it also derives from biblical tradition (Psalm 66:10; Isaiah 48:10).

12-14. *Since fire to its own element ... to the skies*: In Ptolemaic cosmology the upward movement of fire is explained by its natural tendency to return to its source in the outer sphere surrounding the earth (the empyrean).

63

Once again M uses imagery that reflects his professional experience. This difficult sonnet takes the complex relations between fire and stone as a metaphor for spiritual purification and the achievement of immortality through love.

1-4. *Cold stone and inner fire ... stones are bound*: Fire can be struck from stone, but that same fire may then be used to heat the stone until it crumbles into the dust from which lime is made; the lime in its turn is used to bind stones together in buildings that resist time.

7-8. *like some new soul ... from hell to heaven returned*: Referring to the Catholic doctrine of Purgatory where repentant sinful souls are purified. Purgatory was often regarded as a softer version of hell (see 248).

13–14. *I shall be made eternal . . . but of gold*: A return to the kindling image of the opening. That the fire of love in M has been struck out of gold rather than iron indicates the resplendent qualities of the beloved.

64

Probably a poem in itself and not the first quatrain of a sonnet.

66

9. *O flesh, O blood, O wood, O ultimate pain*: Christ is addressed through the images of his passion.

10. *justified*: A theological term: rendered unjust in God's eyes by sin, man can only be justified by the grace that flows from Christ's passion.

14. *so near to death and yet so far from God*: The line has become almost proverbial in Italian.

71

A caudate sonnet, possibly for Giovanni Benedetto da Pistoia; the violent tone seems to go beyond the jocular tradition of Francesco Berni (see note to 85).

12–13. *Think of the Poet . . . about Pistoia*: The Poet is Dante, who inveighs against Pistoia: 'Pistoia, O Pistoia, well were thee / To burn thyself to ashes and perish all, / Whose crimes outgo thy criminal ancestry!' (*Inferno*, XXV, 10–12, in *The Divine Comedy*, vol. 1: *Hell*, trans. Dorothy L. Sayers (Harmondsworth, 1949)).

72

As in 58 and 60, but with greater optimism, M seeks explicit acknowledgement of his passion. The theological resonance of the vocabulary (grace, merit) co-exists with a rare expression of physical desire which is even more explicit in a draft of the poem where he speaks of embracing TC's breast and neck.

10–11. *Let time suspend its days . . . upon its ancient way*: The lover's desire to suspend time can be traced back through Petrarch to Ovid and Catullus.

76

A much-revised poem. The octave presents three hypotheses about the origin of love: a) the soul sees in the beloved a reflection of the light of God; b) the soul loves a memory of something that has been truly seen; c) what the soul loves is something it has not seen but only dreamed or heard of.

12. *my lord*: A change from earlier drafts which had *donna* rather than *signor*. Though much of M's poetry is clearly autobiographical, it is a mistake to assume that every poem has a stable addressee. Poems addressed to a man could be adapted to address a woman and vice versa.

14. *the cause, of course, can only be your eyes*: An almost throwaway colloquial conclusion, as if to dissipate the poem's accumulated perplexities.

77

M seeks to explain why his response to TC's beauty may appear less than adequate.

14. *my partial vision lights a feeble fire*: The fire of my love seems feeble only because my understanding of your beauty is incomplete.

78

An attempt to come to terms with the fact that his love is both spiritual and physical.

14. *who, if I die, could put the blame on you*: If TC's beauty is truly of heavenly origin, he cannot be blamed for the fatal effect it has on M.

79

Written when M was in Florence and using Bartolomeo Angelini (a Roman customs officer, d. 1540) as an intermediary in his correspondence with TC in Rome.

3-4. *and, amid all the joys ... before more noble names*: Angelini had informed M of TC's frequent expressions of esteem and affection: 'more noble names' suggests M's awareness of TC's social superiority.

9. *he who speaks for me*: Angelini.

11. *he who writes*: M.

12-14. *For it would be . . . in their place*: There is not much justifica-
tion for Saslow's suggestion that M is apologizing for the homo-
erotic content of drawings like *Ganymede* or *Tityos*. (For Saslow,
see Further Reading.) M frequently adopts a dismissive tone
when speaking of his own work. The point here is the dispro-
portion between what he has offered (his pictures) and what he
expects in return (the physical presence of TC).

80

3. *my eagle eyes might gaze upon the sun*: The eyes of an eagle were
thought to be strong enough to look directly at the sun.

7-8. *would be as vain . . . and the mind on God*: To cast the mind
on God is vain insofar as God is beyond human comprehen-
sion.

81

A much-revised madrigal where an initially female addressee was
changed to a masculine one (probably TC).

6. *you as sole Sun; and thus the soul's deprived*: With the homo-
phones *sole/soul* I have tried to offer an equivalent for the Italian
wordplay on *sole* ('sun') and *solo* ('alone').

84

The sonnet anticipates 151 (for VC) with the idea that the stone
contains the form and that the artist transforms the experience of
others according to his own temperament.

85

This burlesque verse-letter (in the *terza rima* form known as *capitolo*)
is a reply to Francesco Berni who had written a poem, purportedly
addressed to the painter Sebastiano del Piombo (see note to Letter 19)
in Rome, but obviously intended for M who replies by impersonating
del Piombo and compounds the joke by making himself the supposed
bearer of the letter. Berni, in his poem, had exalted M over contempor-
ary Petrarchist poets: 'he says things, and you say words'.

1-3. *No sooner was . . . to the chosen three*: Carrying out the precise
instructions in Berni's poem.

4.   *The greatest Medico of all our ills*: Pope Clement VII, Giulio de'
       Medici (1478–1534); hence the pun.

7–9.   *The reverend holy man . . . he burst out laughing too*: The pope's
       cousin, Cardinal Ippolito de' Medici (1511–35), 'Medico the
       Less', whom Berni claims to serve both in Florence and in Rome
       (here and there).

10–12. *I haven't seen . . . if he were a priest*: The cardinal's secretary,
       Francesco Maria Molza (1489–1544), poet and humanist.

19–21. *The Carnesecchi . . . you're all he thinks about*: A reference
       to the pope's secretary, Monsignor Pietro Carnesecchi (1508–
       67), whose surname suggests dried meat. The lines now have
       a sinister overtone that M could not have intended: in 1567
       Carnesecchi's body was burned after he had been found guilty
       of heresy and beheaded.

22.   *By Buonarroti you're so idolized*: M himself.

25–30. *and says that he . . . which cannot conquer virtuous renown*:
       M parodies the immortalizing topos. Berni's burlesque manner
       could hardly be expected to call forth such high-flown praise.

32–42. *See votive offerings hung . . . from a painted one*: Replying
       with mock-modesty to Berni's jocular praise of M as someone
       before whom he would like to burn incense and hang votive
       offerings.

54.   *my cowl*: Sebastiano del Piombo had become a friar in 1531.
       Hence also the pun on 'brother' in 57.

58.   *Command me, sir: and then do it yourself*: A comic version of
       the conventional at-your-service ending.

86

Unfinished *capitolo* on the death of M's father.

1–12.   *My heart already was oppressed with grief . . . which affliction
       is the worse*: The death of his father Lodovico comes when M
       has still not recovered from the loss of his brother Buonarroto
       (see 46), hence the need to distinguish between the two griefs.

13–14. *My brother's painted . . . alive within my heart*: The metaphor
       reveals M's preference for sculpture over painting.

15.   *my face stained*: With tears.

28–30. *And even when soul bows . . . to greater grief I fall*: To control
       grief by reason is so onerous that it ends by provoking greater
       grief.

39.   *that false persuader*: The weak flesh, the senses.

40–42. *Ninety times over . . . the heavenly peace*: Lodovico may

actually have been about eighty-seven; in this case M rounds off
his age to ninety for rhetorical effect. The image of the sea
quenching the fire of the sun is puzzling, since it would seem
more appropriate to days than to years.

87

1. *I wish I willed what I will not, O Lord*: As with the opening of
   60, the repetition of the same verb conveys the sense of a vicious
   circle.
2. *ice* and *fire*: One of the most popular Petrarchan antitheses.
13. *to your fair bride*: In traditional Christian metaphor the bride of
    Christ is either the Church or the individual soul.

88

9-11. *How can it be ... that which he has not*: The beauty of the
      beloved paradoxically makes the lover's face ugly with suffering.

89

The first eleven lines work towards a fusion of the *I* and the *you* which
is then brutally undercut by the isolation of the concluding tercet.
1-2. *With your fair eyes ... could never see, being blind*: M modifies
     the conventional formula by making the lover see beauty not in
     but through the eyes of the beloved.

90

7-10. *since your face has made ... some charm or magic sword*: The
      speaker is a target for the arrows of love; but, as in Christian
      mysticism, the wound becomes the sign of his election to a
      specially protected status.
13-14. *and with your mark ... with my spittle*: From the imagery of
       romance and fairy tale M passes to a daring association with the
       miracles of Christ (Mark 8:23 and John 7:33), although the
       Gospel has no record of cures for poison.

93

The 'four tempers' of the poem are sense, heart, soul and reason. The
metaphor is both medical and musical: as with the more familiar

four elements, health and harmony are guaranteed by perfect equality between the tempers. The poem is in the form of a madrigal, set to music by Jacques Arcadelt. (See note to Letter 35.)

94

An unrevised, jocular, and mildly erotic sonnet which develops the theme of envy for the clothes that touch the beloved. The lowly beast of the first quatrain is usually thought to be the silkworm which provides the material for gloves. Later, however, the image shifts to snakeskin and concludes with some kind of hide.

97

9–11. *The art of beauty ... still strives upward everywhere*: The traditional topos of art that surpasses nature and nature that strives towards the perfection of art.

12. *to that*: To beauty.

98

3. *this fate*: The suffering of love.

8. *how there's no good that's worth my misery*: The paradox of a misery that is more highly valued than any good.

14. *the prisoner of a well-armed cavalier*: A play on the name of Cavalieri.

101

The first of four sonnets (101–104) exploring different attitudes towards night. The poems are later than the famous sculpture of *Night* in the Medici Chapel.

1–4. *Since Phoebus does not clasp ... which he does not embrace*: Night is essentially a negative quality, an absence. *Phoebus*: the sun-god.

10–11. *surely she's daughter ... only the other makes it*: Earth is like the womb holding the darkness that has been created by the sun. In Aristotelean theory only the male seed was seen as active in procreation.

103

7–8. *by what's far baser . . . by a glow-worm*: Repeating the idea that concluded 101.

12–14. *but only darkness . . . than any other fruit*: The probably jocular assumption that the procreative act usually takes place at night.

104

1–4. *He who created time . . . the moon that's near to us*: In the Sistine Chapel M had portrayed God separating light from darkness and creating the sun and the moon.

5–8. *From these were born . . . my birth and cradle suited best*: Reflecting the astrological belief that character is largely influenced by the position of the stars and planets at the moment of birth.

9–11. *I copy what I think . . . brings more grief and shame*: An obscure tercet, but the sense seems to be that the speaker makes his situation worse by deliberately acting out what he believes fate has ordained for him.

12–14. *Yet there's one consolation . . . since you were born*: The association of the beloved with the sun is frequent in M, but the last line could point to Febo di Poggio, who, by virtue of his name, had been associated with the sun since his birth. Moreover, the whole four-sonnet sequence starts out with a reference to Phoebus. For Febo di Poggio, see note to Letter 32.

105

1–4. *My eyes saw nothing mortal . . . assails a soul like him*: In the eyes of his beloved M finds the loving God who has created man's soul in his own image and likeness.

8. *the universal form*: The Platonic concept of an unchanging ideal beauty.

12–14. *Uncurbed desire is not love . . . in heaven*: A vibrant affirmation of the spiritual quality of his love.

106

A much-revised sonnet.

2. *earthly jail*: The body.

9–11. *all things high and rare ... at their creation*: The creative
combination of heaven and nature as in 41.

13. *veil*: A frequent Petrarchan and Neoplatonic metaphor for the
body.

107

Madrigal.

9–10. *The noble heart ... but one face*: Recalling the famous 'Love
always comes to the noble heart' by Guido Guinizelli, founder
of the thirteenth-century school of love poetry known as the
dolce stil novo ('sweet new style').

110

Michelangelo the Younger records the story that, halfway up the
staircase of his house in Rome, M painted the figure of death as a
skeleton carrying a coffin on which these verses were inscribed.

111

Madrigal.

4–7. *if then ... to punish such a sin*: A sin committed without doubt
of its gravity would be a mortal sin, punishable by damnation.

9. *the eye that cannot see*: Physical rather than spiritual perception.

120

Madrigal.

12. *he never dies whose suffering never ceases*: Not only is the suffer-
ing of love preferable to death, but it is paradoxically a sickness
that preserves life.

134

Dialogue between an unhappy lover and the souls of the blessed.

15. *short life is still too long for those who serve and suffer*: The
conclusion contradicts that of 120.

140

M plays a witty variation on the Petrarchan theme of the lover's longing to be united with his beloved in heaven. Here the argument is that the beloved will do more good in hell by alleviating the sufferings of the damned than harm in heaven where he/she will distract attention from the Beatific Vision.

1–2. *If at the last . . . its long-loved dress*: The Resurrection of the Dead when souls are reunited to their bodies at the Last Judgement (painted by M on the east wall of the Sistine Chapel).

149

If the lover's response to the beloved's excellence seems inadequate, this is because she raises his soul to heights where his talents cannot follow. A grace less overwhelming might provoke a more effective response.

This is one of a number of poems where the vocabulary suggests the influence of Lutheran views on the irrelevance of good works for the purposes of salvation.

1–2. *I cannot but fall short . . . who takes my life from me*: M may be comparing his own poetry unfavourably with that of VC.

12. *She, full of grace*: Recalling the 'Hail Mary, full of grace'.

150

A development of the theme of 149: it is the beloved's sudden pity that may prove fatal to a fragile temperament ('a power too weak').

151

A sonnet made famous by Benedetto Varchi's discussion of it in his lecture on M to the Florentine Academy in March 1547 (printed 1549). (See also Introduction, pp. xxx–xxxi.)

1–4. *The best of artists . . . the hand obedient to the mind*: The idea is in keeping with the Aristotelian view of art as the fulfilment of nature's unachieved potential, but the sonnet goes on to suggest (ll. 5–14) that the stone hides a plurality of forms and it is the artist's own temperament that determines which of those forms finally emerges. *concept*: Varchi relates the term *concetto* to the Greek *idea*, to the Latin *exemplar* and to the Italian *modello*, 'the form or image that some call intention'.

152

The poem exploits the same sculpture metaphor as in 151, but develops it in a different way. Here the stone is the poet's own soul, in which VC, like a sculptor, may find hidden good works.

5–7. *so, hidden under that excess ... good works*: The soul trembles for its own salvation. In this and other poems there may be a reflection of the controversy over the saving power of good works.

153

The metaphor this time is that of casting a statue in bronze, like M's famous statue of Pope Julius II, which was later destroyed.

11–12. *in me through such small vents ... I must be split and broken*: Following the usual tradition of Renaissance poetry, the beloved's eyes are like the narrow pipes through which the molten metal is poured into the mould. See Introduction, pp. xviii–xix.

156

The poem describes a spiritual ascent so arduous that the poet is torn between conflicting emotions: on the one hand he loves VC precisely because she is set so high above him; on the other he commits the sin of wishing that she could descend low enough to be more attainable.

158

Madrigal; a harsh poem about sensual love in old age.

159

Beneath M's autograph there is a draft letter to VC (see Letter 40), which speaks of his incapacity to give a fitting return for some gift that she has sent him.

9–11. *And now I see ... grace divine*: The theological terms recall the ideas on grace and works that were current in the reformist circles frequented by M and VC. See Introduction, pp. xxvi–xxvii.

161

3.   *this slough, this mortal coil*: The image is used in a very different
      vein in 94.

7–9. *For though these last . . . old habits that still weigh*: The reference
      is to an old proverb 'the fox changes his fur, not his ways', cited
      by Petrarch (*Canzoniere*, 122) and often used, as here, to suggest
      that a man does not change his habits when his hair turns grey.

15–17. *Lord, when my final hour . . . make me one who pleases you*:
      On the autograph there is the beginning of a letter to VC in
      which M promises to send her a crucifix.

162

1.   *Now on my right foot, now upon my left*: Right and left, symbolic
      of virtue and vice.

7–8. *A blank white page . . . for your sacred ink*: VC herself is a
      religious poet on whom M relies for guidance.

14–15. *whether in heaven . . . than superfluous good*: The question
      recalls the parable of the Pharisee and the publican (Luke 18:
      9–14).

164

A double sestet.

3.   *both the arts*: Painting and sculpture.

7–9. *Though foolish and rash judgements . . . move each healthy
      mind*: As in 58 and 83, there is an implicit answer to the scandal-
      mongers.

166

A sonnet praising sight, the only source of spiritual vision, as opposed
to the more earthbound sense of touch.

172

11–15. *my face seems not just old . . . to make her fair*: By contrast
      with his ugliness, she seems even more beautiful than nature
      made her, and in this sense the artist has managed to improve
      on nature.

173

Since the painter inevitably reflects his own mood in his work, it is in the lovely sitter's interest to make him happy.

194

Cecchino Bracci died at the age of fifteen. This and the subsequent quatrains belong to a series of fifty epitaphs that M agreed to write at the request of the boy's uncle, Luigi del Riccio (see note to Letter 43). Frequently the autograph contains a postscript that jars with the tone of the epitaph. Gifts of food are regularly acknowledged. This quatrain bears the comment: 'I didn't want to send you this, because it's a very awkward thing; but the trout and the truffles would force heaven.'

197

M's manuscript provides a puzzling alternative ending: 'show him for whom I once was grace in bed, / what he embraced and what the soul lives in'. The lines might suggest a sexual relationship between Cecchino and some other man, presumably Luigi del Riccio; but M seems eager to exclude that reading since he comments: 'Take these two lines below, which are a moral thing'. It has been argued that sharing a bed, while it demonstrated close affection, did not necessarily imply sexual activity. But why does M go out of his way to raise the question?

198

Accompanied by a postscript: 'For the salted mushrooms, since you don't want anything else'.

199

The postscript reads: 'This awkward thing, already said a thousand times, for the fennel'.

218

With postscript: 'For the fig-bread'.

225

Cecchino's epitaph, like that of Shakespeare, forbids any opening of his tomb. He does not want the pitiful sight of his mortal remains to disturb the abiding image of beauty in the mind of one who loved him.

235

One of the most powerful poems for VC who is seen as possessing the intellectual qualities that the period normally regarded as reserved for men. She resembles both the original androgyne of Plato's *Symposium* and the legendary Sibyl through whom a god speaks to men. Writing to Giovan Francesco Fattucci, M speaks of VC as 'a great friend', using the masculine form, *amico* (Letter 53).

4–8. *I am at last . . . that far self*: The loss of self is the first step towards redemption; pity for that self is shown by abstaining from sin.

11–13. *Lady, who ferries souls . . . never to myself return*: See Psalm 66:12: 'we went through fire and through water: but thou broughtest us out into a wealthy place.'

236

VC's spiritual influence over M is like the power of an artist over his material, which is not a matter of mere manual dexterity. First the artist's intellect, his diviner part, forms a concept and then this concept is given shape as a small clay model or rough sketch to be reworked until it finally resembles the original idea. In the same way VC shapes to her idea of virtue the 'unprized' model of M.

12–13. *If you, being kind . . . away excess*: M's habitual idea of the removal of excess to reveal the form contained in the stone.

13–14. *what penance must await . . . if thus chastised and taught*: In the Catholic sacrament of confession the granting of absolution may be accompanied by the imposition of some self-mortifying act as a penance.

237

This poem is probably the octave of an unfinished sonnet.

2. *first art*: Sculpture, first in the sense of its superiority over other arts.

4.   *wax, clay, stone*: In ascending order of durability.
7–8. *the beauty that first was ... kept for a better place*: A Neo-
      platonic notion: our memory of the idea that preceded the work
      foreshadows the time when our pleasure will no longer be vain
      because it will derive from the vision of eternal beauty and not
      from that beauty's transient physical manifestations.

238

Virtue is the coin that heaven mints for us and that we should para-
doxically both hoard for ourselves and spend in good works.

239

A straightforward sonnet on the immortalizing power of art. It contra-
dicts M's stated disdain for lifelike portraiture. Niccolò Martelli, in
his *Letters* (1547), reports that M defended his idealized figures of the
two dukes (Lorenzo, Duke of Urbino and Giuliano, Duke of Nemours
– see Appendix 2) in the Medici Chapel by saying that in a thousand
years' time nobody would know that they looked any different.
5.   *Cause bows to the effect*: The cause (the artist) is outlived by the
      effect (his creation).

240

Thematically related to 239, it seems to refer to a portrait bust of VC,
although no such work has survived.
9.   *The nobler part is lamed*: The Italian here is very obscure.
11–13. *Who can avenge her ... will steal away her own*: Time
       destroys men who are created by nature, but nature takes revenge
       for this transience of her children by granting permanence to
       their work.

241

7.   *Nature works this way too*: The analogy between nature and the
       artist is a Renaissance commonplace.
14–16. *nor can I say ... or my intense delight*: An ingenious
       Petrarchan conceit. The lover is torn between conflicting emo-
       tions: delight at the vision of perfect beauty and fear that such
       perfection heralds the end of the world.

247

This celebrated quatrain is a reply to a poem by Giovanni di Carlo Strozzi (1517–70) praising M's statue of *Night* in the Medici Chapel.

> The sweetly sleeping Night on which you look
> has all the life an angel's hand could give
> to stone, and thus, because she sleeps, she lives:
> wake her, if you still doubt it; she will speak.

2. *While the oppression and the shame still last*: This line expresses M's distaste for the regime of Cosimo de' Medici (see Appendix 2). That Strozzi was fairly closely associated with Cosimo makes the poem particularly pungent since the statue gives him the kind of answer he cannot afford to hear.

248

1–4. *From heaven he came down . . . in its true light*: The quatrain follows the Neoplatonic view of Dante as a philosopher-poet-prophet who descends from heaven to bring light to men and whose ascent to Paradise is in fact a return. *both the hells*: Hell and Purgatory.

6. *undeserving birthplace*: Florence.

8. *you only*: God.

9–14. *I speak of Dante . . . the happiest state on earth*: Though not, in fact, forced out of Florence, M saw himself as sharing Dante's fate as an artist exiled by his ungrateful city. Comparison with Dante became a commonplace of contemporary praise of M.

249

A political allegory. The lady is Florence, created as a republic and now stolen for himself by Cosimo de' Medici. Not only does Cosimo live in fear, but his state is like that of a lover who loses real desire once he is granted complete satisfaction.

250

Like 248, a sonnet in praise of Dante.

7–8. *the gates that heaven . . . to his just claim kept barred*: A reference to Dante's exile from Florence.

251

Written during a quarrel with his trusted friend and advisor, Luigi del Riccio (see Letter 43). The last line is a quotation from Petrarch, (*Canzoniere*, 231).

259

The poem argues that the love of a human being may help rather than hinder salvation.
6.   *the eternal peace*: God.
13.   *ageing husk or final hour*: Physical decay and death.

260

The sonnet follows the Neoplatonic tradition of Marsilio Ficino in celebrating spiritual love between men as superior to love between men and women which is tainted with sensuality. This poem was written on the back of the same piece of paper as 259.

261

1–4.   *Though long delay ... brief is aged happiness*: There should be greater happiness in a love that has had to wait than in a youthful passion that is quickly satisfied, but this is not the case when love comes in old age.
12–14.   *if love inflames ... a middle of my ending*: The sense is not clear, but the most probable interpretation is that love will make his final years seem like the prime of life.

263

A madrigal.
3–4.   The canonical hours serve as metaphors for youth, middle age and old age. The English pun on *prime* (the first canonical hour) is irresistibly appropriate.
5–7.   *My lifeline and my luck ... peace down here*: The lover's allotted lifespan is coming to an end and love brings him no peace.
12–17.   *He loses most ... won't help him without grace*: The sudden violence with which sexual desire can seize even an old man shows that we are never more in danger of damnation than when we trust in our own strength to resist temptation.

264

Madrigal, possibly written during the last illness of VC.

4. *may Love with privilege print it on the soul*: The phrase *cum privilegio* ('with privilege') frequently appeared on the title pages of books to assert exclusive publishing rights.

7–9. *Through calm ... as a cross against the foe*: The sign of the cross was held to have miraculous powers to ward off evil.

12–14. *where bright angels learn ... with your fair face*: VC's beauty will not vanish with her death because it will be used to dress another virtuous soul.

267

A burlesque portrait of the artist as an old man. Only at the end (ll. 46–55) does the poem's comic verve give way to personal bitterness. The poem is in the *capitolo* form.

4–6. *It takes no time ... his own bobbin at the loom*: A complaint against cobwebs. Arachne challenged the goddess Athena to a weaving contest and was transformed into a spider as punishment for her presumption.

16–21. *Within the body ... escaping through my throat*: The fact that M suffers from both constipation and respiratory problems has the paradoxical consequence of keeping him alive since the soul cannot escape with his breath.

28. *the hag who haunts the feast*: A reference to the *Befana*, a comic witch-like figure who, in Italian folklore, rewards and punishes children on the Feast of the Epiphany (6 January).

29–30. *my house too fits the part ... at such great cost*: M's Roman house was not all that uncomfortable, but may have seemed so by comparison with the luxurious palaces being built in the neighbourhood.

36. *in my bladder there are three black stones*: M suffered from kidney stones.

46. *Love and the muses, bowers of delight*: M's love poetry does not, in fact, exploit the classical and pastoral conventions suggested by 'muses' and 'bowers'.

49. *Making all those big dolls*: a dismissive reference to his own monumental sculpture.

270

My version attempts to preserve the ambiguity of the second line of the Italian '*e vuo' da me le cose che non sono*', which can be understood as 'things that do not exist', 'things that I am not' or 'things that I do not have'.

271

Incomplete octave of an unfinished sonnet.

272

A much-revised sonnet in which the sestet rejects the sentiment of the octave.

1–4. *Bring back the days . . . to the tomb*: A striking contrast between the fury of desire and the serene beauty (possibly of VC) that once inspired it.

274

4. *where I'll catch fire as I did before*: Either 'I shall love God as I once loved mortal beauty' or 'I shall love God as I did in heaven before birth'. The latter reading takes M's Neoplatonism to a heretical extreme.

276

The octave stresses the poet's sensibility to the multiplicity of human beauty. The sestet counters this with the affirmation that the soul's most deep-rooted desire is for something that cannot be satisfied by mortal beauty. The soul that is moved by such heaven-born desire goes beyond what men call 'love' and need not fear the treacherous assault of physical passion in old age.

6. *burdened with cares, and jealousy as well*: The ageing artist is presumably envious of the beauty of the young.

14. *base spoils*: The body.

277

Thanking Vasari for the *Lives*.

1–4. *With pencil or with colours . . . she made lovely lovelier yet*:

The lines exploit the conventional art–nature rivalry. M was, in fact, less than enthusiastic about Vasari as a painter and had criticized his frescos in the Palazzo della Cancelleria in Rome. It is possible that by celebrating literature as 'a nobler art' M was tactfully trying to direct Vasari to a more suitable profession. For more information about Vasari, see Introduction, p. xiv and pp. xxxiii–xxxv.

9–11. *For though some ages past ... their foredestined end*: Some past ages may rival nature in their production of beauty; but, unlike nature, they are subject to inevitable decay.

279

Two quatrains rather than the octave of a sonnet.

280

Possibly the octave of an unfinished sonnet.

282

Written on same sheet as 283 and 285 (with 284 on verso). A bitter realization of the gap between the artist's sacred subject matter and his own intellectual and spiritual weakness. Given its use by Vasari and others to celebrate M's works, the phrase 'things divine' acquires a strong ironic overtone.

284

Either a complete poem or the sestet of an unfinished sonnet. For all the doubts expressed in 282, 283 and 285, art remains the only way in which M can imagine himself serving God.

285

Final version of a much-revised sonnet.

10. *now I approach two deaths*: The 'two deaths' of body and soul.

288

Echoes Petrarch, *Canzoniere* 365, which provided the model for all such recantation poems.

3–4.   *not only I forget . . . with it than without*: By neglecting God's grace the soul becomes more guilty than it would have been if that grace had not been offered.

289

12–14.   *You were not sparing . . . to this other key*: The saving grace that flows from Christ's passion will be of no use without the gift of faith. The emphasis on faith has a Lutheran ring, though M never allows the corresponding denigration of works to overstep the bounds of Catholic orthodoxy.

290

11.   *nor your stern arm be raised against me here*: M's poems rarely take up the imagery of his visual art, but one can hardly forget the uplifted arm of Christ in the Sistine Chapel *Last Judgement*.

292

The octave of a sonnet. Man can do nothing of himself. Salvation is a circular process that begins and ends with God. Even prayer relies on God's prior gift of the power to pray.

293

3.   *I see two deaths approach*: See note to 285, l. 10.

9–11.   *To make me yearn . . . out of nothing born*: In the New Testament redemption is frequently seen as a second creation. In the first creation man is created out of nothing; in the second he is recreated out of sin.

13.   *the high steep road*: See the same image in 288, l. 9.

295

As in 294, M fears that a long life will increase the risk of death finding him in a state of sin that will result in damnation.

296

A much-revised sonnet.

1–8. *Many more years ... greater harm at last*: To those who are
      unafraid, death may seem to come more slowly. But, as the
      sonnet goes on to argue, this is hardly a blessing since those who
      are happy are less likely to adore God and long life increases our
      inclination to sin.

298

6.   *primal stain*: Original sin.
10.   *its own eyes*: The stars. The tercet echoes Luke 23:44–5 and
      Matthew 27:51–2.
12.   *This freed the patriarchs from the shadowy realm*: Alluding to
      the traditional belief that, between his death and his resurrection,
      Christ descended into hell (Limbo) to free the souls of the Old
      Testament patriarchs.

299

A jocular sonnet thanking Vasari for his gifts.

4.   *I leave Saint Michael scales that I can't handle*: The scales as
      a symbol of fair exchange were a traditional attribute of
      St Michael.
5–8. *Too much fair weather ... rough waves toss and dandle*: A
      metaphorical way of saying that too much generosity disarms
      gratitude.

300

Ludovico Beccadelli (1502–72) had recently been appointed Arch-
bishop of Ragusa (now Dubrovnik) in Dalmatia. The appointment
was, in effect, a sentence of exile for this reformist bishop who was an
old friend of M and had once been close to the circle of VC.

9–14. *With wings of thought ... to lodge with him*: M was much
       distressed by the death in December 1555 of his faithful assistant,
       the stone-carver Urbino (*c.* 1512–55), who had served him for a
       quarter of a century.

LETTERS

The chronology of Michelangelo's letters is not always clear. Wherever the date or addressee is lacking in the manuscript I have attempted to supply the missing information in square brackets.

Letter 1

Addressed to a cousin of the Medici (not Lorenzo the Magnificent) during M's first stay in Rome at the invitation of Rafaello Riario, Cardinal of St George (1450–1521). Baldassare del Milanese had bought M's statue of the *Sleeping Cupid* (now lost), and tried to sell it on as a genuine antique. M wanted to buy it back in order to avoid any suspicion that he might be involved in the deception, but Baldassare refused to let it go. Balducci, Rucellai and Cavalcanti are all connected with Florentine banks in Rome. The letter survives only in a copy which has at its foot the name of the painter Sandro Botticelli (1445–1510). M may have used Botticelli as a go-between to avoid advertising his connection with the fallen Medici.

Letter 2

The first extant letter to M's father Lodovico. Lionardo was M's elder brother. (For information about the Buonarroti family, see Appendix 1.) He was also a Dominican friar temporarily defrocked for his adherence to the excommunicated Florentine reformer Girolamo Savonarola (1452–98). Savonarola was executed the year after this letter.

Letter 3

Written a fortnight after M's sudden flight from Rome, where he had been commissioned to make the tomb of Pope Julius II. M's disappointment at the pope's apparent loss of interest in the project is exacerbated by what he regards as humiliating treatment. Giuliano da Sangallo (1445–1516) was the eldest of a famous family of architects and well disposed towards M, unlike his nephew Antonio (1484–1546).

Letter 4

Not the only letter in which M complains about his assistants. He is now in Bologna working on a bronze statue of Pope Julius II (later destroyed). Giovansimone, fourth son of Lodovico and younger brother of M, was a frequent object of M's reproaches. Francesco Granacci, a minor painter, had been with M in the workshop of Ghirlandaio. There is no coinage common to all Italian states in the sixteenth century, but the Florentine florin and the Venetian ducat were gold coins of roughly equivalent value. The broad ducat was slightly more valuable. From about 1540 these were superseded as the standard gold coin by the *scudo*. *Grossi*, *grossoni* and *carlini* were silver coins of variable worth. It has been estimated that an average artisan earned approximately from 30 to 50 *scudi* a year, a successful doctor between 80 and 100; 2,000 *scudi* would buy an elegant town-house and 5,000 a palace. M's frequent complaints about poverty should be taken with more than a grain of salt; he was highly paid by any standards and was able to transfer considerable sums to his family for investment and the purchase of property.

Letter 5

Buonarroto was M's favourite brother, the third son of Lodovico (see Appendix 1). Bernardino d'Antonio, as Master of Ordnance to the Florentine republic, had experience in the casting of artillery. Baccio d'Agnolo Baglioni (1462–1543) was an architect and wood-carver.

Letter 6

Buonarroto and Giovansimone were working under Lorenzo Strozzi in the wool trade. M intended to set them up in a shop of their own.

Letter 7

Gismondo was the fifth and youngest son of Lodovico. (See Appendix 1.) Cassandra, widow of M's uncle, Francesco, had brought a lawsuit against Lodovico and his sons for the recovery of her dowry.

Letter 8

It is not known exactly what Giovansimone had been up to, but the phrase 'set fire in the house' is surely metaphorical.

Letter 9

As always, M is worried about the fortunes of the family in difficult times. After the sack of Prato in August 1512 by their Spanish troops, the Medici re-entered Florence and put an end to the republican government (1498–1512) that had been led by the *gonfaloniere* Piero Soderini (1452–1522). M, meanwhile, was completing the vault of the Sistine Chapel which was unveiled on 31 October. The *spedalingo* (literally 'hospitaller') was the warden of the Hospital of Santa Maria Nuova, which also served as a deposit bank and offered greater security than could be provided by private institutions.

Letter 10

M is relieved to know that Florence has not suffered anything like the shocking massacre of civilians that accompanied the sack of Prato.

Letter 12

M had reason to fear the return of the Medici: he had worked for Soderini and his *David* was widely regarded as expressing the spirit of republican resistance.

Letter 13

The sixty ducats constituted Lodovico's share of the indemnity that the Medici imposed on Florentine citizens as part of the terms of surrender. Giuliano, the third son of Lorenzo the Magnificent, must have known M from childhood. (See Appendix 2 for information about the Medici family.) M would later make Giuliano's tomb in the sacristy of San Lorenzo.

Letter 14

M was about to sign a second contract for the tomb of Pope Julius II (see Chronology) and had called the sculptor Bernardino di Pier Basso (d.1551) to work for him. The house that became M's Roman home and workshop for the rest of his life was in Macel de' Corvi (Ravens' Lane). It was later granted to him rent-free.

Letter 15

From Carrara, where he is quarrying marble for the façade of San Lorenzo, M writes to the pope's agent in Rome. Baccio d'Agnolo had been asked to make a wooden model from M's design, but M found it inadequate and preferred to make his own. In Rome ('down there') the heirs of Pope Julius II are urging him to continue with his work on the ill-fated tomb. Pier Fantini, a proverbially altruistic doctor, supplied ointment and bandages without charge.

Letter 17

Jacopo Salviati (d.1553), a banker and brother-in law of Pope Leo X, was a great admirer of Michelangelo. He belonged to the Wool Guild, which controlled building work at Santa Maria del Fiore. On 22 April 1518 the Wool Guild finally granted M a concession to quarry marble from Corvara and to build a road at Pietrasanta and Seravezza.

Letter 18

The Tribunal of the Eight was responsible for investigating criminal offences. M recovered ninety of his hundred ducats.

Letter 19

Lionardo di Compagno, who was formally inscribed in the Guild of Saddlers, had been urging M to work on the tomb of Pope Julius II. Cardinal Aginensis was also pressing M to fulfil his obligations. M continued to be embarrassed by the 'tragedy of the tomb' until his fourth and final contract with the heirs of Pope Julius II in 1542. For the statue commissioned by Metello Vari see Letter 22. The Venetian painter Sebastiano del Piombo (c.1485–1547) was a good friend of M. He arrived in Rome in 1511 and entered holy orders in 1531. Hence the 'Frate Sebastiano', addressee of Letter 31.

Letter 20

M's commission for the façade of San Lorenzo had effectively prevented him from fulfilling his obligations towards the heirs of Julius. With the commission for San Lorenzo cancelled and the tomb of Julius still unfinished, it is not surprising that M felt bitter and frustrated.

He was also at pains to prove that he had not profited financially from these aborted projects.

Letter 21

A letter recommending Sebastiano del Piombo (Bastiano) as one of the painters who might work on the Vatican apartments after the sudden death of Raphael (1483–1520). Cardinal Bernardo Dovizi da Bibbiena (1470–1520), author of the ribald comedy *Calandria* (1513), had probably known M since the days when they were both attached to the household of Lorenzo the Magnificent.

Letter 22

To M's anger at his father's irresponsible behaviour is added his disappointment with his assistant Pietro Urbano (b.1495), who had been sent to Rome to complete the *Risen Christ* for Metello Vari. Pietro apparently disgraced himself both by whoring and by making a botched job of the statue. M dismissed him immediately.

Letter 23

The dispute involved the investment of money from the dowry of Lodovico's deceased second wife. Lodovico was to be the beneficiary during his lifetime, but the principal was not to be alienated and was to revert to M after Lodovico's death, presumably as a partial repayment of his many loans to the family. Although this is the last extant letter from M to his father, M did not abandon Lodovico, who continued to correspond with his son.

Letter 24

During a stay in Rome Giovan Francesco Fattucci had acted for M in the long and complex negotiations over the tomb of Pope Julius. Back in Florence as chaplain at Santa Maria del Fiore, he remained a trusted advisor of the Buonarroti family and a close friend of M who often refers to him simply as 'the priest'. This letter recapitulates the major stages in M's tumultuous relationship with Pope Julius.

Letter 25

Elected Pope Clement VII in 1523, Giulio de' Medici was eager that M should resume work on the Medici tombs in the sacristy of San Lorenzo.

Letter 26

M exploits his own brand of grotesque humour to ridicule Pope Clement's plan to erect a colossus. The huckster is a biting reference to Figiovanni, overseer of the construction work at San Lorenzo, who had criticized M's plan for the library as being like a dovecot. The postern of the San Gallo gate would obviously have been too small to allow passage for the blocks required to build an eighty-foot statue. M's mockery provoked a testy note from a papal official insisting that the project was no joke, but nothing more was heard of the idea. Giovanni Spina was the Florentine agent of the Salviati bank which arranged for payments to M from Pope Clement VII.

Letter 27

At San Lorenzo M is working on the vestibule of the library and on the Medici tombs in the sacristy. Giovanni da Udine was a specialist in stucco relief and in the painting of animals, fruit and flowers. The 'two captains' are the seated statues of Lorenzo, Duke of Urbino and Giuliano, Duke of Nemours, respectively nephew and younger brother of Giovanni de' Medici, who, in 1513, became Pope Leo X. (See Appendix 2.) M suspected Figiovanni of a deliberate attempt to undermine his authority.

Letter 28

M attributes to an almost supernatural circumstance ('God or the Devil') his sudden flight to Venice during the siege of Florence. By the end of November 1529 he had been convinced to return and resume responsibility for the city's fortifications during the Medici siege of Florence. Giovanni Battista della Palla (d.1531) had been engaged by the French king Francis I to buy works of art in Italy: a Florentine patriot and fervent republican, he died in prison after the return of the Medici.

Letter 29

M had met and fallen in love with the young Roman nobleman Tomaso de' Cavalieri (see Introduction, pp. xxi–xxv) sometime during 1532. The trouble M took with this letter is demonstrated by the fact that it exists in three different versions, one of which employs a highly metaphorical style and hails TC in hyperbolic terms as 'light of our century, peerless in the world'. This more sober version seems to be the one that was eventually sent, accompanied by three drawings: *Tityos*, *Ganymede* and *Phaeton*. The sense of the postscript is not clear, but it may imply that TC is free to choose the drawings that he prefers.

Letter 30

This is a draft for a letter no longer extant.

Letter 31

It is not known which madrigals by M provided the texts for Costanzo Festa and Jean Conseil, composers in the service of Pope Leo X. M continues to complain about the way Figiovanni interferes with his work in San Lorenzo.

Letter 32

Written on the eve of M's definitive departure from Florence. Little is known of Febo di Poggio except that he seems to have had a brief but intense relationship with M in 1534–5. His reply to M's letter asks for money and is signed 'as a son to you'.

Letter 33

Pietro Aretino (1492–1556) had made some suggestions for the scheme of *The Last Judgement* and had also tried to cadge some drawings. The author of such licentious works as the *Ragionamenti*, a dialogue between two prostitutes (1534–6), Aretino later took revenge for M's cautious snub by denouncing the nudes in *The Last Judgement* as indecent.

Letter 34

Niccolò Martelli (1498–1555), a minor poet and founding member of the Florentine Academy, had sent M two sonnets and a laudatory letter on the uncovering of *The Last Judgement*.

Letter 35

The Flemish composer Jacques Arcadelt (c.1505–67) set two of M's madrigals to music.

Letter 36

Pier Giovanni Alliotti, Master of the Robes to Pope Paul III, had been urging M to begin work on the frescos in the Pauline Chapel of the Vatican. M was still awaiting ratification of the fourth and final contract for the tomb of Pope Julius II, according to which he had agreed to deposit the considerable sum of 1,400 *scudi* to pay for completion of the work by others.

Letter 37

While awaiting the last contract for the tomb of Julius II (finally ratified in 1542), M was concerned above all to defend himself against charges of dishonesty. This long self-justifying letter exists only in a copy bearing the indication 'To Monsignore'. It was probably addressed to Cardinal Alessandro Farnese (1519–89), grandson of Pope Paul III, and it deals primarily with the complex vicissitudes of the tomb of Julius II which plagued M during the reigns of five popes (Julius II, Leo X, Adrian VI, Clement VII and Paul III). Initially commissioned in 1505, work on the tomb was first interrupted when Julius himself set M to fresco the Sistine Chapel and then, after M's flight from Rome, by work for the Florentine government (the Signoria). With Julius dead the project was briefly revived, only to be suspended yet again when the two Medici popes (Leo X and Clement VII) preferred M to work on the façade, library and new sacristy of San Lorenzo in Florence. A third contract for the tomb was signed under Pope Paul III in 1532, but the pope's own commission for *The Last Judgement* postponed its completion yet again.

This letter obviously precedes the signing of the fourth and final contract in 1542 and goes over the details of the third contract which resulted from complex negotiations with the heirs of Pope Julius II,

Cardinal Aginensis and Francesco Maria della Rovere, Duke of Urbino (referred to in the letter as 'the old duke'). Refuting accusations that he has failed to fulfil his contractual obligations, M argues that the contract itself had been illegally modified by the duke's envoy, Gianmaria della Porta, in order to make it appear that M had received a larger advance than was actually the case. The second part of the letter recapitulates the story of the tomb from the days of Julius II. It seems that in later life M sought to downplay the idea of a conspiracy against him by Raphael and the great architect Donato Bramante (1444–1514), but rivalry and intrigue were inevitable in a milieu of ambitious projects and lucrative commissions.

Cagli is a small town near Urbino and presumably a byword for rusticity.

Letter 38

M had been seriously ill and was nursed back to health by Luigi del Riccio in the Palazzo Strozzi. M's relations with his nephew Lionardo, though always tense, were not as bad as this letter suggests. As the only son of M's brother Buonarroto (see Appendix 1), Lionardo represented the future of the family, and M never ceased to support him financially and to advise him on everything from property and investment to handwriting and the choice of a wife. The 'priest' is, of course, Giovan Francesco Fattuci.

Letter 39

Evidence that M's poetry could be as difficult for his contemporaries as it still is for modern readers. For M's servant Urbino, see note to poem 300.

Letter 40

The first of the two extant letters to Vittoria Colonna. It accompanied poem 159. The 'things' that she sent him may well have been her own poems (see Letter 54).

Letter 41

Having made a crucifix for Vittoria Colonna, M explains why he does not need to use Tommaso de' Cavalieri as an intermediary. The 'great task' may be *The Last Judgement*. The conclusion is a citation from

Petrarch, *Canzoniere* 206. Poem 162 is written on the same sheet as this letter.

Letter 42

Francis I had written to M expressing the wish to possess one of his works. M had thought of taking refuge in France during the siege of Florence in 1529.

Letter 43

M accuses his trusted friend and financial advisor Luigi del Riccio (d. 1546) of making money from prints produced from an engraved portrait that he disliked because he thought it made him look like a drunkard. In revenge M threatens to destroy work (possibly the *Captives*) that he had promised to give Riccio. The accusation was almost certainly misguided and the quarrel seems to have blown over. M was much distressed by Riccio's sudden death. See poem 251 and Letter 48.

Letter 44

The story of the building of St Peter's is too complex to be recounted here. The clear and elegant design of Bramante (see note to Letter 37) was radically altered by Antonio da Sangallo who envisaged something far more elaborate and grandiose. After Sangallo's death in 1546 M took over, but did not achieve his ambition of leaving the basilica in a state where the design could no longer be modified.

Letter 45

In a rare and reluctant venture into art theory, M gives his opinion on the much-debated question of the difference between painting and sculpture. The book he mentions is the celebrated *Due lezzioni* ('Two Lectures') by the humanist scholar Benedetto Varchi which contains a detailed analysis of poem 151. (For Varchi, see Introduction, p. xvi.)

Letter 46

Luca Martini (*c.*1500–1561), writer and civil engineer, member of Florentine academy. Donato Giannotti (1492–1573), fervent Florentine republican. M figures largely in his dialogues (*Dialoghi*) on

Dante's *Divine Comedy*. The commentary on M's sonnet is obviously
that of Varchi, which Martini must have sent on as a bound manu-
script.

Letter 47

M had sent 550 gold *scudi*: 500 towards the purchase of property and
the rest for charity.

Letter 48

In 1547 Duke Cosimo de' Medici (see Appendix 2) issued a decree
imposing severe penalties on the families of any Florentine citizens
who had dealings with the exiled opposition. Since the Strozzi were
noted political exiles, M insists that he was Riccio's guest rather than
theirs.

Letter 50

The last sentence suggests that M wants Fattuci ('the priest') to believe
that letters addressed to 'Michelagniolo sculptor' simply don't get
delivered.

Letter 53

For Giorgio Vasari, see Introduction, pp. xxxiii–xxxv.

Letter 55

Lionardo and Cassandra had children who survived them, but the
direct line of the Buonarroti family died out in 1858.

Letter 57

Sent with poem 285. Vasari, acting on behalf of Duke Cosimo de'
Medici, had been urging M to return to Florence.

Letter 62

See poem 300.

Letter 68

M was appointed architect of St Peter's in 1547, but the slip that makes him write that he has been working there for seventeen years instead of thirteen turned out to be prophetic. His resignation was not accepted and he remained in charge until his death in 1564.

Letter 69

M is probably thinking of his own changes to Sangallo's plan for St Peter's. The analogy between the parts of the body and the parts of architecture was a commonplace derived from the classical treatise of the first-century Roman, Vitruvius, *De Architectura*, a work that had considerable influence on Renaissance style.

Letter 71

The last extant letter. M died two months later.

GIORGIO VASARI,
'LIFE OF MICHELANGELO' (1550)

1. *in Cimabue, in Giotto, in Donatello, in Filippo Brunelleschi and in Leonardo da Vinci*: Vasari's list is designed to illustrate the three arts that M brought to perfection. Cimabue (*c.*1240–*c.*1302) and Giotto (*c.*1266–1337), often regarded as the founding fathers of Italian painting; Donatello (1386–1466), a major sculptor of the fifteenth century; Filippo Brunelleschi (1377–1446), the architect who created the dome of Santa Maria del Fiore in Florence; Leonardo da Vinci (1452–1519), painter, engineer, scientist.

2. *In Florence then, in the year 1474*: M was actually born on 6 March 1475, in the small Tuscan town of Caprese where his father had been appointed as communal administrator (*podestà*).

3. *for the Simoni have always been noble*: The full name of M's father was Lodovico di Lionardi Buonarroti Simoni, but M always used Buonarroti as a surname.

4. *So Lodovico ... son of Domenico*: Condivi (1553) asserts that Domenico Ghirlandaio (1449–94) was envious of Michelangelo and gave him no help at all. Vasari takes pains to refute the accusation in the 1568 edition of the Life.

5. *And this began to be evident . . . which brought him great fame*: The print in question is actually by Martin Schongauer (*c.* 1550–91). Vasari corrects the mistake in 1568.

6. *the bronze pulpits of Donatello*: Still to be seen in the Church of San Lorenzo.

7. *Domenico sent him . . . Granacci . . . the Torrigiano family*: For Granacci, see note to Letter 4. Pietro Torrigiano (1472–1528), sculptor, whose work can still be seen on the tomb of Henry VII and his queen in Westminster Abbey.

8. *the paintings of Masaccio*: These are the famous frescos in the Brancacci Chapel of Santa Maria del Carmine in Florence. The monumental and expressive figures of Masaccio (1401–*c.*1428) provide a decisive link in the chain that leads from Giotto to the Renaissance. Some of these studies can be found in the Graphische Sammlungen in Munich and in the Albertina in Vienna.

9. *Michelangelo worked on a marble Cupid . . . found this difficult to believe*: For more information on this episode, see Letter 1 and note.

10. *He made the wooden crucifix . . . lunette of the high altar*: Usually identified with the crucifix in white poplar now in the Casa Buonarroti in Florence.

11. *Also in Florence, in the Palazzo Strozzi . . . San Pietro in Montorio in Rome*: Both works are now lost. For Giovan Battista della Palla see note to Letter 28.

12. *Angelo Doni . . . the most finished and the most beautiful*: The Doni *tondo* is now in the Uffizi Gallery in Florence. A *tondo* is a round-shaped painting or relief carving.

13. *When it was finished . . . a hundred and forty ducats*: For an explanation of the monetary terms used (and an approximate value of *scudi*) see note to Letter 4.

14. *a larger-than-life Bacchus with a satyr*: Now in the Bargello in Florence.

15. *As a result, when the French Cardinal . . . on the site of the Temple of Mars*: Now in the first chapel on the right as one enters St Peter's, the *pietà* was, in fact, commissioned by Jean Bilhères de Lagraulas (*c.*1434–99), French diplomat and envoy to the pope.

16. *All beauty and all goodness too . . . his only spouse, daughter and mother*: The somewhat obscure verses are by Giovan Battista Strozzi (1505–71), not to be confused with Giovanni de Carlo Strozzi (see poem 247 and note).

17. *Pier Soderini, then gonfaloniere of the city*: This was the highest position in the Florentine republic, held by Soderini from 1502 until the return of the Medici in 1512. See note to Letter 9.

18. *but unfortunately a certain Simone da Fiesole ... on a giant figure*: The block of marble had not, in fact, been botched by Simone da Fiesole, but by Agostino di Duccio (1418–81) or his assistant.

19. *But Giuliano da Sangallo and his brother Antonio*: For Giuliano and Antonio da Sangallo see Letter 3 and note.

20. *neither the Marforio in Rome ... nor the giants of Monte Cavallo*: Famous examples of classical sculpture, still visible in Rome.

21. *When the statue was finished ... was erected in the year 1504*: The statue that now stands before the Palazzo della Signoria is a copy; the original is in the Accademia in Florence.

22. *a marble tondo for Taddeo Taddei ... for Bartolomeo Pitti ... gave to his friend Luigi Guicciardini*: The Pitti tondo is in the Bargello, Florence, and the Taddei tondo in the Royal Academy, London.

23. *Yet again at that time ... of Santa Maria del Fiore*: Originally intended as one of a series of the twelve apostles, the statue is now in the Accademia in Florence.

24. *It so happened that while ... as his subject the Pisan War*: Leonardo depicts the Battle of Anghiari (1440) where Florentine and papal troops defeated the Milanese. M chooses an episode before the Battle of Cascina (1364), a Florentine victory over Pisa. Though M's cartoon has been destroyed, a number of preparatory drawings have survived. In the collection of the Earl of Leicester at Holkham Hall, Norfolk, there is a copy of the cartoon's central section by Bastiano da Sangallo (1481–1551). Bastiano, better known as Aristotile, was the nephew of Antonio and Giuliano da Sangallo.

25. *The pietà, the giant statue of David ... have him build his tomb*: Through a series of interruptions, modifications and revised contracts, this immensely ambitious project was to poison M's life for forty years. The final much-reduced version was erected in 1545 in the Roman basilica of San Pietro in Vincoli (St Peter in Chains).

26. *At the same time he began ... in his house in Rome*: one of the *Victories* is preserved in the Palazzo Vecchio in Florence. There were actually six *Captives*: the four that Vasari mentions remained, in fact, unfinished and are now in the Accademia in Florence; two finished figures are in the Louvre.

27. *He also completed ... nor by any ancient either*: Now part of the tomb of Pope Julius II in San Pietro in Vincoli.

28. *Francesco Maria, Duke of Urbino*: For Francesco Maria della Rovere, Duke of Urbino, see Appendix 2.

29. *In the meantime the pope ... the Bentivogli ... San Petronio*: In 1506 Julius II, an aggressively military pope, conquered Bologna and expelled the ruling Bentovogli family. San Petronio is the cathedral church of Bologna. For M's casting of the bronze statue see Letters 5 and 6.

30. *They say that while ... a fine pair of ignorant botchers*: Francesco Francia, Bolognese painter (*c.*1450–1518); his companion could not have been Francesco del Cossa, who died in 1478. Vasari is probably thinking of the Ferrarese painter Lorenzo Costa (*c.*1460–1535), who had worked for the Bentivogli.

31. *This statue was later destroyed ... in the duke's wardrobe*: The head also has now disappeared.

32. *The pope ... should now be painted*: The Sistine Chapel takes its name from Pope Sixtus IV, uncle of Julius II, who commissioned its construction in 1475. The legend that M painted the whole vault without assistance has now been laid to rest, but the achievement is still enormous for an artist in his thirties who had relatively little experience of fresco. Vasari's description should be read with the help of a good guidebook. Here it should suffice to note that the vault portrays: a) nine episodes from Genesis, moving from the Creation to the Fall and concluding with the Flood; five of these scenes are flanked by large nude figures known as the *Ignudi*; b) a series of prophets (Jonah, Jeremiah, Daniel, Ezekiel, Isaiah, Joel, Zechariah) and sibyls (Lybian, Persian, Cumaean, Erythrean, Delphic); c) the ancestors of Christ (Jesse, Solomon, Rehoboam, etc.; d) episodes where Israel is saved from destruction (Punishment of Haman, Brazen Serpent, David and Goliath, Judith and Holofernes).

33. *It seems that Bramante ... being assigned to Michelangelo*: This is more plausible than the 1568 version which follows Condivi in asserting that Bramante actually proposed Michelangelo for the task, in the hope that, as a sculptor lacking experience in the technique of fresco, he would produce inferior work and lose the pope's favour. For Bramante's relations with M, see Letter 37 and note.

34. *Pope Julius was very keen ... he really thought he had injured*: This account of M's flight from Rome is very inaccurate. It actually occurred in April 1506, before he began working on the

Sistine Chapel, and was provoked by the pope's insulting refusal to grant him audience. See Letters 3, 24 and 37.

35. *When Michelangelo arrived ... to a perfect completion*: The 1568 version sets this episode in Bologna, which was in fact where, after his flight from Rome, M was summoned to work on the bronze statue of Julius II.

36. *others holding up festoons ... its present strife and misery*: Rovere (oak) is the family name of Pope Julius, and the acorn had long been symbolic of the Golden Age.

37. *Designs were proposed ... for the architecture*: Baccio d'Agnolo, woodcarver and architect (1462–1543); for Antonio da Sangallo see note to Letter 3; Andrea Sansovino, sculptor and architect (*c.*1470–1527). The Casa Buonarroti in Florence has a wooden model and a number of drawings for the project.

38. *Jacopo Salviati*: See Letter 17 and note.

39. *For the Medici Palace ... perforated copper shutters*: The windows are those of the Palazzo Medici-Ricardi. For Giovanni da Udine, see note to Letter 27. Giovanni di Baldassare, known as Piloto (d. 1536), a prominent goldsmith. Their work on the Medici Palace has not survived.

40. *So Michelangelo left Rome again ... but not better*: Brunelleschi's project for San Lorenzo dated from 1418: the lantern was raised in 1427, but the façade remained unfinished.

41. *Inside the sacristy ... and Duke Lorenzo, his nephew*: M originally intended a free-standing monument with four Medici tombs: Lorenzo the Magnificent and his murdered brother Giuliano, together with Giuliano, Duke of Nemours, and Lorenzo, Duke of Urbino, respectively son and grandson of Lorenzo the Magnificent. But the tombs of the brothers were abandoned and the other two were eventually placed against the chapel wall flanked by the figures of *Dawn* and *Dusk*, *Night* and *Day*. For the Medici family see Appendix 2.

42. *Vitruvius*: For Vitruvius see note to Letter 69.

43. *At that time Michelangelo sent his pupil ... beside the main chapel*: Urbano (b.1495) botched the job and then disappeared from M's life. The *Risen Christ*, which can still be seen in the Dominican church of Santa Maria sopra Minerva, Rome, was completed by Federigo Frizzi (*c.*1470–1522). Antonio Metelli is better known as Metello Vari. See note to Letter 22.

44. *One of these is of Our Lady ... perfection of the whole*: The statue now stands on the marble sarcophagus that holds the bodies of Lorenzo the Magnificent and his brother Giuliano.

45. *or vernacular rhymes such as these by an unknown author*: In fact, the Florentine academician, Giovanni di Carlo Strozzi. See note to 247.

46. *But the work was denied . . . island of Giudecca*: Vasari is less than accurate here. M was placed in charge of the fortifications in April 1529 (not 1530); the visit to Ferrara in July of the same year was a perfectly official affair that allowed M to study the city's defences; he did not flee to Venice until September and was back in Florence at the end of the year, before the restoration of the Medici. Antonio Mini, M's assistant for nine years, left for France in 1531 and died there in 1533. There is a portrait of Alfonso I d'Este (1476–1534) in the New York Metropolitan Museum, but the attribution to Titian is doubtful.

47. *he went back to Florence . . . whom he had greatly offended*: It is more than likely that M would have sought to regain the favour of Pope Clement VII by contacting Baccio Valori (d.1537), the senior papal representative in Rome. The *Leda and the Swan* has disappeared, though there is a copy by Rosso Fiorentino (1495–1552) in the National Gallery, London. The statue that M made for Valori was not an *Apollo* but a *David*, which is now in the Bargello, Florence.

48. *And his genius was such . . . sustained him in his poverty*: As a faithful servant of the Medici, Vasari makes it clear that he does not approve of M's republican opinions; but M's habitual caution about expressing political opinions makes it unlikely that he would have envisaged anything as risky as the insulting drawings suggested here.

49. *It is said . . . Baccio Bandinelli*: Baccio Bandinelli (1493–1560), a major sculptor, rival and inveterate enemy of M.

50. *Dante's words . . . the living seemed alive*: Purgatory, XII, 67, in *The Divine Comedy*, vol. 2: *Purgatory*, trans. Dorothy L. Sayers (Harmondsworth, 1972).

51. *Charon, his eyes red . . . and beckons with his hand*: Inferno, III, 109–11 in *The Divine Comedy*, vol. 1: *Hell*, trans. Dorothy L. Sayers (Harmondsworth, 1949).

52. *a pietà at her request*: Now in the Gardner Museum, Boston.

53. *Michelangelo has often produced beautiful drawings . . . that could not be more harmonious*: Gherardo Perini was a young man from a banking family with whom M seems to have been in love in the early 1520s. There is a drawing of *The Rape of Ganymede* in the Fogg Museum at Harvard University; *The Punishment of Tityos* is in the Royal Library at Windsor Castle.

54. *Also to be seen are his cartoons . . . by Jacopo da Pontormo*: The *Venus* is usually identified with a painting in the Accademia attributed to Pontormo (1494–1557). Altoviti and Bettini were bankers. *Noli me tangere* ('Touch me not') are Christ's words to Mary Magdalene when he appears to her after the Resurrection (John 20:11–18). The scene was very popular with Renaissance painters.

55. *one with St Peter, where Christ gives him the keys*: In fact, *The Crucifixion of St Peter*. Vasari corrects the mistake in his 1568 edition of the *Lives*.

56. *Thus in a short time . . . with the statue of Moses between them*: In the tomb of Pope Julius II *Moses* is placed between *Rachel* (the contemplative life) and *Leah* (the active life). These are the only statues in the tomb completed by M; the others are by sculptors Raffaello da Montelupo (*c*.1505–66) and Tommaso Boscoli (1503–74).

57. *a Deposition of Christ*: This is the *pietà* now in Santa Maria del Fiore in Florence.

58. *the tomb of Cecchino Bracci for his friend Luigi del Riccio*: See Introduction, p. xxviii.

59. *which he designed for Urbino to make*: For Urbino see note to poem 300.

60. *He said something similar . . . it really was pitiful to see*: Playing on the double meaning of *pietà* as 'pity' and as a representation of the Virgin with the dead Christ in her arms.

Index of First Lines

PENGUIN CLASSICS

LA VITA NUOVA (POEMS OF YOUTH) DANTE

'When she a little smiles, her aspect then
No tongue can tell, no memory can hold'

Dante's sequence of poems tells the story of his passion for Beatrice, the
beautiful sister of one of his closest friends, transformed through his
writing into the symbol of a love that was both spiritual and romantic. *La
Vita Nuova* begins with the moment Dante first glimpses Beatrice in her
childhood, follows him through unrequited passion and ends with his
profound grief over the loss of his love. Interspersing exquisite verse with
Dante's own commentary analysing the structure and origins of each
poem, *La Vita Nuova* offers a unique insight into the poet's art and skill.
And, by introducing personal experience into the strict formalism of
Medieval love poetry, it marked a turning point in European literature.

Barbara Reynolds's translation is remarkable for its lucidity and
faithfulness to the original. In her new introduction she examines the
ways in which Dante broke with poetic conventions of his day and
analyses his early poetry within the context of his life. This edition also
contains notes, a chronology and an index.

Translated with a new introduction by Barbara Reynolds

PENGUIN CLASSICS

THE DECAMERON   GIOVANNI BOCCACCIO

'Ever since the world began, men have been subject to various tricks of Fortune'

In the summer of 1348, as the Black Death ravages their city, ten young Florentines take refuge in the countryside. They amuse themselves by each telling a story a day for the ten days they are destined to remain there – a hundred stories of love, adventure and surprising twists of fate. Less preoccupied with abstract concepts of morality or religion than earthly values, the tales range from the bawdy Peronella hiding her lover in a tub to Ser Cepperallo, who, despite his unholy effrontery, becomes a Saint. The result is a towering monument of European literature and a masterpiece of imaginative narrative.

This is the second edition of G. H. McWilliam's acclaimed translation of *The Decameron*. In his introduction Professor McWilliam illuminates the worlds of Boccaccio and of his storytellers, showing Boccaccio as a master of vivid and exciting prose fiction.

Translated with a new introduction and notes by G. H. McWilliam

---

PENGUIN CLASSICS

THE BOOK OF THE COURTIER
BALDESAR CASTIGLIONE

'The courtier has to imbue with grace his movements, his gestures, his way of doing things and in short, his every action'

In *The Book of the Courtier* (1528), Baldesar Castiglione, a diplomat and Papal Nuncio to Rome, sets out to define the essential virtues for those at Court. In a lively series of imaginary conversations between the real-life courtiers to the Duke of Urbino, his speakers discuss qualities of noble behaviour – chiefly discretion, decorum, nonchalance and gracefulness – as well as wider questions such as the duties of a good government and the true nature of love. Castiglione's narrative power and psychological perception make this guide both an entertaining comedy of manners and a revealing window onto the ideals and preoccupations of the Italian Renaissance at the moment of its greatest splendour.

George Bull's elegant translation captures the variety of tone in Castiglione's speakers, from comic interjections to elevated rhetoric. This edition includes an introduction examining Castiglione's career in the courts of Urbino and Mantua, a list of the historical characters he portrays and further reading.

Translated and with an introduction by George Bull

PENGUIN CLASSICS

DANTE IN ENGLISH

'All in the middle of the road of life
I stood bewildered in a dusky wood'

Dante Alighieri (1265–1321) created poetry of profound force and beauty that proved influential far beyond the borders of his native Italy. This new collection brings together translations from all his verse, including the *Vita Nuova*, his tale of erotic despair and hope, and the *Commedia*, his vast yet intimate poem depicting one man's journey into the afterlife. It also contains extracts from many English masterpieces influenced by Dante, including Chaucer's *Canterbury Tales*, Milton's *Paradise Lost*, Byron's *Don Juan*, T. S. Eliot's *The Waste Land* and Derek Walcott's *Omeros*.

Edited by Eric Griffiths and Matthew Reynolds, this anthology explores the variety of encounters between Dante and English-speakers across more than six centuries. Its detailed notes enable even readers with little or no Italian to appreciate translations that range from the hilarious to the inspired. Eric Griffiths' introduction explains how intricately Dante's work is tied to his own time, yet still speaks across the ages. This edition also includes an account of Dante's life and a list of further reading.

Edited with an introduction and notes by Eric Griffiths

and Matthew Reynolds

Penguin Classics

THE NEW PENGUIN BOOK OF ROMANTIC POETRY

'And what if all of animated Nature
Be but organic harps, diversely framed'

The Romanticism that emerged after the American and French revolutions of 1776 and 1789 represented a new flowering of the imagination and the spirit, and a celebration of the soul of humanity with its capacity for love. This extraordinary collection sets the acknowledged genius of poems such as Blake's 'Tyger', Coleridge's 'Khubla Khan' and Shelley's 'Ozymandias' alongside verse from less familiar figures and women poets such as Charlotte Smith and Mary Robinson. We also see familiar poets in an unaccustomed light, as Blake, Wordsworth and Shelley demonstrate their comic skills, while Coleridge, Keats and Clare explore the Gothic and surreal.

This volume is arranged by theme and genre, revealing unexpected connections between the poets. In their introduction Jonathan and Jessica Wordsworth explore Romanticism as a way of responding to the world, and they begin each section with a helpful preface, notes and bibliography.

'An absolutely fascinating selection – notable for its women poets, its intriguing thematic categories and its helpful mini biographies' Richard Holmes

Edited with an introduction by Jonathan and Jessica Wordsworth

---

PENGUIN CLASSICS

THE COMPLETE POEMS
ANDREW MARVELL

'Thus, though we cannot make our sun
Stand still, yet we will make him run'

Member of Parliament, tutor to Oliver Cromwell's ward, satirist and friend of
John Milton, Andrew Marvell was one of the most significant poets of the
seventeenth century. *The Complete Poems* demonstrates his unique skill and
immense diversity, and includes lyrical love-poetry, religious works and biting
satire. From the passionately erotic 'To his Coy Mistress', to the astutely political
Cromwellian poems and the prescient 'Garden' and 'Mower' poems, which
consider humankind's relationship with the environment, these works are
masterpieces of clarity and metaphysical imagery. Eloquent and compelling, they
remain among the most vital and profound works of the era – works by a figure
who, in the words of T. S. Eliot, 'speaks clearly and unequivocally with the voice
of his literary age'.

This edition of Marvell's complete poems is based on a detailed study of the extant
manuscripts, with modern translations provided for Marvell's Greek and Latin
poems. This edition also includes a chronology, further reading, appendices, notes
and indexes of titles and first lines, with a new introduction by Jonathan Bate.

Edited by Elizabeth Story Donno

With an introduction by Jonathan Bate

PENGUIN CLASSICS

THE COMPLETE POEMS   JOHN MILTON

'I may assert Eternal Providence
And justify the ways of God to men'

John Milton was a master of almost every type of verse, from the classical
to the religious and from the lyrical to the epic. His early poems include
the devotional 'On the Morning of Christ's Nativity', 'Comus', a masque,
and the pastoral elegy 'Lycidas'. After Cromwell's death and the dashing
of Milton's political hopes, he began composing *Paradise Lost*, which
reflects his profound understanding of politics and power. Written when
Milton was at the height of his abilities, this great masterpiece fuses the
Christian with the classical in its description of the Fall of Man. In
Samson Agonistes, Milton's last work, the poet draws a parallel with his
own life in the hero's struggle to renew his faith in God.

In this edition of the *Complete Poems*, John Leonard draws attention
to words coined by Milton and those that have changed their meaning
since his time. He also provides full notes to elucidate biblical, classical
and historical allusions and has modernized spelling, capitalization
and punctuation.

Edited with a preface and notes by John Leonard

PENGUIN CLASSICS

SELECTED POEMS AND LETTERS
ARTHUR RIMBAUD

'I know dusk
And dawn, rising like a multitude of doves.
What men have only thought they'd seen, I've seen'

Arthur Rimbaud was one of the wildest, most uncompromising poets of his age, although his brief literary career was over by the time he was twenty-one and he soon embarked on a new life as a trader in Africa. This edition brings together his extraordinary poetry and more than a hundred of his letters, most of them written after he had abandoned literature. A master of French verse forms, the young Rimbaud set out to transform his art, and language itself, by a systematic 'disordering of all the senses', often with the aid of alcohol and drugs. The result is a highly innovative, modern body of work, obscene and lyrical by turns – a rigorous journey to extremes.

Jeremy Harding and John Sturrock's new translation includes Rimbaud's greatest verse, as well as his record of youthful torment, *A Season in Hell*, while the African letters unveil a portrait of the man who turned his back on poetry. The edition also includes an introduction examining Rimbaud's two very different careers.

Translated with an introduction by Jeremy Harding and John Sturrock

THE STORY OF PENGUIN CLASSICS

Before 1946 ... 'Classics' are mainly the domain of academics and students; readable editions for everyone else are almost unheard of. This all changes when a little-known classicist, E. V. Rieu, presents Penguin founder Allen Lane with the translation of Homer's *Odyssey* that he has been working on in his spare time.

1946 Penguin Classics debuts with *The Odyssey*, which promptly sells three million copies. Suddenly, classics are no longer for the privileged few.

1950s Rieu, now series editor, turns to professional writers for the best modern, readable translations, including Dorothy L. Sayers's *Inferno* and Robert Graves's unexpurgated *Twelve Caesars*.

1960s The Classics are given the distinctive black covers that have remained a constant throughout the life of the series. Rieu retires in 1964, hailing the Penguin Classics list as 'the greatest educative force of the twentieth century.'

1970s A new generation of translators swells the Penguin Classics ranks, introducing readers of English to classics of world literature from more than twenty languages. The list grows to encompass more history, philosophy, science, religion and politics.

1980s The Penguin American Library launches with titles such as *Uncle Tom's Cabin,* and joins forces with Penguin Classics to provide the most comprehensive library of world literature available from any paperback publisher.

1990s The launch of Penguin Audiobooks brings the classics to a listening audience for the first time, and in 1999 the worldwide launch of the Penguin Classics website extends their reach to the global online community.

The 21st Century Penguin Classics are completely redesigned for the first time in nearly twenty years. This world-famous series now consists of more than 1300 titles, making the widest range of the best books ever written available to millions – and constantly redefining what makes a 'classic'.

The Odyssey continues ...

The best books ever written

PENGUIN CLASSICS

SINCE 1946

Find out more at www.penguinclassics.com